IN GRATITUDE FOR ALL THE GIFTS:
SEAMUS HEANEY AND EASTERN EUROPE

MAGDALENA KAY

In Gratitude for All the Gifts

Seamus Heaney and Eastern Europe

UNIVERSITY OF TORONTO PRESS
Toronto Buffalo London

© University of Toronto Press 2012
Toronto Buffalo London
www.utppublishing.com
Printed in Canada

ISBN 978-1-4426-4498-4 (cloth)

Library and Archives Canada Cataloguing in Publication

Kay, Magdalena
In gratitude for all the gifts : Seamus Heaney and Eastern Europe /
Magdalena Kay.

Includes bibliographical references and index.
ISBN 978-1-4426-4498-4

1. Heaney, Seamus – Criticism and interpretation.   2. Heaney, Seamus –
Knowledge – East European poetry.   3. East European poetry – History
and criticism.   I. Title.

PR6058.E2Z57 2012   821'.914   C2012-900596-7

This book has been published with the help of a grant from the Canadian
Federation for the Humanities and Social Sciences, through the Aid to Schol-
arly Publications Program, using funds provided by the Social Sciences and
Humanities Research Council of Canada.

University of Toronto Press acknowledges the financial assistance to its publishing program of the Canada Council for the Arts and the Ontario Arts
Council.

 Canada Council   Conseil des Arts   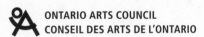 ONTARIO ARTS COUNCIL
for the Arts   du Canada   CONSEIL DES ARTS DE L'ONTARIO

University of Toronto Press acknowledges the financial support of the
Government of Canada through the Canada Book Fund for its publishing
activities.

Contents

Acknowledgments

I would like to thank the Faculty of Humanities at the University of Victoria for awarding me a Humanities Faculty Fellowship for the 2010–11 academic year, which greatly helped me to finish writing the manuscript. I would also like to thank the Department of English for awarding me an Internal Research Grant that helped me compile material for this project.

I am grateful to Richard Ratzlaff at the University of Toronto Press for his encouragement and support of the project.

A shadow presence in these pages is Helen Vendler, whose undergraduate seminar on Seamus Heaney stimulated my lifelong passion for Heaney's work. Her early encouragement of my student work emboldened me to pursue a career as a professor and literary critic. Thank you, Professor Vendler, for all the gifts you may not even realize you have given me.

Love and thanks are due to my family. To K, who watched this book come into being and inspired me, my deepest love and gratitude.

IN GRATITUDE FOR ALL THE GIFTS:
SEAMUS HEANEY AND EASTERN EUROPE

Introduction

Since the beginning of our new millennium, readers have been proffering summative assessments of Seamus Heaney's work, perhaps because major calendrical changes reinvigorate our taste for deaths and entrances, and for critical revaluations; the beginning of a new century seems a good vantage point, and is readily seen as the beginning of a new era. During the previous fin de siècle, it made sense to think so. Today, we are still seeking to articulate the major changes occurring in the last two decades of the previous century, which proved revolutionary in the two Irelands and in Eastern Europe. A newly peaceful Northern Ireland and an Eastern Europe free from the shackles of Soviet communism emerged. Our interest in politics, ideology, and the complicated life of once-subjugated nations, however, remains strong. Major literary events such as the so-called Northern Irish Renaissance, or what we may call a Polish Renaissance characterized by a group of extraordinary poets, remain unparalleled – we have not come up with a new Renaissance quite yet.

This book is not a summative assessment or a survey but, I prefer to think, an analysis that is also a celebration of a crucial moment in the career of Seamus Heaney, a figure who links these two phenomena by virtue of his intensive reading of Eastern European poets at the same time as he deeply engages Irish history, politics, and culture. I call this moment his visionary turn. It gathered momentum in the 1970s, solidified in the 1980s, carried over to the 1990s, and was a complicated matter all the way along. When a poet renowned for concreteness and tactility of language turns his focus to abstract ideas, moral questions, 'nothings' instead of 'somethings,' as it were – but does not abandon his previous mode, merely adapts it, changing its guiding principles – then questions will be asked and judgments passed. Now, if we can view this 'turn' as the entrance into a space of complex dialogue with a whole new group of poets – that is, poets new to Heaney, poets whom he had not grown up reading, from outside the English- and Irish-language traditions – then new questions arise. The contention of this study, then, is that Heaney's visionary turn exists in response to poetic developments on the other side of Europe. Reading the poetry of Eastern European writers, albeit in translation, was an experience whose importance for Heaney cannot be overemphasized.

The topic of literary influence, however, becomes controversial when we cease to deal with direct allusions and quotations and when we attune ourselves to echoes, discern formal borrowings, or detect an align-- ment of voice with that of another writer. Such is the case here. Heaney does not know any Slavic languages, nor has he been trained in the study of Slavic literatures. His interest in Eastern European poets is not premised upon the sort of literary-historical knowledge that he brings to bear upon British or Irish poets, nor can he draw upon a lifetime of reading, as he does with figures such as Wordsworth or Auden. This cannot happen with Czesław Miłosz, Zbigniew Herbert, Osip Mandelstam, or Joseph Brodsky. Heaney's interest in these latter writers therefore thrives without the kind of educational and cultural ballast that we usually consider necessary for deep understanding, namely, a knowledge of local history, local literary history, and original language. The last point is the most potentially troubling. Heaney modestly admits that he lacks extensive knowledge of Polish or Russian literary traditions; this knowledge, though, is not necessary to assimilating the influence of individual poets. What he lacks in breadth he certainly compensates for in depth, and his essays on these writers are cited with admiration by scholars of Slavic literature. Heaney's ear is sharp and subtle enough to pick up frequencies that could easily elude others. The matter of local language is more troubling, since Heaney himself frequently insists upon its primacy. He mentions the admirable translations of these poets' work, but the fact remains that he will never hear them in the same way as he hears poets writing in English.

For those who insist upon 'the original' as the only text worth reading, and eschew translated poetry altogether, this will not be an acceptable situation: if there must always be loss in translation, then let us not read translations. This sort of attitude, however, closes the door to vast realms of legitimate pleasures in legitimate texts. The seriousness with which poets often approach the matter of their own translation validates the enterprise on the most basic level, that of communicative possibility. The seriousness with which translation studies have entered academia as a bona fide branch of literary studies extends the import of the translator's task. The enormous impact that a new translation can have upon the reading public reveals the potential competitiveness of the field and most readers' basic openness to reading in translation.[1] Facing-page editions of translated work prove popular in the country of origin as well as the host country – local readers can be curious to know how 'their' poet sounds in a different language. The translated text necessarily bears the imprint of the translator's own idiom, but it is not quite right to postulate that a poet-translator will refashion a foreign poet in her own image; this is assuming too much egotism. One continuous line of inquiry in this book will be the difference between Eastern European and Anglo-American poetic idioms. Eastern European poetry in translation sounds different from Anglo-American work: its translators are not simply imposing their own speech patterns upon those of the poets they translate.

The fact is that there are not enough native speakers of Polish – of Russian, there are more – in England or the United States that Miłosz and Herbert could have had a significant impact in their original languages, although the size of the émigré community may contribute to the amount of translations available. Their popularity is premised upon their availability in English. As a prefatory consideration, we should bear in mind that the model of influence operative here will be quite different from Harold Bloom's agonistic model or the Eliotic 'traditional' model with which Heaney is so familiar. Heaney struggles *to* assimilate the influence of Eastern European poets, seeking linkages between their vision and his, and he does so in order to write in a new manner. His task is to bring together different poetic languages, not least in the literal sense, and to see whether an exceedingly 'other' mode of writing *can* be emulated; his project is not based upon clear affinities and a confident sense of commensurability. This type of influence has the most shaky of foundations. It is based upon the reading of translated text, upon radical divergence from one's 'home' traditions (for Heaney, English and Irish), and it often works *contrary* to these traditions and to the scholars working within them. This type of influence is based upon a postulate by no means universally accepted – that one *can* emulate a foreign idiom.

The terms 'ethics' and 'morality' will figure prominently in the discussion (their difference is explored in chapter 3), and it is apposite to question what sort of methodological ethics are at work in this analysis. A choice of methodology is not merely an academic choice, nor even simply a heuristic one; it is an ethical choice, since it attempts to align itself fairly with the interest of the authors and texts at hand – to do the work justice. It soon runs into the quicksand of intentionalism – should authorial intent even be part of our deliberations? Heaney provides clear guidance regarding reading practices – the man was, after all, a teacher, a trainer of teachers, and a professor of both creative writing and literature. He privileges close readings of carefully chosen texts, and is willing to grant the texts a good deal of power. *The Redress of Poetry*, a collection of lectures delivered between 1989 and 1994 while he served as professor of poetry at Oxford, establish the obligations of readers and writers in the age of ideology: '[poetry's] integrity is not to be impugned just because at any given moment it happens to be a re-fraction of some discredited cultural or political system' (7); poetry can function as a form of redress. It is an interpretive crime to deny poetry its 'self-delighting inventiveness,' its joy in its own energies, be they formal, linguistic, imagistic, or narrative. 'Leave / To poets a moment of happiness, / Otherwise your world will perish,' writes Miłosz (*New and Collected Poems* 76); Heaney would add that we leave the poem its own self-delight. Paraphrasing Yeats, he states that

> the will must not usurp the work of the imagination. And while this may seem something of a truism, it is nevertheless worth repeating in a late-twentieth-century context of politically approved themes, post-colonial backlash and 'silence-breaking' writing of all kinds. In these circum-stances, poetry is understandably pressed to give voice to much that has hitherto been denied expression in the ethnic, social, sexual and political life ... But in discharging this function, poets are in danger of slighting an-other imperative, namely, to redress poetry *as* poetry, to set it up as its own category, an eminence established and a pressure exercised by distinctly linguistic means. (*Redress* 5–6)

The critic is put in a difficult position: the duty to read an author as he wishes to be read may work against a countervailing pull to proffer critical novelty, to break a critical silence. It is my contention that we can heed both duties by attending to the 'distinctly linguistic means' for exercising and resisting pressure, but this of necessity entails a modicum of close reading, which is not a methodology approved of by all critics. Despite the fact that literature professors usually be-lieve close reading should be taught in literature courses, in our own critical work, overmuch attention to 'distinctly linguistic' phenom-ena may be deemed old-fashioned or even critically naive, exposing our unconsciousness of better, more theoretically or technologically so-phisticated methodologies.[2]

The critical model dominating Heaney criticism remains historically inflected close reading: we are convinced, it seems, that this viewpoint has greater explanatory power than other models. The 'drift toward other discourses' in which famously 'distant reader' Franco Moretti situates his own project (*Graphs* 1) has not taken hold of Heaney schol-arship to any large extent. Readers are fascinated with Heaney's influ-ences and his travels, but it can still be challenging to situate him on the map of world literature, especially in the more theoretically driven reaches of this very broad and flourishing field. In short, the bound-ary between comparative literature and world literature is permeable. Heaney's work has achieved international fame, and yet it is not fre-quently used for theoretical arguments of any kind, whether they be post-structuralist inquiries (Eugene O'Brien is a salient exception), ap-plications of world-systems theory, or bird's-eye views of the travel of cultural forms ('formalism without close reading,' to Jonathan Arac). The exception may be postcolonial theory, yet even in this case, liter-ary issues are paramount when Heaney's work is under analysis. Eco-nomic considerations have entered Heaney scholarship, but usually in historical terms, as his marvellous initial contract with Faber and Faber is situated within a consideration of editorial connections and publish-ing patterns.[3] Even if we accept that there is no *necessary* homology between political systems, economic systems, and literary production, such an absence is surprising.

Is this a problem at all? Probably not. Heaney's work has not been enclosed in a New Critical urn – although let us recall that the much-maligned New Critics could also be alive to the existence of a history beyond the urn. It has been scrupulously linked to its historical context. There are timelines of Heaney's life and times, biographies (Michael Parker's remains compelling), and countless allusions made to events in his life, so that Heaney's work is richly historicized. Due to the ex-cellence of his compatriots' writing, new perspectives on Heaney have emerged as a result of scholarship on poets such as Derek Mahon and Michael Longley. One of the commonest errors made about close read-ing is that it necessarily scants the writer's context. Scholarship on Irish poetry generally proves this pattern wrong (as, for example, in Michael Wood's *Yeats and Violence*, 2010). It would be a grave mistake to pre-suppose that the literary could be read symptomatically, or merely as a sign of the times. But *how* exactly to balance the claims of history, so often viewed in demonic terms, and poetry, so often viewed as a benign effusion, is a question which can only be answered by critical praxis.

Heaney sees 'the actual' as a gravitational pull (*Redress* 3), a refreshingly secular metaphor. If literature is to rise above its historical situation so that its existence does not depend upon the allure of its historicity, then it must be strong enough to resist this pull. Great literature is, and does. Even when it engages historical events directly, its voice stays clear, separate from though involved with the confused din of history. Only by attending to the nuances of form and diction can we recognize its voice; otherwise, a poem becomes yet another historical document, and there are more straightforward historical documents than poems. Poetry will not give us reliable images of history. It will also not be reliably historical.

A poet such as Miłosz presents an even greater conundrum than Heaney, since he sometimes appends a place and date to his poems, prompting a rereading that is a re-situation. 'Berkeley, 1980' carries a very different charge from 'Warsaw, 1945.' Are we obligated to read them as occasional poems, or at least as situated poems? Is the lack of a date then significant, prompting a different reading practice? The question in back of these – which can only be answered on a case-by-case basis – is whether we must choose between historical and ahistorical reading practices, given that the second does not really exist. Forms are social and historical, and formalist inquiry is underlain by history; states of mind are historical, and biographical inquiry has always to call upon historical events, just as psychoanalytical inquiry has to utilize historical and material details of the writer's life. If we attend to a writer's development, then history structures our very modus operandi. It is inescapable, and often (as with 'In Warsaw,' marked 'Warsaw, 1945') makes for tough reckoning, but the qualities that make a poem worthy of much painful reading, to paraphrase Frank Kermode, inhere within the poem itself, not its context. Miłosz openly states that poems with historical but not artistic merit may not be worth preserving. Their value is local and ephemeral, to give comfort, to allow the suffering to speak. They may be outshone by poems written in less interesting conditions.

Some of these phrases may be contentious: 'less interesting,' for example, or 'worth preserving,' since evaluation is such a fraught business that even critics as exacting as Michael Wood wish to cordon it off from serious inquiry, yet he, too, refers to excellent work, masterpieces, et cetera. Evaluative terms have a way of sneaking into our speech. So does interpretation, and so does comparison, even if 'comparative literature' is considered its own discrete field. The question of how studies of influence can *not* proceed comparatively seems to have been proven rhetorical by debates about transnationalism, the global and the local, the universal and the planetary. Perhaps this shows that comparative literature's conclusions have become everyone else's premises, as Haun Saussy believes (Saussy 3). Writers' reading lists are not nationally bounded, and as we connect a writer to a network of precursors, rivals, and followers, we find ourselves moving between countries, continents, and even language families. Twentieth-century writers do not greatly respect national borders.

This study is therefore a hybrid book, poised between categories, acutely aware that translations do not exist in a vacuum: they are the product of one culture meeting another, sometimes with a third acting as mediator or eventual recipient. When an American writer translates an Eastern European, and the translation travels throughout the anglophone world, several potentially relevant matters arise, even if not all may be applicable to the argument at hand. There are lifetimes' worth of stories to be told about Osip Mandelstam, Joseph Brodsky, Zbigniew Herbert, and Czesław Miłosz, the poets most important to Heaney. One needs to pick and choose discriminately – and perhaps rather ruthlessly. The possible context for such a study is almost infinite.

Heaney's reading list also appears infinite. Given that he cheerfully recalls reading stacks of books by various and sundry authors at any one time, attending poetry festivals near and far, there is more than enough material to consider. It is imperative, however, to separate enjoyment from influence. Heaney dipped into the work of Anna Akhmatova, Marina Tsvetaeva, Miroslav Holub, Janoš Pilinszky, and Vasko Popa; he re-translated a cycle of songs by Leoš Janáček, entitled *Diary of One Who Vanished*. Each encounter, no doubt, added to Heaney's imaginative store, and subtly inflected his view of poetry. There is a difference, however, between reading for pleasure and reading for influence, between taking pleasure in masterful verse and having it sink into the mind and enter the bloodstream, so that it audibly changes one's own writing. That honour is reserved for a very few poets: Czesław Miłosz chiefly, Zbigniew Herbert secondarily, Osip Mandelstam and Joseph Brodsky well after those. There is another category, too: the *composite* influence of much reading is powerful, and a composite Eastern European influence is frequently evident in Heaney's work. The spatio-temporal specificity of these writers' work cannot be definitively established, but must be individually, idiosyncratically assessed: why, for example, does Heaney write that Janáček's songs, 'for all the Moravian ... local colour,' have their 'true setting' in 'the clear and passionate land of "once upon a time" '? (Janáček viii). By establishing the universal reach of great art, Heaney may seek to minimize the (possibly great) distance between us and the turn-of-the-century Czech Janáček, who may seem rather distant from Heaney in 1999, when he publishes his 'version' of Janáček's songs. Heaney is hardly one to scant the deep importance of 'local colour' and setting, however, especially given his concept of a poet's individual 'voice-right.' As we examine the major and minor, individual and composite influences of Eastern European poets upon his work, we must constantly negotiate between a view of literature as *inescapably* bounded by time and space – even while it may seek egress from them – and literature's circulation in an idealized universal 'land of "once upon a time." '

Considerations of context readily cross the boundary into cultural studies, a field usually correlated with popular culture instead of so-called high culture, although it is noteworthy that translations of 'high cultural' Eastern European poets enjoyed a great deal of popular success. Heaney is so widely read and known that this distinction is almost untenable for him as well. These constitute two different sorts of popularity, however: Heaney's is a fairly direct matter, resulting from his excellence – though excellence is not, unfortunately, a sufficient guarantor of popularity – but also, less saliently yet still notably, the prestige of his publisher, his assimilation into school and university curricula, his presence in anthologies, and his accessibility, not to mention his warm and generous personality. The success of these Eastern European poets, though, is due to different factors, since they are dissident poets at odds with their countries' governments, relying on clandestine circulation of their manuscripts – in Mandelstam's case, on the memory of his wife Nadezhda – and living in exile or emigration for much of their lives. Their popularity at home has to do with their excellence but also their principled dissidence, and, in the case of a poet such as Brodsky, connections to a milieu of scholars, artists, and writers; their popularity abroad involves their status as dissident poets who hail from exotic and tragic lands. Clare Cavanagh has provided an admirably wide-ranging view of this phenomenon in *Lyric Poetry and Modern Politics: Russia, Poland, and the West* (see her substantial introduction, 2–44).

In order to understand how Heaney would read these poets, then, this cultural context is central, since it makes its own impress upon his mind. The project of ascertaining how and why he was influenced by Eastern Europeans and maintained a literary friendship with Miłosz takes place against a significant backdrop, conditioning the way in which Heaney responds to these poets, even if it is not in a foreseeable manner. A corollary question lies behind this study: Heaney *could* have been influenced by any number of contemporary poets writing in his own language, so why did he venture so far afield? It is not easy to explain an ellipsis of influence, to use David Damrosch's image, while asking why certain authors are excluded from it; the focus of these chapters, both historical and analytic, will be upon the positive fact that Heaney was excited, provoked, and inspired by certain Eastern European poets, leaving us with a rich field of inquiry, and not the negative fact that he left other books on the shelf, so to speak. Nobody could ever accuse Heaney of reading too little.

This study will focus upon the practical matter of a particular cross-cultural relationship and the culture in which it developed, but the question of how to read comparatively, what sort of presuppositions and aesthetic ideologies may inform our interpretive acts, will always be foundational. It may arise in faintly ludicrous form: Miłosz insists that he wants to be seen as a poet, not a political scientist. Since when would this be a problem? The answer is, since Miłosz published a book entitled *The Captive Mind* in 1953. It is not a question we in the humanities are wont to ask – if anything, we usually wish that policymakers found our work more 'relevant' to their realms of activity. *The Captive Mind*, however, proved too much so, garnering Miłosz the reputation of a political thinker, somewhere between a political scientist and sociologist, and is still probably his most popular single book. 'Social scientists who want to be relevant on contemporary issues will find this book a launching platform for exploration of uncharted areas,' writes Daniel Lerner in the *American Sociological Review* (488). There is nothing wrong with such praise, and it helped to make a name for the Polish writer, but when Ewa Czarnecka reminds him of his fame he retorts, 'What sort of fame? I prefer a different sort of fame … I find it far away from my real interests' (Czarnecka and Fiut 145). He compares himself to Boris Pasternak, whose *Doctor Zhivago* helped to garner him the Nobel Prize, but 'he got the prize for a novel, not for the poetry that was his life' (146).

When reading a writer in isolation, these matters are easily clarified, and we can do our part to restore the sort of fame that the writer would desire – that is, if we consider our ethics of reading to be structured by authorial intention. With authors such as Miłosz and Heaney, statements of intention abound, and so do statements proclaiming the relative, not absolute, status of material conditions on behalf of virtually every poet here under consideration: historical circumstances *may* call forth literary works whose place is best understood against their backdrop, either because they are not indicative of the poet's work as a whole or because their chief merit is in their responsive or reactive function. Readers shake their heads at Osip Mandelstam's abortive attempt to praise a hydroelectric dam in verse, recognizing this as proof of his opposition to Stalinist aesthetics. There are, however, many ways of shaping a canon, including an individual's canon, which may run counter to public taste. The example of Miłosz's *Captive Mind* illustrates the oddity of reputation making: known as a poet in Poland, Miłosz entered literary life abroad under what he sees as false pretences. Zbigniew Herbert bemoans the misapprehension of comic irony in his poems (Herbert in Weissbort 327), based on cultural misunderstanding. Heaney, meanwhile, is acutely aware that his encounter with these poets' work is mediated, and that he, too, is caught up in the machinery of canon making, as one of the 'Ulster Renaissance' poets, the star of Philip Hobsbaum's 'Group,' a poet of the Troubles (and, after 1972, one who 'escaped from the massacre' by moving from Belfast to Dublin), and, perhaps most pertinently, as a poet of concrete imagery and local experience. We are curious of a poet's development, but often wish for it to proceed along foreseeable lines. In the case of Heaney in the 1970s, it may even seem perverse and counterproductive to turn from the enriching influences of William Wordsworth, Patrick Kavanagh, and Robert Lowell to the difficult influences of Herbert and Miłosz. The nature of his talent becomes more difficult to discern once we must reckon with voices coming from outside our established canon of influences. When Heaney – a writer firmly rooted in the English language, with its mix of Anglo-Saxon and Latinate vocabulary of which he makes such stunning use – starts to use 'foreign' models (of which Dante, we should note, precedes Herbert and Miłosz), we have to start reading transnationally.

Heaney's work enables multi-perspectival discussion of the relationship between Eastern European and English-language poetries, as he maintains his concern with the matter of history at the same time as he reads poetry formally. Formal readings can also be ethical readings, and attention to a poet's cultural context can help explain formal choices. When Peter McDonald argues that form bears its own authority (*Serious Poetry* 5), connecting it to a poem's originality, he does so within an argument for poetry's capacity to work against opinion in an often eccentric way. Brodsky emphasizes this capacity in a different context, that of poetry's power to stand against oppressive politics *by means of* its eccentricity – its refusal to don the common uniform, in Heaney's metaphor ('Joseph Brodsky' 32). Brodsky also emphasizes the formal work of the poem as its site of resistance. Expecting it to proclaim forthright dissent would be naive, which is what distresses Miłosz when he meets anti-war activists in Berkeley in the 1960s and 1970s. To add Auden's voice to the chorus, a poem may illuminate but it will not dictate. Let us examine, then, the quality of its illumination, its source of light, as well as the phenomena that it makes visible.

Verse is not solely an intellectual medium or solely a sensual medium: it is both. Poems must be allowed their sensuality even in scholarly discussion, and to treat them as statements that are curious for their obliquity or their fine feeling, but not to recognize – or, better yet, to savour – their textures and contours would be deplorable. Engaging a poem's sensual dimension need not lead us into a morass of sloppy language in which we exchange thinking for feeling. On the contrary, attending to poetry's complexities of sense and thought leads us into rich conceptual terrain. The verbal texture of the poem will always exceed the theoretical statements, generalizations, or summative expositions that we seek to make of it. For this reason it is especially important not to overlook poetic texture and voice in favour of purely historical considerations or theoretical conclusions. These considerations will account for neither the poem's aesthetics nor its process of thinking, which will not allow itself to be summed up in a single thought. In order to understand the way a poem thinks through historical events or its own historicity, we need to be alive to its ideational narrative, as it were, and not hasten to freeze it in a single idea. Single ideas are easier to deal with than narratives, but few poets would wish to be associated with a single idea, even a positive one such as heroism, witness, or dissidence. Nowhere is this more true than in the case of the poets under consideration.

There is often more poetry than can fit within a single reputation; it may not be facetious to speculate that poets may be discussed in terms of multiple reputations. For example, despite Brodsky's insistence that poetry and politics have no more in common than their first two letters, his reputation as a poet and especially an essayist owes much to the effect of politics upon his life and thought. Should we, then, separate his political reputation, as one who resisted totalitarianism, from his poetic reputation, or, even more complicatedly, admit that this political reputation may combine fruitfully with his expository work but *not* his verse? Miłosz recognizes that his own poems can be grouped into miniature canons from which different reputations could arise, such as that of a politically engaged poet – we simply have to pick and choose certain poems and overlook others ('Separate Nations' 3). What of the fact that Miłosz often uses passive constructions to speak of his engagement in history, stating that history forced his hand, or that he describes poems coming in moments of daimonic inspiration – does it make sense to coalesce these moments into a single narrative with its implication of continuity? For instance, we may describe Miłosz's wartime experiences and years of poverty as preconditions for later wisdom; this narrative would imply a steadily developing consciousness. His work, however, fascinates by its quick flashes of bewilderment, anger, or despair when the poet *cannot* find his way, or in radiant moments of happiness that is inexplicable to him and to us. We cannot always share, only admire, great wisdom; the objective correlative of the poem can, on the other hand, make us share flashes of feeling, non-logical and non-progressive.

Eastern European poets often find themselves bearers of memory, as the individual's experience is readily taken as a synecdoche for collective experiences. Meanwhile, a memory becomes increasingly symbolic as our distance from it increases. Cavanagh considers the position of Eastern European poets as 'acknowledged legislators,' and the distinction between an individual, caught up by events and trying to live through them as best he can, and an acknowledged legislator, is easily effaced. It may not be fair, though, to take a poet as a legislator when his concern is with survival or recollection (Cavanagh is well aware of this problem). Heaney is extraordinarily sensitive to this issue. His own conscientious consciousness is always mediating the claims of the many against the life of the individual. Although he recognizes one's inevitable subsumption into various collectives – for instance, into the mass of English-language readers, whose opinions and presuppositions can sometimes be generalized – he also recognizes its inevitable unfairness. The individual may feel bullied by the blunt force of generalizations. Yet we accord an individual's words weight by associating them with a collective. We add weight to historical experience by attributing moral significance to it, so the preservation of memory is connected to the cultivation of a moral sense. The call to 'never forget' reminds us that our ethics are formed in the crucibles of historical events. Our attempt to learn from the past is not just tactical. Nowhere is this more evident than in the work of Eastern European poets, and it is of great value for Heaney. We are, however, led back to questions of comparative methodology when we ask how a writer from a foreign culture *can* be a historical and moral example; while Heaney does not appear overly troubled about this question, his critics are. I will explore this comparison from different angles – culturally in the first two chapters, where I will explore Anglo-American readers' expectations for Eastern European poetry in chapter 1 and the 'heroic' examples that these poets offer in chapter 2, then concretely and comparatively in the successive three chapters, wherein I will elucidate the influence of Zbigniew Herbert (chapter 3) and of Czesław Miłosz (chapters 4 and 5). At all times, Heaney's life and poetry will guide the discussion.

The first chapter will assume the greatest distance towards the phenomenon at hand – namely, the critical and creative vogue for Eastern European writing that swept over Great Britain and the United States during the Cold War. It was most pronounced in the 1980s, and Heaney's *Station Island* (1984) and *The Haw Lantern* (1987), as well as his expository *The Government of the Tongue* (1988), form its high-water mark. This chapter situates these volumes in a transatlantic context that is both cultural and political, given that the cultural fascination with Eastern Europe had a political basis. It was not unnoticed on the 'other side' of Europe, and the much-esteemed Eastern poets sometimes took part in a cynical backlash against this fascination, even while the backlash itself kept these poets in the middle of scholarly discussion (*plus ça change* ...). Heaney did not turn cynic. Instead, he welcomed the general interest in poets he had been reading for many years, and took part in the critical re-evaluations of Anglo-American literature that were stimulated by these foreign poets' presence in English translation.

There is a distinction to be made between those poets *creatively* inspiring Heaney to write poems in dialogue with or emulation of theirs, and those who stand as 'heroic names' in the book of honour. This is the topic of chapter 2, which examines these names, the stories behind them, what they are called upon to do, and how they work together. Some of them do, in surprising ways; some do not, even if a few intrepid critics have sought out unusual alignments. One factor here is the romance of heroic narratives, which may be compounded by a differently rooted – but no less potent – opposition to scientific modernity on the part of certain of Heaney's precursors. Whereas Heaney himself does not belabour this point (though he cites certain passages on the topic with admiration), it must be kept in the background if we are to understand the spirit of his admiration for these writers. Concrete, verifiable narratives (such as that of Osip Mandelstam's suffering and death, or Brodsky's dramatic exile) have a great impact, but so does an insubstantial, unverifiable feeling of alliance with some personalities over others.

The effect of Zbigniew Herbert upon Heaney, however, is quite concrete, although it is never obvious, and this is the focus of the third chapter. In Herbert, we see a poet whom Heaney emulates in a complicated manner, never actually copying a poem into his own form, yet taking on his key motifs and postures. 'The Pebble' and 'The Knocker' exert the most powerful effect upon Heaney's work, both in terms of their central trope – object as bearer of judgment – and, more complicatedly, by their dramatizations of self-judgment. This is the theme of Heaney's *Station Island*, the volume on which Herbert exerts his greatest influence. Behind the matter of poetic influence lies reputation, yet here Heaney demonstrates his independence from public opinion: without overtly rebelling against the public image of Herbert – and Herbert is a poet with an often-overbearing public image – Heaney brings Herbert into his own sphere, and modifies his view of the poet as his own poetic focus changes. Is this literary opportunism? Does it 'misread' Herbert's reputation, and are we obligated to take the public view of a poet into account while responding to him privately, to suit our own poetic, psychological, and cultural needs?

The questions are rhetorical insofar as art is necessarily opportunistic, and its success does not depend upon accuracy or judiciousness.[4] When we consider creative influence, however, such questions are inescapable. In this context, they necessitate bringing together critical and poetic voices from four countries: Ireland, Poland, England, and the United States. They all inform Heaney's relationship with Herbert and Miłosz. The fourth chapter will approach Heaney's long literary relationship with Miłosz from a cultural, historical, and poetic point of view. Since his unusual life fascinates Heaney, a brief biographical interlude will allow us to see where Miłosz was, literally and figuratively speaking, when Heaney encountered him and started reading his work in earnest in the early 1970s. It is several years, though, before Miłosz enters Heaney's *poetry* – thirteen, to be exact. *Station Island* allows us to see how Miłosz enters Ireland, as it were, in the guise of a Yeatsian master. Heaney incorporates Miłosz's prose as well as verse into his work, and the autobiographical *Native Realm* exerts considerable influence upon him. In fact, it would be inadequate to say that Miłosz is merely another poetic influence; Heaney's intense interest in the elder Pole's life, circumstances, philosophy, morality, and poetic work begs to be called friendship or tutelage, depending on how much we wish to stress his view of Miłosz as, in his own words, the 'Master' or 'my hero,' or whether we view it as a relationship of equals, fellow-craftsmen.

The terms we use to discuss Miłosz, or any other poet for that matter, are the subject of a spirited argument explored in chapter 5 between A. Alvarez and Miłosz, which affects Miłosz's self-positioning and Heaney's changing response. Literary history is not a neutral playground for discussions of influences and alliances. Whereas Heaney quietly maintains his lifelong sympathy for the English Romantics who have continuously nourished his imagination, Miłosz maintains a lifelong quarrel with Polish Romanticism. When it comes to individuals, though, he tries to present Adam Mickiewicz – with whom he is sometimes compared – under a different label to American readers. This historical discrepancy between Heaney and Miłosz's views becomes pivotal when we consider the way Heaney reads Miłosz, and how it affects Heaney's own writing. The central distinction is that between expressivism and obliquity or irony. They need not be diametrically opposed, but the difference of these techniques, grounded in different approaches to literary history (here the influence of T.S. Eliot on Miłosz is key), underlies the discrepancy between Heaney and Miłosz's work. Heaney attempts a bold unification of their themes and perspectives in *The Haw Lantern* and then, brilliantly, in his recent (2006) elegy, which definitively tilts the scales in favour of a visionary rather than a sternly didactic Miłosz.

The nature of Heaney's allegories, written under the aegis of Miłosz and of Herbert, is not easy to define, and even less easy to judge. Heaney experiments with a type of poetic language that is new to him. In order to take a synoptic view of Heaney's intersections with Eastern European poetry, we must take cognizance of the responses his own work occasioned, to see how others have assessed this complex stage of his career. The Conclusion appraises Heaney's work at this stage by taking on some of his most outspoken critics. Asking whether we can, in fact, view Eastern European poets as part of a group, and whether we can view their influence as a discrete phenomenon in Heaney's career, this section ends by assessing the legacy of Eastern European poetry. Given that it is so often discussed in terms of content, my final line of inquiry sets the demands of content against the force of form, a dichotomy that Heaney upholds while insisting that poetry's survival is guaranteed by the latter and not the former; to assess how Heaney negotiates poetic influence, we must assess how its inflection of content is matched or opposed by its inflection of poetic form. The irreconcilability of music and meaning disconcerts Herbert and Miłosz. Learning to hear this discordance, this strain, leads to the creation of a radically different kind of music in Heaney's work than we have heard before.

1 Looking Eastwards

Noble feelings are very dangerous for literature.

Czesław Miłosz

Embarrassing Words

The fact that Seamus Heaney has been influenced by Eastern European poetry is beyond the need of justification. The way in which he has been influenced, the why and the wherefore, not to mention the degree, remain curiously ill-defined. There is, however, a rich context to his interest, one that is not unfamiliar but that is rarely viewed from Heaney's perspective, placing his work in the foreground, his voice as our guide. Heaney's very insistence on the exemplary quality of Eastern European work provides us with the best way to begin such a definition, since he readily delineates the problematic motivating a cultural turn eastwards. The diplomatic and good-natured poet-critic allows himself some emotional breadth when he summarizes the effect of Eastern European poetry upon English-language readers such as himself, moving between the first-person singular, plural, and the distancing third-person 'poets in the west,' a group from which he wishes to temporarily exempt himself. The manner in which he asserts – *aggressively* asserts – the value of Eastern European poetry in the West, particularly in the English-speaking world, must be reckoned with:

It seems to me that the ultimately powerful thing about the major poets of Russia and Eastern Europe in our time is not their courageous, necessary and fiercely local work of resistance to a totalitarian ideology but their verification of words which poets in the west have become almost too embarrassed to utter: words like faith, hope, justice, spirit, love, words which were abandoned as a precaution against falsity and inflation but whose abandonment has resulted in a kind of cultural and spiritual debilitation. Admittedly, the ways in which they got spoken in the poetry of Eastern Europe were usually elaborate and fiercely guarded, but the economy and strictness of the expression by no means diminished the reality of the things expressed. In our situation, in a politicized context where the word 'humanist' is spoken with venom and employed as a term of abuse, where the unmasking of covert forms of oppression within the language has rendered the majority of academic critics incapable of making the canonical poetry of their own cultures valuable to the young, there is something hugely encouraging about the poetry in translation which one has been reading with such respect and gratitude for decades now. (Heaney, 'A Poet's Europe' 159–60)

Heaney's affirmation begins with negation: power, he asserts, does not inhere in political utility alone. This type of power is noteworthy but not 'ultimate,' not the power that will last until the end. For readers of his verse, this is not a surprising statement; Heaney has always insisted on the word's ultimate ability to release energies that act within and upon both the individual and the community. The word does not simply mediate but creates, performs, makes present. In his above-cited formulation, the word verifies. It verifies the content of other words, words that have come to be viewed with suspicion. What happens here is that Heaney's statement of admiration becomes a disquisition on abstraction and, more precisely, the words we use to denote abstract values (faith, hope, justice) and abstract entities (spirit).

His desire to affirm the importance of this poetry is, moreover, preemptively deprecated as 'chic,' a term threatening to trivialize deep analysis. Heaney declines to furnish a list of his most admired Eastern poets, stating that 'the more comprehensive it becomes, the more chic it begins to sound: which is what we are up against, of course, this tendency of affirmative statement to go hollow' (160). Following the 'chic' may lead to hollowness, as personal choice is overshadowed by mass desire, which empties out the pointed, poignant statements Heaney could make (and does make elsewhere) on the particular poets who are meaningful to him. The compulsion to affirm, then, must take into account our distrust of the hollowness that may accompany affirmation yet need not. Yet hollowness results not just from the vagaries of fashion but from the conditions deprecated by Heaney earlier in his statement – exaggerated fear of bombast, embarrassment, stultification, and the over-politicization of the academy. Whether this hollowness is a 'tendency' in our contemporary culture is, meanwhile, a not incontestable point. Heaney delivers this summative assessment in 1991; its cultural context will serve to underscore its originality, even while 'embarrassment' over what was perceived as the current weakness of Anglo-American poetry was surprisingly widespread.[1]

Thomas Parkinson points out a similar tendency in contemporary culture as Heaney does, yet he speaks in 1979, at the time that Eastern European poetry was most visible and celebrated.[2] What Heaney refers to as 'our culture' is, presumably, the same scholarly and artistic Anglo-American culture of which Parkinson (a Yeats scholar and an Americanist) speaks. He holds that this culture's 'stress on the definite and the specific,' and corollary valuation thereof, causes us to embrace 'the concept of the concrete as being desirable as an end in itself' (Parkinson 661) in contemporary poetic practice. He connects this circumstance to the rise of free verse and a widespread view that poetic form should not be rigidly prescribed, but should organically take the shape of the unique experience it seeks to capture (660); yet such a view ignores the fact that the *most* definite and specific facets of life (statistics; data of all kinds) may prove irrelevant, not to mention boring, if they enter a poem. It also ignores the fact that some of the most famous lines in modern poetry are not specific or definite at all: Stevens's 'Death is the mother of beauty' does not offer an image, concrete experience, or psychological state to the reader. What, then, should we call such lines? The word 'abstract' is the obvious antonym to choose, yet the word seems hardly fitting. Parkinson uses the term when he posits that 'language is by its very nature vocal in its tonal structures and abstract in its reference' (661). By this he means that words cannot actually present an object to the addressee; they can intend to present it and emphasize the objective, but cannot 'actually' heal the rift between signifier and signified content.

The necessity of looking sceptically upon the injunction to ground ideas in things must be emphasized, since it lies behind Heaney's enthusiasm for Eastern European poetry and at least partly behind his aloofness towards some contemporary American poetry, particularly towards Charles Olson and the Objectivist group. He is more sympathetic to the Confessionals than to the Objectivists, whose poetics are equally far from those of Zbigniew Herbert and Czesław Miłosz, but he is simultaneously attracted to the language of value – 'faith,' 'hope,' 'justice' – that must be called abstract. A sort of 'cultural and spiritual debilitation' ensues when we insist too much upon concreteness, which Heaney tacitly links to modesty and decorum. This latter term is used by Parkinson in his paper to indicate the necessity of referring the chosen signifier *back* to a hierarchy of values which determine the function of the word in the poem as a whole. Decorum may be viewed a matter of form, not of subject. This notion is crucial to Heaney's sense of the Eastern Europeans' salutary openness to an abstract language of values.

The impact of such remarks on Heaney, who was on the same conference panel as Parkinson, and who had already spent considerable time in the American academy, would not have been lost. His later words show that he has reflected on the ability of a foreign poetry to change the terms in which we assert poetic value. Heaney's statement grounds itself in his cultural situation, though this does not serve to qualify its claims; Heaney pre-empts criticism of cultural relativism – Eastern European poetry fulfils a locally specific function, and as such is incomparable with English-language poetry – by asserting that the value of this work cannot be reductively categorized in terms of its dissident value and safely labelled as exotic. The foreignness of its language is the key to its relevance; it exposes the 'debilitation' of our own literary language by means of its contrastive force. Heaney's words thrum with pent-up indignation: our disparagement of humanism and glorification of anti-humanism, our mad hunt to uncover oppression within the language, and our conviction that the canon is now suspect, if not indefensible, are seen as results of the politicization of our 'context' (i.e., literary culture). The negative charge of '*academic* critics' suggests that our rage for politics is the rage of academics who are not active participants in the world of telegrams and anger (in contrast to the grand example of Yeats, poet and politician). Heaney's hypothetical contemporary critic, presumably fed a diet of post-Foucauldian theory, tragically silences herself when it comes to communicating value. If a critic's task is to communicate value – which certainly appears to be Heaney's own view – then one must beware of political agendas that may compromise one's ability to do so. This belief will be crucial to our examination of Heaney's responses to Eastern European poetry.

His statement mounts a post factum defence of the poetry 'which one has been reading ... for decades now' at the moment when contemporary theory dominated the literary academy. The difference of its terms from those of contemporary theory – and, by extension, criticism, which applies these terms – paradoxically helps to establish its continuing importance. Although Heaney's most intense exposure to this poetry occurs earlier, in the 1970s and mid-1980s, its influence perseveres, as his 1991 remarks make evident, justifying a certain oppo- sitional perspective towards the British and American literary scenes. His remarks also retrospectively illuminate the function that Eastern European poetry is and was called upon to perform. This function can be subdivided by its application to three concentric arenas of influence: that of Heaney's poetic development, of English-language poetry taken as a whole, and of contemporary intellectual culture.

Slavic Chic

However Heaney may decry the sudden 'chicness' of Eastern European work in the late twentieth century, it is undeniable that this vogue is responsible for bringing him face to face with the poetry in the first instance. The reasons *for* it are complex, but include a fascination with the Iron Curtain, the astoundingly high quality of poetry being pro- duced behind this curtain, the popularity of Daniel Weissbort and Ted Hughes's *Modern Poetry in Translation* journal, the widespread view that the English-language masters Yeats and Eliot were, and would re- main, unparalleled, and the championship of Hughes and A. Alvarez. In his famous introduction to *The New Poetry* in 1962, Alvarez decries the 'negative feed-backs' that motivate each new generation of British poets and calls for a 'new seriousness' that will abolish – or, rather, ren- der ineffective and frivolous – the preponderance of 'gentility.' This is a quintessentially English quality, and Alvarez calls for a turn towards the United States and towards continental Europe; shortly after this, he remains true to his word by editing the Penguin series of Modern European Poets in translation. Despite its exaggerations, the intro- duction usefully links poetry's seriousness to 'a sense of being chal- lenged by its own history, which includes being challenged by history' (Longley, *Poetry and Posterity* 220). Fran Brearton goes so far as to hypoth- esize that this series of 'negative feed-backs' played a part in stimulating the poetic resurgence, dubbed the 'Northern Ireland Renaissance,' oc- curring in the 1960s and 1970s (Brearton in Matthew Campbell 94–112); this 'Renaissance' is marked by the rise of Heaney himself as well as his friends Derek Mahon and Michael Longley. This is also the time when the Northern Irish Troubles break forth, so that the 1960s bring both violence and poetry to the forefront of discussions about culture. Just as Heaney was starting to search for a means to symbolize his native country's predicament, he was also reading newly translated work by Eastern European poets such as Miroslav Holub (1967), Zbigniew Herbert (1968), and Vasko Popa (1969). *Modern Poetry in Translation* was publishing work by these poets and others in an attempt to counter 'the inertness of the English scene at the time, and the American scene too, as it seemed to us,' Daniel Weissbort recollects, and the journal allowed poets themselves to encounter each other's work (see Amichai in Weissbort 305–12). New readerships and new sympathies were quickly formed.

Heaney echoes Alvarez and Weissbort's sentiments two decades later as he attempts his own diagnosis of British poetry in 'The Impact of Translation,' claiming that the 'geopolitical phantasmagorias' of early Auden and the visionary, though 'low-wattage,' poetry of Edwin Muir point to a road not taken by mid-century verse (*The Government of the Tongue* 41). Instead, the turgid rhetoric and spilt Romanticism of Dylan Thomas was followed by the long legacy of tight, formally chaste, thematically straitened verse associated with the literary group dubbed the Movement (a major proponent of Alvarez's 'gentility'). Neither introduced the note that Alvarez and Heaney wished to hear sounded.[3] Meanwhile, Heaney was trying to respond to the explosion of violence in Northern Ireland, a phenomenon that separated him from the Americans and the English. Neither turgid rhetoric nor gentility would do. Asked by an *Irish Times* reporter whether he envied the 'quiet lives' of American or British poets, Heaney controversially replies, 'Well, no, I actually don't. The Americans are at bay in prosperity and freedom ... [;] the poet in America for a long time has had great difficulty in escaping from the arena of the first-person singular. In England, I think the poet has great difficulty in escaping from the civility of the literary tradition itself' (Heaney in O'Donoghue 66–7). This civility did not obtain in Eastern Europe, where gentility is a quality for which to fight (see Zbigniew Herbert's darkly ironic 'A Question of Taste'). American and English poetry are seen, by Heaney, to be mired in their respective traditions, despite their claims to cutting-edge contemporaneity. The Irish situation was different. So was the Polish.

In the 1970s, then, English poetry was seen to be entering a doldrums after the triumph of the Movement aesthetic, whereas Polish poetry was at a high point. Heaney had already worked through the influence of Ted Hughes and Geoffrey Hill, the two contemporary Englishmen most amenable to his own aesthetic. Irish poetry from the Republic maintained a presence in Heaney's mind, but he was, at the moment, interested in reaching beyond the island, and connecting the work of past masters Dante and Wordsworth (constant presences in his work) to contemporary masters, and of setting his voice beside – sometimes against – the voices of Northern Irish compatriots and acquaintances.[4] American poetry was strong, but not very influential for Heaney aside from the work of Robert Lowell, who is a shadow presence in *Field Work* (1979). Interestingly, Heaney's time in the United States served to stabilize his own aesthetic more than to introduce new influences into his poetry. This unusual point demands further exposition. Heaney's first extended trip to the United States took place in 1970 to 1971, when he was a visiting assistant professor at the University of California at Berkeley. He had been living and working in Northern Ireland (as a teacher and then a lecturer at Queen's University); the academic year in Berkeley introduced him to a culture he called 'weightless,' a word perhaps inadvertently echoing Czesław Miłosz's *Visions from San Francisco Bay*. In a telling metaphorical opposition, this gravity-less culture actually 'put the screws on my own aesthetic' (Heaney in Brandes 17). The young poet, then, tightened and fixed his own aesthetic *in opposition to* the loose forms he encountered in the United States. Heaney's apologetic defence is telling: 'There comes a point when honesty to your own prejudice is as proper as attempts to overcome it,' he tells his interviewer, conceding that 'sometimes I think that the thing I want to hear is not even sought after' (17). The problem, then, hearkens back to Parkinson's remarks about Anglo-American poetry's valuation of particular virtues at the (necessary?) expense of others. This valuation affects the Confessional movement, which, to Heaney, exaggerates an underlying tendency of American verse: 'People are driven in on their First Person Singular in a distressed way and, of course, this makes them yearn for the kind of collective identity some other countries have; yearn for conditions of extreme duress, even' (Heaney in Beisch 167). In its embrace of open forms and the inward gaze, American poetry did not furnish Heaney with the sense of 'something that has come through constraint into felicity,' the 'preciousness ... of wise feeling become eternally posthumous in perfect cadence' that could best be found in 'poetry that contains and practices force within a confined area' (17). Instead, it presented him with the big open howl of the Ginsbergian, to use his own terms, which, while powerful, did not strike the note he wished to strike himself.

The question begged by this situation is how and why a country embracing the influence of Williams and Pound, celebrating Ginsberg and Olson, would also participate in the enthusiasm for Eastern European poets that straddled the Atlantic Ocean, bringing together formalists and non-formalists alike in their appreciation of Czesław Miłosz, Zbigniew Herbert, Miroslav Holub, and Osip Mandelstam, to name four poets specifically admired by Heaney. Given that the dominant poetic practices in Great Britain, the two Irelands, and the United States were various enough that terms such as 'specificity' and 'concreteness' barely do enough work to bring them together, we must query the cogency of non-poetic reasons for the 'Slavic chic' of the later mid-century. The most obvious is the mystery created by the metaphor of the Iron Curtain itself: Slavic countries were seen as definitively 'other' and took on the mystique of inaccessibility. More importantly, the high quality of the 'Old Masters' (as Miłosz, Herbert, Wisława Szymborska, and Tadeusz Różewicz are called in Poland today) was indubitable, as was that of several other prominent Eastern European poets (Mandelstam, Holub, Popa), and *they*, too, underscored the separateness of their poetic tradition, particularly from that of the United States. The middle term in the West-East binary turns out to be history. Asked why Eastern European poetry tends to be spiritual and moral, not psychological, Miłosz replies thus:

> It may be indicative of our whole set-up in my part of Europe, the terrible pressure of historical events, the constant historical spasms. And so it directs attention away from one's purely personal problems. In American poetry, there is a lot of subjectivity and the internal world of the poet, which is not the case with poetry from our area. There is a sort of tendency to objectivize more. And so psychology – well, let us not divulge too many secrets ... There is an anthology of Polish aphorisms by an author who says, 'Never confess your dreams. What if the Freudians come to power?' (Interview with Mona Simpson in Haven, *Czesław Miłosz* 9)

The difference of modern Eastern European history from that of the wealthy West impels Eastern poets to write differently, so that the *West*, with its confessionalists and what Heaney calls 'reflexive talents' folded into themselves, points up a road not taken to the *East*. This is how we

could have written, Miłosz implies, had we not had so much historical upheaval. History has forced us to direct our gaze elsewhere, away
from the 'internal world' of the singular self. Miłosz clearly does not
want to sound disparaging; instead, he turns, with delicate comicality,
to a seemingly offhanded reference that points up exactly the difference
at the centre of this argument: the typically Eastern humour involved
in the question of who might hold the reins of power in the future is a
humour predicated upon a sense of historical absurdity, which is based
on the real experience of totalitarian rule. History has forced the hands
of the Eastern Europeans. They respond by adapting their writing so
that it parries the thrusts of historical conflict.

It is a dangerous point. Miłosz's delicate sense of humour is not
echoed by others who espouse the same basic tenet. In a provocative
article, Chris Miller places what he deems the 'resignation of thematic
ambition' in post-war poetry in English and the vogue for Eastern Europe side by side (14), adducing important corollary facts such as the
enormous print runs of state-financed poetry in the Soviet Union and
the dark glamour of Soviet-era suffering: 'The drama of [Eastern European poets'] lives was such as to make the life of the average English
poet seem somewhat insignificant. Here were poets in the thick of history' (24). He is quick to add that 'there is something necessarily fallacious ... about the appeal of their horribly interesting times, though the
courage of the lives they lived is self-evidently attractive.' This courage
attracts Heaney, of course, and his admiration is evident in every remark devoted to the subject, yet it need not be *aesthetically* interesting.
Miller comes closer to the mark when he posits the adequation of these
poets to the turbulence they survived (24). The status of the poet rose as
a result of this turbulence. A fascination with oppression also dictates
the selection principle behind Alvarez's *Under Pressure*, which seeks to
showcase the experience of 'total war' and totalitarianism, yet is also
guided by the rather separate principle of translatability.[5] Adam Czerniawski, considering Alvarez and others, stresses the role of political
turmoil even more forcefully: 'However interesting and innovative a
literary phenomenon, ... it will not attract wide-spread recognition unless there are already political forces at work which focus attention on
the author's country' (72–3; Alvarez makes a similar point in his later
book *Where Did It All Go Right?*). Miller, like Czerniawski, identifies the
Movement's detrimental effect on English poetry, curiously viewing it
as post-traumatic fallout from the Second World War. This phenomenon separates the United States from Great Britain, yet writers and

scholars in both countries are fascinated by Eastern Europe, even where there is no trauma to be vanquished. We may add the point, alluded to by several of the writers here mentioned, that the status of the poet is, and has been, notoriously low in England and in the United States. The joke that poets are viewed so highly in the Soviet bloc that they are killed for their work is relevant to the issue, if rather distasteful in its own voyeuristic adequation of pain with value.

Part of this high status of the Eastern European poet is due to the important fact that, in Miller's words, 'the poetry reader in the East identified the non-official language of poetry with truth, a literally Edenic condition for the Western poet: that she should set down words that define reality' (16). Heaney's comment about words we are embarrassed to utter comes to mind. In a social context where the press routinely lied, however, this situation smacks less of pretension than of desperation – not an Edenic condition, perhaps, but a comprehensible one deserving of respect. The identification of poetry with clandestine, necessary truth may run counter to contemporary views of literary language, but this identification may also account for its appeal to academic readers who covertly longed for egress from a hyper-sophisticated, linguistically suspicious view of literature. Miller points to 'affirmation' as the salient quality in Soviet-era poetry that won over Western readers, by which he means 'the ability to state positive values in a form poetically convincing' (23) – in other words, a form that lacked sentimentality or imprecision. One of the most striking qualities of Herbert and Milosz's verse is its lucidity. Their position as undisputed masters of the craft, as well as their irony, held embarrassment at the promotion of 'positive values' at bay. Their affirmative morality is not tiresomely catechetical because of its hard-edged clarity. Here is a germinal irony: poets such as Herbert or Holub do not describe the suffering of Eastern Europeans in language whose goal is to elicit pity or to terrify with stark realism. Their clarity is not that of the documentary filmmaker but of the ironist. They still, however, take their place silhouetted against the backdrop of their suffering under totalitarian law, and this backdrop is crucial for understanding their reputations west of the Iron Curtain.[6]

We may conclude that Eastern European poetry struck Western readers because of its difference, not similarity, and that this difference had its roots in politics and its branches in the more rarefied air of affirmative abstractions (truth, hope, justice, the good). There is a danger, however, in underscoring the difference of this poetry. It inheres in an implied disparity between the different and the influential. The gap between these concepts, and the way in which those who participated in the 'chic' for Eastern European poetry started to critique it in the late 1980s and beyond, is illuminated by Heaney's own public comments. Speaking at the same 1979 conference panel as Parkinson, Heaney examines Ted Hughes's fascination with the conditions of Eastern European poetry: 'I think it was Miłosz, the Polish poet, who when he lay in a doorway and watched the bullets lifting the cobbles out of the street behind him realized that most poetry is not equipped for life in a world where people actually do die.' These are Hughes's words as recalled by Heaney, who then remarks that the 'disappointment at the inadequacy of art is born perhaps from a too great expectation of art' – a modest disclaimer – 'yet it surely awakens a sympathetic response in the Western reader and the Western writer.' This is the same Heaney who, elsewhere, quotes Miłosz's lines 'What is poetry which does not save / Nations or people?' He shares Miłosz's excessive expectation for art as 'surely' as he shares Hughes's admiration of it, and as readily as he extends it to us, who find ourselves sharing his admiration in large part because it responds to the dire context from which Miłosz spoke. Heaney justifies this extension by participating in the general diagnosis of English-language poetry's insufficiency:

> Our attraction to these extreme statements and images suggests that somewhere within us there lurks an assumption that the poetry of Britain, Ireland, and America is somewhat otiose in comparison with what it should or might be ... the impatience we have with talkiness, linguistic slackness, metrical wooliness, arbitrary forms and line endings, the unease we experience when faced with a too complacent surrealist inventiveness, the irritation we feel at a self-regarding poetry, a poetry of the orphaned self, the enclosed psyche – all this implies an assumption that our poetry has failed to live up to E.M. Forster's imperative, 'Only connect,' ... connect the literary action with an original justifying vision and with the political contingencies of the times ... Much contemporary poetry assumes that it is no match for telegrams and anger and so keeps to the exquisite, the private, the good cause. ('Current Unstated Assumptions' 646)

In such a straitened poetic climate, 'certain kinds of assumption are looked upon as presumption.' The central assumption about poetry, though, that still obtains, is that the poet's ambition will reach higher than mere aestheticism or histrionics, and that poetry will retain both a 'public force' and its own 'private rights' (650). The main question that remains is which kind of assumption is presumption. Does Eastern

European poetry prove so exciting to English speakers because it happily crosses the boundary into presumption ('What is poetry which does not save / Nations or people')? Heaney implies that presumption is thematic and vocal – the arrogation of power – and can be linked to subject-matter but also to audience: a voice presumes that it can speak *of* and *to* the times in which it lives, including times when 'telegrams and anger' dominate its social context. The stultified vision of overly modest, non-presumptive contemporary poetry does not, however, go hand in hand with formal tautness, as it could. This poetry sins by 'talkiness' as well as formal imprecision ('slackness,' 'wooliness') and even arbitrariness. Heaney's indictment of contemporary Anglo-American verse points to the misfit between ungoverned voice and overly modest content ('the orphaned self,' 'the enclosed psyche'); his sights seem to be set on post-confessional, creative-writing-class poems, invariably written in free verse without inherent formal logic, about and for the self. To it he opposes Eastern European writing.

Heaney's process inverts Alvarez's: instead of naming the qualities that led 'us' to value Eastern European verse, he uses the valuation as proof of deficiency in English poetry. His statement of unfulfilled potential implies that certain conditions might bring that potential to fruition, yet he is too subtle to participate in the fascination with horror that Miller describes; instead, Heaney straightaway suggests what poets can learn from their own attraction to the Eastern Europeans. Admiration leads to advice. 'Otiose,' derived from the Latin 'otium' (leisure), communicates impatience with 'our' poetry's lack of consequence, a point that will be utilized very differently almost a decade later. Heaney never invalidates his 1979 statements, but does signal an end to his own attempt to assimilate the purposeful (un-otiose) charge of Eastern European poetry into his own work, claiming that his process of learning from a poet such as Zbigniew Herbert had, eventually, come to a natural end, and warning against the *merely* 'useful' function of poetry in his renewed defence of the poetic pleasure principle:

> Well, Herbert I think is a finished writer, in the good sense. I don't think anybody can learn much from Herbert ... His is a kind of writing shared by many language groups ...[;] writing in which the poetry is in the plotting, where the poetry doesn't seem to reside in the dwelling upon a privileged moment of insight or joy. The poetry dwells more in the laying bare of patterns in a reality beyond the poet ... It's the truth-seeking dimension of poetry. And yet, I do think that in poetry just being useful is a bigger sin than just being pleasurable. (Brandes 10–11)

Heaney speaks these words in 1988, after the publication of *Station Island* and *The Haw Lantern,* perhaps justifying his eventual turn to other poetic models. Of course he is not correct. He has learned immensely from Herbert on both the level of 'plotting' *and* on a higher level, in which the relationship of poetic subject to metaphorical object is established. Heaney's striking statement opposes writers who are 'finished' ('in the good sense') to writers from whom we can learn. This undefined quality – which almost presages an early death for Herbert, as a poet who *had* 'finished' his service to the lyric – lets Heaney conclude that he cannot have Herbert serve as a lifelong mentor because he is, perhaps, too exotically, unapproachably 'finished.' The subsequent generality assumes that nobody for whom Herbert is absolutely different, therefore unassimilable, can learn much from him. This is a slightly ungenerous way to lay Herbert to rest, at least momentarily – he will formally elegize him ten years later.

Heaney's comments, however, offer one way to consider the influence that Eastern European poets do have: 'laying bare' trumps the Romantically 'privileged moment of insight,' truth takes the upper hand over inspiration, and a new conflict, of utility and pleasure, comes to the fore. Heaney is speaking in the final years of Slavic chic, the late 1980s, which will soon become historical once communism falls in 1989 and the most obviously 'useful' dimension of this poetry becomes unnecessary. His qualified warning that 'just being useful' may be a grave literary sin registers his own dissatisfaction, perhaps, with the fashion for 'useful' Eastern European poetry, though the obvious fact that this poetry may *also* 'just [be] pleasurable' for aficionados is not granted its weight. Utility may be a key component of our fascination with this poetry, and this quality inevitably refers to context. Unusually for Heaney, his statement affirms value through composition ('plotting') and context (utility) rather than feeling or pleasure, and therein lies its tacit critique. The voyeuristic underside of the fashion for Eastern Europe – its fascination with the *conditions* of poetry – shows us the reason why it waned.[7]

Slavic Chic Critiqued

The effect of this fascination with oppression is, according to Miroslav Holub, that attention to context displaces attention to content: 'From many anthologies and learned essays we, who are labeled east-European authors, even gain the impression that we are specialists in suffering and bitterness rather than in words' (Holub 22). Again we are confronted with a subtle humour flashing out from one of these so-called specialists – Holub alerts us to the alienating quality of the Anglo-American image of poets such as himself. Of course, the danger of distortion is present in all scholarship on the arts, which does not hold a mirror up to its objects but shapes them to fit the dictates of intellectual argument (or, at worst, ideology or academic fashion); Holub knows this. He directs his pique not at the scholarly establishment per se but at the blindness to artistry that it manifests. In the same piece, though, he warns that poetry 'needs some pressure ... from the environment so as not to evaporate, as we know from the physics of postmodernism ... In that respect we were for a long time at a great advantage' (22). Perhaps the critics were right in one respect: by fetishizing the dire conditions of poetry production, they tacitly recognized that poetry, to be valuable, cannot be mere play. Alvarez's metaphor of being 'under pressure' is modified to great effect by the scientific Holub.

Miłosz makes a more pointed comment about this pressure: 'Communism has given Polish literature an incredible chance. Always historically oriented, but preoccupied only with Poland's history, suddenly it was confronted with a universal theme. Few writers drew the appropriate conclusions' (Miłosz, interview with Mona Simpson in Haven, *Czesław Miłosz* 7–11). Few writers could make the pressured situation universally applicable, we may conclude, and satisfy the desire for translatability of experience as well as language, yet we may recall Miłosz's approbation of historical awareness. Stanisław Barańczak begs to differ: Communist Poland 'could rightly be described as a country where poetry was needed,' wherein people had great expectations of poetry, yet 'by and large' it met those expectations (Barańczak, *A Fugitive from Utopia* 4). The need that Barańczak discerns is a local condition, like the 'chance' to which Miłosz refers; by positing the larger value of these local situations, Holub allows us to hypothesize the translocal significance of Eastern European 'pressure' without claiming it as a necessary and sufficient condition for good work.

Geoffrey Hill also begs to differ. His essay 'Language, Suffering, and Silence' is the most damning indictment of literature 'under pressure' available, published well after the vogue for this poetry had run its course (1999). Hill quotes the same passage as Heaney, quoting Hughes, had identified as an indictment of literature's insufficiency to address certain realities. The question at stake is which sort of experiences constitute proof of value, and if we agree that certain experiences do. The passage comes from Miłosz's *The Captive Mind*, suggesting that art's worth is ultimately proved at the moment one is threatened with death, and using as dramatization an image of 'a man' lying on the cobblestone street of a city under fire, watching bullets lift the cobbles. Such 'naked experiences' survive disillusionment and the 'elimination of emotional luxuries' that took place in Eastern Europe (*Captive Mind* 41). The man is obviously Miłosz, and whereas the passage intends to establish an inclusive perspective, Hill reads in it 'the elitism of the man-of-the-moment' (Hill 251) who holds that 'arbitrary extreme experience' constitutes a sort of baptism for art. Hill's anger, which seems as 'hectoring' as the tone of the passage he isolates, weakens his credibility, but his argument gains strength both in its counter-examples – Dickinson, Whitman, and Shakespeare's sonnets are adduced as works that do not depend upon 'extreme experience' for their value – and in its most general effect, as a reaction against what Hill sees as a certain prescription for literary success. Miłosz is not prescriptive, nor would he uphold Arnold's rejection of passive suffering as a theme for poetry in the stringent spirit Hill attributes to him, but Hill is associating him with the prescriptions (and proscriptions) *implied* by a whole cultural field. He is actually reacting not against Miłosz but against the excesses of 'Slavic chic,' in the derogatory sense of 'chic' as superficial and transient excess of enthusiasm for something whose value cannot be extended. Miłosz does not state that suffering has intrinsic value. The excessive celebration of 'specialists in suffering,' in Holub's terms, begins to imply that it does, if only because it is difficult to find another term by which to link poets as various as Holub, Miłosz, Herbert, Brodsky, and Mandelstam. Hill's essay judges those who hold one type of experience as a guarantor of merit; in fact, Miłosz's aesthetics are not antithetical to Hill's own.

Bruce Murphy's argument represents another sort of criticism, breathing the same air but standing on different ground. The target is, again, Miłosz, possibly because of his prodigious output, but more probably because of the unusual nature of his expository work, which – despite the popularity of certain of its themes – appears to project 'Christian metaphysics or nihilism' as the only possibilities for poetry and, indeed, for human belief (Murphy 168). As if this were not bad enough, Miłosz's longing for neat dichotomies such as that of good and evil, truth and falsity, that would dictate the establishment of 'absolute criteria,' is elucidated in a series of public lectures (*The Witness of Poetry* 50, 56, 48), his contention that art *must* believe in an objective reality is reiterated throughout, and his opposition to all manner of relativism proclaimed. Never mind the continuous contextual (often historical) qualifications Miłosz sets around these pronouncements, which are taken as dicta by Murphy and by Hill – these two commentators oppose the spirit of Miłosz's work more than its content, and this offers their critiques wider resonance: those who experience world-historical events are wrong to make such experience the precondition of artistic excellence or wisdom, those who oppose relativism are naive to think ancient religious values could have universal modern currency, and those who believe 'absolute criteria' for art or morality might be defined are, simply, begging to be discredited in the late twentieth century. It is hard to disagree. An essential difference in cultural fields is being exposed by these critiques: within each field, different experiences may be common, different temporalities may obtain, and the notion of 'absolute criteria' may be contextually situated in a manner that would irk a proponent of complete universalism. Knowledge of context may, paradoxically, *ensure* the translation (perhaps universalization?) of work that may otherwise seem archaic or, even worse, self-promoting.

Once 'Slavic chic' had become an undisputed phenomenon, then, the terms in which it functioned came under scrutiny and summative assessments were ventured, as if this era could be definitively cordoned off. What comes to the fore in these self-scrutinizing discussions is the intent behind terminology: Fran Brearton and Justin Quinn call it 'a certain Western sentimentality about suffering' that leads to eventual fatigue with the question of politics; once this sentimentality had been exposed, there is nothing left to discuss (85), and the poets 'under pressure' cannot live up to the pressure placed upon them by Western readers, and can only disappoint (86). Brearton and Quinn, meanwhile, have kept the Eastern poets as a reference point for their own scholarly work despite this statement of disappointment; they provocatively insist that discussions of Eastern European literature had nowhere left to go after the late 1980s (a much-discussed point in contemporary Eastern European scholarship), and yet this was precisely the time during which the meaning of 'Slavic chic' became a topic eliciting an exciting variety of assessments and extensions, beginning with Heaney's remarks quoted at the beginning of this chapter. The topic now 'under pressure' is surely the social, literary, and psychological needs that this 'chic' answered, beyond the manifestation of a certain voyeuristic sentimentality.

If one motivating factor is a widespread disaffection with English and American poetry of the 1960s and 1970s, then perhaps this phenomenon was fated to end when its effect had been fully registered and absorbed. More ironically, once the terms used to describe the chic poets started to appear repetitively sentimental, the work of these poets was no longer groundbreaking; the hard-edged, unapologetic quality that attracted Heaney was being described in distressingly 'wooly' and platitudinous language (to use his term). Even writers as cosmopolitan as Daniel Weissbort allow themselves to slip into hyperbole: 'The writers who, through the difficult and often tragic times, continued to keep distinctions alive, to insist on individual values in the face of collectivist pressures, to expose the unscrupulousness ... of rulers, surely played an essential part ... in educating, inspiring, and finally empowering the reformers.' Such poets demonstrate 'the resilience of the human spirit' (Weissbort 15, 18). This is certainly true. Yet given that Western readers did not face the same pressures as Eastern poets did, how long could a poetry that was seen in terms of perseverance continue to hold interest on these terms alone? The project of reforming a faraway society may be absorbing, but its relevance to the society of Western readers needs to be demonstrated in order for the poetry to hold their long-term interest. Passionate exposure of unscrupulousness is not enough. If Western poets are to be influenced by their Eastern European contemporaries, then they must seek out terms of commonality as well as difference. Conceptual and poetic links must be forged, alternate paths indicated, affective ties reliant on more than pity and horror established. This is why Heaney's eventual 1991 comments on the *potential* of Eastern European poetic language to show us a path less travelled yet nonetheless available are essential to our understanding of Eastern European literature's relevance.

The key term of Weissbort's statement proves to be 'distinctions': these exotic writers keep certain distinctions alive. Implied is an opposition to other – perhaps, Western – writers (Weissbort published his book in London). They are, by implication, distinctions between right and wrong in the face of tragic pressures to align oneself with a totalitarian regime, individuality and collectivism, unscrupulous action, and hypocritical rhetoric – such as the rhetoric of utopian equality measured against the brutality of real communism. These are straightforward enough. The distinction that fascinates Heaney, however, is complicated: it is between different relations to language, 'verification' of words that denote values and 'embarrassment' or lack of ambition ('A Poet's Europe' 159). Once Eastern European poetry is reduced to a laying bare of patterns (merely *utile*), it becomes less useful to the Western writer than if it is viewed from a greater critical distance as a verification, and this is where a critique of 'Slavic chic' may turn into an affirmation of its continued potential for influence. The distinction between *utile* and *dulce* changes when it is superimposed onto that between verification and embarrassment, and turns into a distinction between 'encouraging' health (with indubitable use-value) and 'debilitation.'

Heaney's 'truth-seeking dimension' of poetry is, perhaps, the dimension where we can speak of universal, and continual, applicability and accessibility ('universalism' has had a poor academic career recently, but the word begs to be used in this context). Its truth may have a local value that leads to sentimental readings, but its value extends far beyond the local, and leads Heaney to ponder the relation to language that such writing encourages:

> [Eastern European writers] are the ones who toed the line, not just the verse line but the line where courage is tested, where to stand by what you write is to have to stand your ground and take the consequences. For these poets, the mood of writing is the indicative mood and for that reason they constitute a shadow-challenge to poets who dwell in the conditional, the indeterminate mood which has grown characteristic of so much of the poetry one has grown used to reading in the journals and new books, particularly in the United States. (*Government* 39)

To Zbigniew Herbert, the line where the private individual tests himself against the oppressive powers-that-be also separates indicative from conditional moods:

> The languages of politics and of literature are entirely different and so are the mentalities. Politicians are concerned with 'far-reaching' goals, personal games, gangster-style tricks. What interests me is human fate ... We use two different styles. I have tried to use the conditional. I hesitate. I appeal to conscience ... I don't like imperatives, exclamation marks, black-and-white divisions. I just don't. (Herbert, trans. Michael March, in Weissbort 322)

Does Heaney misread? Does he misinterpret Herbert's poetry, which possesses a strongly articulated intent? The issue goes beyond translation, though Heaney also lets us know that 'whether we can truly know the driven brilliance of [Eastern European] work through translation is not a question I wish to address here' (*Government* 38). Yet the issue surpasses mere literalness of translation: to both poets, verbal mood is a metaphor for communicative philosophy. It is ethical. Mood separates fact from desire (conditional) and speculation (subjunctive; conditional in English). For Herbert, their difference aligns with the difference between social (political) and individual concerns. Politicians rely on the future indicative: this is the language of 'far-reaching' goals (a cliché usefully ironized by quotation marks), propaganda, and campaigning. It is a performative mode that allows the populace to glimpse a future that they are to believe *will* come to be. The language of conscience is the language of assessment, of ethics, and of the hesitation that must occur while one assesses. Because it is allied with ethics (the study of what we would and should, which are not always aligned), it disclaims the imposition of 'black-and-white divisions' communicated by the indicative. We can only reach the imperative (what we must do) through the conditional. Some of Herbert's most famous poems use the imperative, and rather ostentatiously at that (see 'The Envoy of Mr Cogito'). Herbert's remarks, therefore, cannot be read as a guide to his writing but as a statement of alliance: this is what the poet *would* do. In the background, of course, lurks the real (present-tense indicative) menace of 'gangster-style tricks' played by the communist regime.

Heaney's ability to generalize the attraction of Eastern European poetry is certainly not always accurate when measured against the statements of these poets themselves, just as his statement of Herbert's 'finished,' non-influential quality, is problematic. Yet his accuracy in describing the attraction of these poets for Western audiences is not. His ability to let us know what he desires to see in their work transcends the issue of misreading. Holub's critique of Western reading strategies points to the importance of determining *style* as the crucial and unexamined term in our consideration of the fashion for Eastern Europe. In his comment Herbert is concerned primarily with ethics, which he metaphorizes as a matter of style. In his comment Heaney is concerned primarily with style, which he metaphorizes as a matter of ethics. He cannot restrain his own stylistic exuberance, as his punning ('toed the line') is slightly out of place in this patently serious context but, immediately upon reading, this ceases to matter, as his voice rises and swells. Heaney's sentences achieve some of the 'vault-filling resonance' that he discerns in Miłosz; his lectures and essays on Eastern Europe often achieve this passionate resonance, and whereas it is easy to cavil at their sweeping statements, it is also important to recognize their accurate portrayal of his own desire. These are manifestoes. As such, their insistence on the indicative mood as the mood of challenge to indeterminacy – which is implicitly allied with solipsism, 'wooliness,' and lack of thematic ambition – works on the hortatory level. Heaney's need to communicate what is missing in Anglo-American poetry, and why Eastern European writing can furnish the antidote, impels him to make statements that may not always seem analytically accurate, but advance his project of diagnosis and curative renewal. The extraordinary difference between Heaney's and Herbert's statements, however, points up the necessity of briefly considering Heaney's career in Poland.

Mutual Regard

The focus of this study is on Heaney's response to Eastern European and particularly Polish poetry, since it proved most influential for his own work, but a brief glance at responses to Heaney from this 'other Europe' interestingly highlights the very terms here under scrutiny. A reading of Heaney's poems 'astounds one with a legion of details,' writes Ola Kubińska. Most striking is the minuteness ('drobiazgowość') of Heaney's descriptions, which, Kubińska hastily adds, is surely not a matter of accident but of design, since for Heaney description is an analytical mode (Malcolm and Kubińska 98). Her seemingly obvious statement reveals the deeply felt difference between concretely descriptive, experiential poetry and the poetry of parable and 'aerated' abstraction that Heaney finds so astounding. Details that, to mid-century British and American critics, provide necessary grounding and cogency to the lyric, seem like so many grains of sand, beautiful yet minute and innumerable, to a Polish reader.

The poet and critic who has done most to disseminate Northern Irish writing in his native Poland, yet desiring international scope, is Piotr Sommer. Sommer is a poet himself as well as a critic, translator, and editor, and brought Northern Irish poetry to the Poles' attention in his influential journal *Literatura na świecie* (*Literature in the World*). Arguing that this writing may appear apolitical only on the surface, Sommer encourages non-Irish readers to be attentive to the possibility of hidden or doubled meanings. Speaking from a vantage point clearly influenced by his own reading of Eastern European poetry, he encourages Polish readers to beware of the oversimplification that may result from direct statements on current events (he singles out Michael Longley as a poet who will not be pushed into political rhetoric at any cost). Hence the details that may seem innocuously descriptive may carry a latent charge. Heaney, however, is guilty of being overly 'declarative,' Sommer states, as opposed to the allusive Derek Mahon (Sommer, *Po stykach* 139); paradoxically, this quality links up with those Heaney admires in Eastern European work ('standing one's ground'), and is antonymic to those for which he impugns himself (hesitancy; excessive 'government' of one's tongue).

Sommer clearly prefers certain types of poetry, which is natural in an independent reader but provocative in a translator who introduces new poets to his home culture. This accounts for the delay in translating Heaney. In a retroactive apology of sorts, Sommer writes, in a 1998 essay, that Heaney initially appeared to flirt with sentimentality and to focus too closely on pastoral to interest a Polish reader, given that pastoral ('literatura wiejska') was an officially sanctioned genre under communism, and therefore struck a false note; in the same line, Sommer explains that mid-century literature of the British middle class – probably that of the Movement writers, though Sommer does not specify this group – worries over an ethos and mores uninteresting to Poles (ibid. 139). He posits that poets in communist Poland were ready to feel empathy for Northern Irish poets, and sought a literature of 'real life.' After *Wintering Out* (1972), Heaney began to sound interesting to him (140). The '"multidimensional belonging"' ('"zwielokrotniona przynależność,"' 147) that characterizes Northern Irish poets interests Sommer, and in this regard Heaney's bog poems are exemplary for their complexity. The 1970s in Poland were an overpoliticized time ('przepolityzowany'), and a poetry that summoned politics without reducing conflicts in order to control them more effectively, and without reducing the reader to the status of pupil, was attractive (ironically, at the same time Irish critics were faulting Heaney's *North* for reductionism and determinism). Further irony ensues when Sommer writes that in the 1980s, he lost interest in Heaney, sensing that ethics and not aesthetics were his primary interest, and that Heaney himself was forcing their demarcation (ibid. 150). This is, of course, exactly when Heaney was writing under the influence of Eastern European poetry. Imitation, then, does not guarantee reciprocity. In both Heaney and Sommer's case, interest in foreign poetry is founded upon a sense of parallelism but set in motion by its difference, its revelation of a road not taken by writers of the home country.

Heaney's poetry first appears in Poland in the January 1975 issue of *Literatura na świecie*; he is not singled out, though, as particularly worthy of notice in this special issue devoted to contemporary poetry in English. A year later, in the same journal, Sommer focuses attention on the two Irelands and their extraordinary literary output, but only includes one poem by Heaney, 'The Tollund Man'; the same issue includes an essay by Seamus Deane entitled 'Irish Poetry and Irish Nationalism.' Heaney is, therefore, immediately positioned in a politicized context within the journal. His poems appear piecemeal in various periodicals after this, and his reputation is fairly slow to build; Danuta Kłopocka usefully reminds that most contemporary English-language poetry was virtually unknown until the 1980s (Kłopocka in Malcolm and Kubińska 137), so this is not unusual. Sommer's 1982 anthology of new British poets (*Antologia nowej poezji brytyjskiej*) contains Heaney, as does his more selective anthology of six Northern Irish poets (*Sześciu poetów północnoirlandzkich*, 1993). At this point, when Sommer's interest in Heaney flags, veteran translator and poet Stanisław Barańczak takes over the task of bringing Heaney into Poland: *44 Poems* (*44 wiersze*) appears in 1994, and 1996 is the year Heaney takes Poland by storm, in the form of two volumes, one of essays and one of poems, both translated and edited by Barańczak (all published by a major Cracow publisher, Znak; the same house has just published Miłosz's collected works in their final, posthumous version); a volume of essays by Polish critics on Heaney's work appears in 1997 and Sommer brings out a volume of selected translations (*Kolejowe dzieci: Wiersze i prozy*). Jerzy Jarniewicz becomes the only Polish – indeed, the only Eastern European – critic to write a scholarly book on Heaney (2002). Another selection of essays (a Polish version of *Finders Keepers*) is published, also by Znak, in 2003, translated and edited by Magdalena Heydel and Agnieszka Pokojska, and Barańczak brings out *Electric Light* (as *Światło elektryczne*) in the same year.

This is a triumphant, if delayed, debut. Several questions remain: most obviously, why such popularity in Poland? Heaney has attended poetry festivals and has given readings in a variety of locations, yet we do not find anything near this amount of translational and scholarly activity in other countries. It may be chance. It may have to do with the energetic work of two well-known poet-translators – Sommer and Barańczak – to bring Heaney into Poland. It may also have to do with Heaney's personal interest in Poland, which is rooted in his fascination with Miłosz primarily and Herbert secondarily, and perhaps with his collegial working relationship with Barańczak, a colleague at Harvard for many years, thirdly. It is not based on reciprocal influence – Heaney has not had great influence upon Polish poets. This is, again, due to a situation whose irony is only superficial: as Heaney's work appeared (tardily) in Poland, his attempts to write allegorically, in parables, summoned exactly the kind of writing from which Polish writers were seeking to free themselves.[8] They did not need Heaney to teach them allegory. After the fall of communism in 1989, once it became permitted to write openly about history and politics, it also became less important – there was no brutal regime to which one must register one's opposition. It seems that Heaney's poetry arrived in Poland in the wrong forms at the wrong times to exert a strong influence.

More fruitful than the search for reciprocal influence is a consideration of the overarching phenomenon by which we can bring together Irish and Polish – indeed, all Eastern European – poetry: namely, the politicization of the lyric. Just as Polish poetry faced certain expectations to respond to current politics, so Irish poetry, particularly Northern Irish, faced such expectations after the outbreak of the Troubles. Heaney actively sought to incorporate his community's predicament into his poetry; other poets, such as Michael Longley and Derek Mahon, addressed it less directly than he. Sommer admires Irish poets for avoiding the overpoliticization to which Polish poets fell prey; as we have seen, Miłosz faults the Poles for not using the 'opportunity' to make their work as serious and deep as possible. The Northern Irish poets are noteworthy, *pace* Sommer, for their ability to write between the two extremes of overtly opportunistic 'public' poetry and the opposite, apolitical 'private' verse. Such terms must be viewed a bit sceptically, at least for the moment, because the extent to which they imbricate each other is the subject of an emotional ongoing debate.

Politics and Poetry

In Ireland and England, scholars and poets were questioning the relation of political tragedy and literature in order to come to grips with the Northern Irish Troubles and their possible connection to the poetic excellence of the Sixties generation. Northern Irish poetry and the Troubles 'emerged from an intensity, a root, a common emotional ground,' Heaney notoriously proclaims, though there can be no talk of 'direct or obvious connection.' Seamus Deane, in an early interview with Heaney, presses for a statement of exigency: 'Do you think that if some political

stance is not adopted by you and the Northern poets at large, this refusal might lead to a dangerous strengthening of earlier notions of the
autonomy of poetry ... [and, by correlation,] to the sponsoring of a literature which would be almost deliberately minor?' Heaney tentatively
responds, 'I think it could ...' (ellipsis in original) (Deane, 'Unhappy
and at Home' 66–72). Heaney's insistence that poetry will always burst
through 'corseted' notions of decorum owes a great deal to Alvarez,
coming as it does in this 1977 interview, yet it is worth noting both the
zeal with which Deane seeks a statement of political obligation and the
tentative yet finally firm manner in which Heaney refuses it. Heaney
had committed himself to addressing the Northern Irish 'predicament'
after Bloody Sunday in 1972, which served as a turning point for his
relation to politics, but does not wish to follow his compatriot in asserting that apolitical poetry might be 'deliberately minor.' What we see in
this early interview is Heaney trying to pick a course between ideology
and deliberate apoliticism, and acting out Herbert's hesitant appeal to
the conditional far more than a desire to stand one's ground in the indicative. Heaney is concerned with balance. An overtly engaged position would upset the delicate formal and thematic balance for which
he strives; his statement, in the same interview, that 'the conciliatory
nature of art is in direct relation to the rage which produced it,' echoes
Adorno's basic thesis (most directly articulated in 'On Lyric Poetry and
Society,' and complicated in *Aesthetic Theory*) regarding the inevitably
social quality of art that must necessarily seek autonomy and create an
illusory image of autonomy. For Heaney, conciliation is pre-eminently
valuable. It need not signal indecision or complaisance.

Heaney has, however, frequently been faulted for avoiding the Troubles by moving south, though these rumours circulated at the same
time as he was crafting the volume that would earn him the title of
'laureate of violence' (*North*, 1975). The political motives of Heaney's
move from the North to the Republic in 1972 have been the subject of
speculation on the part of scholars and of media reporters (see Corcoran in O'Donoghue 165–77). He insists that it was not for political but
for professional reasons, having taught full-time for ten years. The offer
of Glanmore Cottage in County Wicklow and a life devoted to writing was extraordinary, even while he was unsure if he would stay in
the south. Heaney's move to the Republic did not, of course, detach
him from Northern Ireland psychologically or poetically – the poetry
he wrote during the Glanmore years was some of the most political
verse he had yet written. His realization that everybody in Northern

Ireland is 'infected' by tribal mentality, and that even the most rational humanist cannot detach herself from patterns of thinking underlying the sectarian conflict, produces poetry that consciously troubles its moral waters.

In this long, serious, agonizing attempt to invoke the marvellous as well as the murderous, Eastern European poets are legislators and guides. Not only are they willing to dive into the clouded waters themselves, they are willing to castigate themselves for their own perceived failures to live up to the humanist ideal that Heaney sees as both necessary and impossible. Asked about poetic responses to the Troubles, Heaney replies, 'I like to quote the great Polish poet Czesław Miłosz: "What is poetry that does not save nations or people?" Most poets don't really think about that. In a war situation or where violence and injustice are prevalent, poetry is called upon to be something more than a thing of beauty' (Heaney in Kim, n.p.). Most Polish poets *do* think about that. The famous lines from 'Dedication' are Heaney's touchstone for discussions of poetic responsibility (as frequently, it should be noted, as Yeatsian notions of responsibility). They are not taken literally – Heaney does not grandiosely see himself as a saviour of nations or people – but serve as a yardstick against which to measure his work. In the context of the 1970s and 1980s, we can see how Heaney's reading of lines such as this would have shaped his view of what poetry could and should do. He volubly quotes from Miłosz's prose as well as verse in his defence of his socio-political views: 'Let me quote my hero, Miłosz: "Poetry below a certain level of awareness does not interest me." I think there's a problem with political poetry that is howling that it's aware' (Heaney in Leith, n.p.). Poetry may save nations or people, then, without howling for awareness, perhaps precisely in the way suggested by Adorno's theory of art's social function (connecting rage to conciliation, in Heaney's terms). Poetry without this 'certain level' is negligible, though we should note that Heaney slightly distances himself from the peremptoriness of the statement by quoting rather than paraphrasing Miłosz.

Heaney, then, has proclaimed an obligation to respond to political situations, and is consistently judged in politicized language, even though a Polish critic may applaud his private tone, his lack of historical 'opportunism' (Sommer, *Po stykach* 160–1). There is no question that the Troubles influence Heaney's writing and his interest in Eastern Europe, but the question is inevitably one of degree and of causality. Opportunism represents one pole of excessive engagement; this is what

Heaney fears in his 1977 interview with Deane, and why he tends to take a step back from questions of engagement; before the time of the interview, he had remarked, 'We live here in critical times ourselves, when the idea of poetry as an art is in danger of being overshadowed by a quest for poetry as a diagram of political attitudes. Some commentators have all the fussy literalism of an official from the ministry of truth' (*Preoccupations* 219–20). It is hard not to read this into the context of Deane's interview or the critiques of *North*. His words are more than clear, and gesture towards the language of *The Haw Lantern*: the critic who condemns the politics of a poem arrogates to himself a function that is based on a false superiority and a false detachment from the subject at hand. Better the republic of conscience than the ministry of truth. Heaney is interested not in statement making but in the examination of roots and motives. His concern is how to respond to the demand that poetry engage politics, and how he may fuse the demand he makes of himself with the demands of others. Poetry's *ability* to take part in political discussion is a given.[9]

The starting point for discussions of poetry and politics too often rests upon unquestioned assumptions: 'East European poets, like Irish ones, tend to be regarded as political unless proved otherwise,' writes Dennis O'Driscoll, with the result that 'bad poems may be elevated into good ones on the grounds of their newsworthy subject-matter, their susceptibility to journalistic paraphrase' (O'Driscoll, 'The News' 14). Written in a 1987 review, such statements communicate the weariness of a reader who has read one too many politically, but not artistically, significant poems. His implied urge to judge art by aesthetic criteria is praiseworthy; more surprising is the fact that he voices these sentiments in a review of work by Zbigniew Herbert, Adam Zagajewski, and Marin Sorescu. The philosophical questioning of Zagajewski, the ironic parables of Herbert, and the humorous indirection of Sorescu are ill suited to 'journalistic paraphrase,' which does not seem much of a danger in their case. They consciously shape their work to render such paraphrase ludicrous: 'My cat washes / with her left paw, / there will be another war' (Sorescu 35). Sorescu is mocking the prophetic and 'newsworthy' qualities that may elevate a lesser poem to stardom. The crucial point is that these writers, among others, craft poems that appear, on the surface, to *disclaim*, not proclaim, their own importance. These may not be precisely the 'bad poems' of which O'Driscoll is thinking, but they are examples of verse (by the poets he reviews) that is deeply aware of the necessary division between poetic and political discourses.

A paradoxical situation ensues: major Eastern European poets make it clear that the discourse of poetry must be separate from the discourse of politics, yet their Western readers keep viewing them in political terms, and they serve as (unwilling) touchstones in the ongoing debate regarding politics and literature. The 'newsworthy subject-matter' we may discern in their poetry is implicitly public, not private. Anglo-American verse, however, has a marked preference for poetry of private experience, focused on the personal self. The effect of poetry's politicization is that Eastern European verse is easily called down from its pedestal: either it is allied with journalism (O'Driscoll) or with responsibility: 'Poets such as Zbigniew Herbert, Różewicz, Holub remind us that in Eastern Europe, the poet has a responsibility both to art and to society, and that this responsibility is single and indivisible,' writes Tom Paulin in his introduction to *The Faber Book of Political Verse* (1986). They remind Western readers that their carefully constructed theory of the basic privacy of lyric might be false; we must remember our responsibilities. Paulin's statement is slightly ominous: there is no 'domestic sanctuary' in a totalitarian state, he maintains, but 'each action has a political significance which cannot be evaded' (17, 52). His tone is as significant as his words, and one may read a slight rebuke into such statements. Paradoxically, they help us to understand why the vogue for Eastern Europe eventually tapered off. Whereas Miłosz's call for a 'certain level of awareness' is open enough to encompass a concern with the private self, and is internalized by Heaney, Paulin's portentousness induces fear ('… which cannot be evaded').[10]

The difficulty of labelling a poet 'political' is compounded when we consider the way in which politics are interwoven with religion in both Eastern Europe and Northern Ireland. Jerzy Jarniewicz points to the way in which the Catholic church, in both Poland and Ireland, is identified with the nationalist cause, the 'peasant culture with its concern with place,' and even a 'cult of the earth' which, to Jarniewicz, has become something of a cliché (Jarniewicz in Crowder and Hall 108–9). Although he underestimates the degree to which Irish Protestant writers are 'concerned with place' just as much as Catholics, rural or urban, Jarniewicz's linkage alerts us to the necessity of recognizing the extent to which any discussion of politics and community must also involve discussion of religion, particularly when countries such as these are at stake. Heaney's concern with politics is, at its root, a concern with community, and the extent to which his individual voice can or should attach itself to a communal project; he finds a similar concern in the work of Eastern European poets.

A Long-Distance Comparison

One Polish critic writes: 'When we read Heaney, we receive the impression that Ireland – with its stormy history and the drama of partition, resembling the fate of partitioned Poland – never ceases to haunt the poet's thoughts' (Sławek 401). The main point, certainly, is obvious, but the glancing comparison here is astonishing, partly because Poland's eighteenth-century partition at the hands of Russia, Prussia, and Austria is so different from the self-division of Ireland following its civil war, and partly because it is so difficult for Western critics to justify, let alone to make, such a comparison. Heaney implies such a comparison – though he hardly ever actually undertakes it – in his *Government of the Tongue* essays. Not only does it appear unsupportable, but the very urge to compare Ireland to Eastern Europe is seen as epistemologically and culturally suspect:

> Despite Heaney's thoughtful and sensitive reading of eastern European poets, the question arises; is there not to be found in places like Italy or Spain a more apt connection with Ireland, with the cultural dominance of an ultra-conservative church, a society politically divided by civil war, parochially partisan ... ? Perhaps a Pasolini or a Lorca may have more to offer by way of artistic and critical analogy than a Mandelstam or a Miłosz. In terms of 'the North,' with which *The Government of the Tongue* begins, are not imaginative contexts more readily available closer to home, in Scotland, for example, rather than in Zbigniew Herbert's Poland? For the problem of cultural identity in Scotland relates directly and historically to the conflict between political nationalism and religious patriotism on a scale more in keeping with our history than, say, the struggles of Poland. (Dawe 248)

It is difficult to imagine Heaney employing the neo-realist style of Pasolini, much less participating in radical politics as the Italian poet and filmmaker did, and Dawe's own analogy is problematic. The surreal element of Lorca does not quite mesh with Heaney's verse, either, yet the offhand comparisons most significantly reveal Dawe's surprise at, and apparent lack of sympathy for, Heaney's motives in seeking out writers such as Mandelstam and Miłosz. Not only does Heaney rarely make direct analogies between the politics of Ireland and Eastern Europe (the exceptional example is cited below), but his aim, as supported by his essays and his poems, is not to seek mirror-images of Irish political realities but to write a different kind of poetry. Mirror-images are certainly not to be found; Scotland is indeed 'closer to home' than Poland. For Heaney's aim, imaginative affinities are more important than direct political parallels, though the presence of a conservative Catholic church, which creates its own culture as well as pervading the nation's culture, is an important parallel to bear in mind. Ultimately, Heaney does not seek analogy but inspiration, and his reference to Miłosz as his 'Master' pushes away direct analogy, inviting instead a study of how the older Polish poet served as teacher to the younger Irishman in spite of their differing backgrounds.

Dawe continues to expose the imperfect analogies between Ireland and Eastern Europe, pointing out that the poets Heaney admires, such as Mandelstam, Herbert, and Miłosz, relate oppositionally to their home cultures, whereas contemporary Irish poets are 'essentially *insiders* since little separates them from the cultural idealism of which their poetry and the historic Irish nation are assumed to be part' (248). Phrased this way, however, the former are cultural 'insiders' as much as the latter, taking on a tradition of heroic idealism which is as much a part of the cultures of Eastern Europe as of Ireland, even if many of its practitioners live in exile. Such poets position themselves very carefully vis-à-vis their native cultures, and Miłosz's ferocious attacks on Polish national myths are mounted from the perspective of one who is located – mired, even – within the culture he takes so much pleasure in analysing from his émigré position. Dawe dangerously conflates political opposition to the regime with opposition to national culture – and the difference between these two is crucial to Eastern European life under communism. Cultural roots, meanwhile, can be both shallow and deep, straight and tangled; Miłosz's ambivalence regarding Polishness has much to do with the ideological superstructure erected upon a local culture in which he discerns obdurate, lasting value.

Dawe sensibly points to the difficulty of drawing stylistic inspiration from poets working in foreign languages, yet Heaney is exceptionally sensitive to the type of language, imagery, and speaking persona pervading the poem, even while the poet's local idiom is lost in translation. The usage of abstract concepts is one technique *not* lost or obscured, and it fascinates and provokes Heaney. Even within the English-language tradition, he is often drawn to poets who are different from him – Lowell, early Hughes. Dawe's critique ultimately hits the most common point of contention about Heaney's verse: 'Whatever unease he may or may not feel about the Ireland we live in does not surface in his poetry. There is an acceptance of this place as it is that ranges from the stoical to the faithful' (252). Similar sentiments are voiced by David Lloyd and Thomas Docherty (in Allen, ed. 147–54);[11] when seen against the backdrop of admonitions by Stan Smith and Seamus Deane to opt for political engagement not to be 'deliberately minor,' such critiques may be seen as indictments of Heaney's putative ability to submerge 'unease' in 'acceptance.' When seen against a theoretical backdrop, they become complaints that Heaney does not incorporate enough (necessary?) disruption and aporia into his work, that he places too much confidence in communication (Lloyd is an exacting post-structuralist) – a point that a careful reading of *North* would ultimately disavow, reliant as it is on the continual disruption of communicative codes, uncertain where it should 'trust the feel' of material history, Christian metaphysics (which would 'consecrate the cauldron bog'), or self-styled legend (in the face of 'unmagical invitations' from 'pathetic colonies'). Yet even when we concur that Heaney accepts Ireland and his belonging in it, Dawe's critique contains provocative questions but does not offer answers to the fact that, in his own words, 'young writers I knew [in the 1970s, in Northern Ireland] were looking abroad for answers: to the Russian poets like Mandelstam, Akhmatova; eastern European writers such as the Polish poet Zbigniew Herbert, Vasko Popa from the former Yugoslavia, and the German Hans Magnus Enzensberger ... During the same period, Irish writing has been read worldwide as a laboratory within which the interpenetration of history, cultural nationalism, and postcolonialism can be studied' (Dawe 100–1). This excerpt from a later (2002) essay strikes a nostalgic note towards the phenomenon previously decried in Heaney's work, but it also indicates the answer to Dawe's earlier question: the 'interpenetration of history, cultural nationalism, and postcolonialism' present in the 1970s helps to explain why so many young writers would look towards countries with strong traditions of cultural nationalism, complicated colonial relations, and uneasy borders, where history was a common subject for poetry as well as everyday debate. The sense that poetry must address, and possibly redress, history in Northern Ireland, would have been a topic extensively treated by Central and Eastern European

poets before the Troubles occasioned a new sense of urgency in Northern Irish culture.

Thomas Docherty takes the indictment of Heaney's comparison further by opining – similarly to David Lloyd – that Heaney is motivated
by a search for identities, so that while he is drawn to Eastern Europeans, he seeks to make them recognizable in Irish terms: Gdańsk is seen
as Derry, Voronezh as Belfast (Docherty in Allen, ed. 150). He couches
these uncomfortable equivalences, which Heaney never openly asserts,
in the now-familiar opinion that Heaney's rejection of difference constitutes the 'blind spot' in his relation of politics and aesthetics, so that
he reduces alterity to identity. In other words, Heaney will not let the
writers he admires be different from him – he must seek parallels that
we must reject. In Docherty's most radical statement, Heaney's parallels betoken an 'imperialism of thought' that resembles the very imperialism under which writers from the Eastern bloc have suffered (149);
he commits the very sin against which we must direct our pious anger.
Docherty is convinced that Heaney has one-to-one correspondences in
mind, choosing not to address the figurative dimensions of Heaney's
implicit parallels and hinting, by the strength of his pronouncements,
that comparative projects are doomed to fail, based as they may be on
'imperialism of thought' – better to stay within the local, we must assume, rather than risk such nefarious complicity.

This essay comes under scrutiny by Justin Quinn. Docherty's notion
of the 'radical incomprehensibility' of Eastern Europe shunts the entire
region into a realm of total alterity. More fitting, Quinn holds, is Neil
Corcoran's criticism that Heaney is motivated by an abject sense that
the locus of greatness is shifting eastward; there is, however, another
major problem underlying such opinions – namely, Corcoran's broader
notion of 'something too vulgarly prone to think in terms of competitive
"greatness"' (Corcoran, *The Poetry of Seamus Heaney* 212) and Heaney's
treatment of exemplarity. Quinn surmises that Heaney listened to his
own critics by deciding not to include his essays on Eastern Europeans
in *Finders Keepers*. He singles out Mandelstam as the only Eastern European worth mentioning in detail, though he understandably cannot
make Mandelstam fit the parameters of an influence argument, insight-
fully asserting that his work is 'less an influence than a confirmation' of
Heaney's own aesthetic principles. He does not spend time considering the Polish poets from whom Heaney does, subtly yet pervasively,
take influence, concluding that Heaney ultimately 'does not try to bring
such models to bear on his own poetry' (Quinn in O'Donoghue 92–105).

Heaney begs to differ. He ventures into dangerous territory with a bold comparison provoked by life in Belfast: 'It hasn't been named martial law but that's what it feels like. Everywhere soldiers with cocked guns are watching you – that's what they're here for – on the streets, at the corners of streets, from doorways, over the puddles on demolished sites. At night, jeeps and armoured cars groan past without lights; or road-blocks are thrown up, and once again it's delays measured in hours, searches and signings among the guns and torches' (*Preoccupations* 30–1). Written in late 1971, the piece presages *The Government of the Tongue* and *The Haw Lantern*'s turn to Eastern Europe. The comment belies Heaney's growing frustration with life in the North. Written around the time he decided to emigrate to the Republic, it reveals a man whose life has been forced to change by a de facto civil war and who is searching for means to communicate and extend his predicament. Literalist condemnations of Heaney's search for parallels in Eastern Europe fail to account for the crux of his effort: regarding his own situation, it is a *figurative* effort, a search for metaphors that may function as symbols. They are crafted in order to extend lines of communication, to explain 'what it feels like' without becoming mired in atavism or fleeing into escapism. His fascination with poets who lived under extreme socio-political conditions is a search for exemplars rather than doppelgangers, for guiding lights rather than mirror-images.

The Poet as Bard and Outsider

It is easy to raise questions about possible parallels between Irish and Eastern European literature because it is correspondingly easy to view Ireland as utterly separate, an anomalous state on the margin of Western Europe with a native culture tucked away behind centuries of linguistic and cultural domination. This is true, but it is also restrictive. Dennis O'Driscoll holds that a touristic element persists as a real pitfall for Irish writers: 'The danger for Irish writers is that they will live up to the expectations of foreign audiences by producing a kind of coal-effect literature, artificially heated to the required blaze of extravagance and colour' ('The State of the Language' 32). The keywords here are 'expectations' and 'artificial.' These expectations mirror those governing Anglo-American literature, as Heaney and Parkinson have identified them, only the demand for concreteness is here intensified by a demand for blazes of local colour. Heaney has amply considered the uniqueness of Ireland, its legends and mythic tropes, and its picturesque backwaters. He has been critiqued both for portraying an implausibly old-fashioned rural society *and* for broadening his vista beyond it. Heaney laments the 'myth of separateness' prevailing in Ireland, which is responsible for the bragging claim that the Romans never conquered Ireland, that 'the Renaissance never touched us,' and that Ireland possesses the oldest vernacular literature in Europe ('A Poet's Europe' 157). All of this combines to form a 'naïf pride' in being cut off.

If the myth of Irish separateness creates a naif pride, however, so does the myth of an individual's separateness from the conflicts surrounding him. The detractors who accuse Heaney of holding himself aloof from the Troubles misconstrue one of the most basic features of his oeuvre:[12] his sense that the conflict without is rooted deep within the self, which is grounded in its environment, both physical and socio-cultural. This is a basically Romantic posture: the state of the environment enters the individual self. As Heaney slowly comes to terms with this grounding, he also recognizes the need to think through the subliminal values informing the work of Eastern European poets, however abstract and aerated their language may seem.

A crucial element of Heaney's socio-political identity conditions his interest in Eastern Europe: although he is fascinated by the difference of its poetry, while attempting a fleeting, embittered parallel to the 'martial' order of Belfast in 1971, he also admits that his own minoritarian position within the culture must be taken into account. It is not a point he makes very often, despite his offhanded comments about the 'aggravated young Catholic male' persona present within him. Heaney does, however, offer one memorable formulation, which hinges on his unusual position within the culture: he is attracted to the Eastern Europeans' 'resistance, defensiveness, and generally being short on the uplift factor ... [;] hedging the philosophic bets and so on. That attracts me very much, the sense that these are well-disposed but hard-bitten imaginations. The sense that you can't expect much from things. I think it's an appeal that is specifically to the minority part of myself, the minority of Northern Ireland part' (Heaney in Tell 42). The comment serves as a useful reminder that analyses of the difference between Ireland and Eastern European countries frequently subsume the poet in question into the culture from which he speaks, so that a study of his interest in Eastern Europe becomes a study of Northern Ireland itself, as if the poet could serve as a synecdochic cultural representative. The 'minority part' of Heaney, though, calls out for recognition.[13] The 'sense that you can't expect much from things' is often given short shrift by his critics. He continues by connecting this 'minority part' to its cultural context, thus qualifying his experience of community.

Heaney, however, views the poet as cultural insider – almost, not quite, a bard – even while the culture from which he speaks is minoritarian. He does not speak on behalf of the majority, but for an embattled group. Yet he insists on his communal roots. The particularities of this positioning – communal yet minoritarian, attentive to the voices of others while insisting upon the un-ideological, non-partisan nature of the voice – constitute what is perhaps the strongest, most specific link between Heaney and poets such as Herbert, Mandelstam, and Miłosz, namely, the deployment of a voice firmly rooted in a community. It is typically an individual voice that speaks *to* people, sometimes *for* people, and does not exist in pure isolation or in confessional solipsism. The social character of Heaney's voice is present in more than his subject matter or his specific forms (despite his much-quoted desire to pursue 'a more social voice' in the long lines of *Field Work*). It is present most obviously in his prose: as Edward Mendelson notes, 'Heaney writes as a man speaking to friends, or to students who are also friends, not as a man working in solitude' even while his work testifies to an 'essential loneliness' beneath his desire to act rightly in the social sphere (726). The problematic point here is that the friendly demeanour is underlain by anxiety, which may upset the basis of his poetic identity. Mendelson astutely senses the anxiety motivating Heaney's 'search for the right course of action for a poet' and worry that he might err, which is a key component of his essays, *Station Island*, and *The Haw Lantern*. Despite his sardonic note that Heaney never reports an instance when he did *not* make 'a sympathetic and admirable choice,' Mendelson proceeds to sketch out a crucial feature of Heaney's aesthetics: while insisting upon the poet's individuality and independence, he concomitantly insists upon his moral obligation and exemplarity, testifying to a deep belief – or desire to believe – that the poet *is* a bard, no matter how loudly he proclaims himself an outsider. Mendelson notes with some exasperation that Heaney speaks of Yeats and Pound without mentioning that they have allied themselves with less-than-admirable political causes (726); against these he sets Mandelstam and Miłosz, although he does not note that the latter also underwent a brief flirtation with Marxism, for which he later repented.

If we are to understand Heaney's insistence on the exemplarity of the Eastern Europeans, then, we must reckon with this recalcitrant, un-modern view of poetry as bardic utterance, which works as a subterranean and subliminal link between them. What separates the socially situated poet from the bard? The question is relevant on both sides of Europe: even Dawe concedes that 'in Ireland, too, there is a widely held perception of the poet as some kind of public figure who, in regard to both his social life and beliefs, voices on behalf of "the people" an accessible articulation of their spiritual and cultural beliefs' (27). 'Accessible' is a term that may smirk at Heaney's popularity, yet the point is also made by poets themselves: asked by Piotr Sommer about the status and function of the poet in Ireland, Derek Mahon replies, 'Probably it isn't very different from the status of the poet in Poland. People actually listen to what the bard has to say no matter how idiotic it is. I gave an interview for the *Irish Times* to a journalist who wanted to know what I thought. What I think has very limited consequences, and they thought it might have some effect on the life of this Province' (Mahon in Sommer, *Zapisy* 224). With his typical double-edged sarcasm, Mahon affirms and mocks the idea that a journalist should attribute social efficacy to the poet's thoughts. At the same time, beneath the sarcasm there is a gladness that 'people actually listen.' The sarcasm is occasioned by the effacement of a boundary between 'the poet' and 'the bard,' a boundary that Mahon emphasizes by means of his conspicuous effacement of it.[14]

In order to ground and extend this point in the cultural space of Ireland and Eastern Europe, this bardic quality must be mentioned as a fact underlying the status of the poet. The ways in which individual poets – such as Herbert, Miłosz, and Brodsky – respond to this quality will be detailed in future chapters. Crucial to note here is a related fact that Heaney's sceptical assessors tend to overlook, which is the deep communal rootedness of the paradigmatic poet in both Ireland and Eastern Europe. Irish literature is predominantly a literature of community. It has a public dimension, and the individual psychology often appears to grow out of a communal psychology. The same situation obtains in Herbert and Miłosz's Poland.

Although the poet *most* important to Heaney – Miłosz – strongly rejects bardic status, he has come to be associated with the bardic role. Miłosz, within Poland, functions as an arch-poet and as a historical sign, according to Marek Zaleski (Zaleski 251); whether he likes it or not, Jerzy Jarzębski posits, Miłosz takes upon himself the obligations of the Romantic bard (Jarzębski 246), and serves, in his individual capacity, as a 'synthesis of the nation's fortunes.' The specific parallels essayed between Miłosz and the premier Polish Romantic poet, Adam

Mickiewicz, as well as between Mickiewicz and Yeats and, equally surprisingly, Miłosz and Yeats, will be considered in the next chapter. The
Polish bard is noteworthy for his position within an oppressed culture.
The Romantic bard is different from the medieval one in his socio-
political function, yet Heaney is attracted by the fact that Miłosz's biography encompasses the medieval as well as the Romantic and the
modern (see Brandes 9–10); within his person, then, this singular poet
lends his reader access to *several* local communities (rural and urban;
intellectual and national); revealing his deep roots in each. This is why
Heaney can state that in both Poland and Ireland private consciousness
'grow[s] like a growth ring in the tree of community,' and this proves
true to his own experience (Brandes 8).

To be considered part of a community is to participate in a risk: 'For
any poet to risk the communal incarnation of his experience today is
at the same time to risk confronting the strain between communal and
individual values which lurks at the heart of that endeavour,' writes
Timothy Kearney in 1979 (470). The Troubles cause every resident of Ireland to question how her individual values do or do not strain against
communal ones, but for a poet, communal incarnation of experience
is a risk. Heaney is not one to shy away from confronting this risk in
Wintering Out and *North*. Once he begins to poetically process the influence of Eastern European poetry, the 'strain between communal and
individual values' becomes far more complex, though, since it occurs
not only between him and his home community, but between him and
the community of Polish poets whom he reads, and the community
of readers to which he belongs, so that the degree to which Heaney's
response diverges from that of his readerly community becomes another possible source of strain. Heaney's insistence that his reading of
Eastern European poetry is *not* focused upon politics but upon poetics –
specifically, upon the relation of language to value – positions him at
a slight slant to the community of Anglo-American readers who, *pace*
Alvarez, concentrate upon historical 'pressure.' His remarks (quoted
at the beginning of this chapter) about this poetry's eccentricity to the
Anglo-American academy subtly acknowledge his valuation of this
eccentricity.

The shadow side of community is exclusionary or extremist group
thinking, and the most relevant instantiations of such thinking to the
poets at hand are Messianic nationalism and sectarianism. The overarching similarity uniting Ireland with Eastern European countries
is the construction of a potent myth of martyrdom. Yeats famously

worried over his participation in this myth making; decades later, Heaney is tempted by it as he begins crafting images equal to his community's predicament. 'I could risk blasphemy, / Consecrate the cauldron bog,' he worries in 'The Tollund Man,' in order to 'make germinate' the bodies of the dead in a 'blasphemous' resurrection (*Wintering Out* 48), thereby sanctifying the corpse-ridden land. Will this prevent the bog from becoming an inverted wasteland, whereby its preserving waters keep alive not just dull roots but sharp animosities? The question points to the problematic way in which the grand myth of Christianity mediates the Catholic poet's relationship to communal history. Although Heaney consciously troubles his myth making (often in the very poems that undertake it), he is not immune to the lure of martyrology when it is conjoined with heroism.[15] The difference of Eastern Europe allows Heaney a greater degree of attraction to the martyrological mystique than he allows himself – or can morally stomach – on his home ground. Heaney does not explicitly connect the mythic and Messianic dimensions of communal membership, which are so central to the vatic dimension of poetry in Eastern Europe during the Romantic era, with their roots in a communal religious sensibility. He is, however, strongly attracted to this sensibility.

The Religious Unconscious

Heaney states, 'I am developing this notion that I am closer to translation from Polish because it gives cultural space to my sub-cultural Irish Catholicism, and that in some sense Polish poetry in translation is more intimate and hearth-grown to me than English poetry' (Heaney, 'Poets' Round Table' 46). This is a more tentative statement of a previous contention that 'in both America and England the religious sensibility has been bred out of poetry' (Heaney in Corcoran, *The Poetry of Seamus Heaney* 39). This sensibility provides poetry with a structure, a geometry, a trustworthy form (44). Religion, then, links together two of the elements responsible for Heaney's interest in Eastern Europe: the desire to give full voice to the minoritarian sensibility mentioned above, and the urge for poetry to possess a formal 'geometry,' to exercise force within a contained area. The tentative nature of the later comment ('I am developing ...,' 'in some sense') may derive from Heaney's own knowledge that his sense of closeness to Polish may seem far-fetched to his audience, or from the presence of the sharp-tongued Joseph Brodsky at the same table. In 1989 he had already developed the parallel to its fullest.

The most striking aspect of his comment is its conjunction of 'cultural space' with the 'intimacy' of work written in a language foreign to him.

When we play the two metaphors off of one another, Heaney's words gain even more gravity: if the 'religious sensibility' is compared to an undesirable genetic characteristic, something *consciously* 'bred out' by the arbiters of taste, and is pervasively present in the 'sub-cultural' minority, then the metaphor is menacing indeed. The abolition of 'cultural space' for this sensibility corresponds, tacitly yet insistently, to eviction and expropriation; the eugenic propagation of secular imaginations seeks the eventual extinction of this undesirable minoritarian weakness. In contrast, Poland is seen as a country where this characteristic has persevered. Heaney is speaking here of literature that testifies to the existence of a 'cultural space' where poetry and religion can coexist without a diminishment of the former. This recalls the repressive 'embarrassment' that English speakers feel at the utterance of words such as hope, truth, and justice: a similar embarrassment may result from the expression of a 'religious sensibility.' 'Sensibility' has a broader and vaguer reach than 'belief,' and Heaney knows it. He is not speaking of belief, which would be a much more black-and-white matter, but of a perception of sacredness that constitutes a sort of linguistic immanence that is welcome to him. His terms – 'intimate,' 'hearth-grown' – indicate a consolatory quality in this sensibility, conjoining it to intimacy with a language that has not been subjected to eugenic experiment.

Polish literature allows him to envision a healing of the rift between the 'common unconscious' in Ireland, which is still religious, and the language used to communicate it: the unconscious of the English language has been secularized, Heaney holds, and this creates an incommunicability, a basic lack, within the Irish reader. In one deft stroke, he brings together Ireland's linguistic colonization with its peripheral position vis-à-vis English (a position shared by Eastern European countries vis-à-vis Western Europe) – it is 'a marginal society,' and 'for someone like that [i.e., from a marginal society], the reading of poetry in English doesn't satisfy those needinesses which must be satisfied in the biggest poetic experiences. But when I read, even in translation, the poetry of the Poles, I find sub-cultural recognitions in myself which are never called up or extended by English poetry. I just find an experience of fullness and completion which is new and refreshing to me' (Heaney in Brandes 10). Heaney is speaking generally here, hazarding a bold subsumption of his own taste into the needs (albeit diminished into 'needinesses') of people 'like that.' It is quite different from his previously cited statements about the power of Eastern European poetry to refresh the entire English-language literary scene. It insists that we account for a need that is nourished by communal membership, and this need has little to do with fashion or even with the desire to hold one's ground in the indicative. It is not, we should note, fashionable. In these statements, Heaney addresses a need that is local – a result of minoritarian status – and personally specific – a result of his unique desire; the general value of Eastern European work, and its possible significance for English-language poets, is another matter. Nor can we deduce that this specific need is satisfied by all manner of Eastern European writing: Heaney singles out Polish poetry, and the two Poles he has read most deeply and thoroughly are Herbert and Miłosz. Of these two, Miłosz is certainly more likely to embody the Catholic religious sensibility than the classicizing Herbert. Even Herbert, though, who submits religious iconography to the same ironic treatment as society, writes poetry that has 'a pointed, more-than-secular intensity' (Paulin, *Minotaur* 206). It is a matter of tone and pitch rather than statements of belief; such are the sub-cultural reverberations that foreign poetry can set in motion.

Heaney takes great care to stress the values to be found beneath the surface of language and beneath the surface of culture. This is why he essays so few comparisons of Ireland to Poland or of himself to any of the Eastern European poets. It would be a futile endeavour, prompted by a desire to find superficial analogies, whereas the core of his fascination with these poets lies much deeper. The *difference* of Eastern Europe remains a major element of the vogue that brought these poets to the forefront of cultural discussions, and Heaney does not attempt to change the general perception of their difference. Instead, he directs our attention to the religious substrate of 'the biggest poetic experiences,' and elsewhere to the language of abstract and universal values used to communicate them – in other words, to the substrate *and* the superstructure. In order to understand the desires impelling Heaney's 'sub-cultural recognitions,' we must bear in mind his wish to verify abstract words that embarrass the Western poet at the same time as this wish is fuelled by a Western 'chic' for the writers using these words; we must consider Heaney's passionate interest as a stage in a developmental narrative, unromantic as it may be, at the same time as the roots for his passion – communal roots, religious roots – continue to nourish his work thereafter.

2 Heroic Names

Heroic Names

The fascination of a writer's life cannot be underestimated, especially when the life in question is judged to be heroic. Heaney gives voice to his own fascination, again in the plural but with a great degree of personal emotion, which comes close to awe:

> How often, in epigraphs to essays and poems, or as the subject of essays and poems, ... do we not nowadays come upon the names of Tsvetaeva and Akhmatova and the Mandelstams and Pasternak? These, and many others – Gumilev, Esenin, Mayakovsky – have become heroic names ... Yet in the case of the heroes, it is not so much their procedures on the page which are influential as the composite image which has been projected of their conduct. That image, congruent with the reality, features a poet tested by dangerous times ... In the professionalized literary milieu of the West, the poet is susceptible to self-deprecation and skepticism. The poet in the United States, for example, is aware that the machine of reputation-making and book distribution ... is indifferent to the moral and ethical force of the poetry being distributed ... [This] produces also a subliminal awareness of the alternative conditions and an anxious over-the-shoulder glance towards them. (Heaney, *Government* 39–40)

There are also certain poets whose procedures on the page are of paramount importance to Heaney, Zbigniew Herbert and Czesław Miłosz. Then there are those who become heroic names in the book of honour, those whom Diogenes's lantern would reveal as just. They do not exert much of a literary influence on Heaney, but their lives compel his interest, even envy, and they help him form the notion of honour and heroism that is central to his view of Eastern Europe. Heroic writers, he states, need not be viewed as *literary* exemplars, but as moral ones (perfection of the life is their legacy). This chapter will explore this latter category of poets.

Heaney's remarks point to several key nodes of feeling which structure his ruminations on these heroic names. For one, they are counterpoised to the same Anglo-American literary milieu that we have set against Eastern Europe in the previous chapter. Here it is 'the West,' a heady generalization for Heaney, and it is connected to a professionalization that brings with it scepticism and self-deprecation, presumably because poetry is less capable of being professionalized than other, more popular, forms of culture. Dwelling in a professionalized milieu produces scepticism about the poet's calling. Several years later, Heaney will adduce the ascent of an anti-humanist academic culture, one that is thoroughly suffused with scepticism towards the work it exists to teach, as another debilitating condition of life in the West. Here he focuses on the marketplace, which offers him an easy contrast to the communist East (though we must recall that in contemporary Northern Ireland, too, 'reputation making' is a blood sport). His comment strains at the seams as it implies that the 'anxious over-the-shoulder glance' recognizes a positive aspect (the valorization of ethics in poetry) to a dark reality (totalitarian rule and censorship of precisely such ethically watchful poetry). This glance, as we have seen in the previous chapter, is often made with touristic intent, to look upon an exotic and exciting reality; she who makes the glance is well aware that her life is more comfortable than those lived in 'alternative conditions.' Yet what is most crucial here is Heaney's presentation of self-deprecation and scepticism as negative qualities that exist because of an inexorable machine of marketing and distribution. He tacitly implies that poets in the East need not possess these qualities, gifted as they are in possessing a culture with a strong bardic tradition (as is Ireland, but that is not at issue for Heaney at the moment) and with an audience ready to read their poems as serious ethical propositions. Eastern Europeans such as Miroslav Holub and Zbigniew Herbert, however, are nothing if not sceptical and self-deprecating in their poems. Heaney's hero of certainty and self-confidence is Joseph Brodsky, though he proffers a 'composite image,' not an individual likeness. Later in the same essay, he points to another term that reveals the divide between East and West: 'Our own recent history of consumerist freedom and eerie nuclear security seems less *authentic* to us than the tragically tested lives of those who live beyond the pale of all this fiddle' (*Government* 43, emphasis mine). Certainty, confidence, authenticity, and ethical force: these are the qualities that Heaney foregrounds. As we will see in the chapters to come, the first three are shaken to the core by Herbert and Miłosz in order to sensitively communicate the fourth.

The composite image to which Heaney refers, however, depends upon the summation of these poets' very diverse experiences – of imprisonment, of exile to labour camps, of exile from the country, of voluntary emigration, of perseverance in the homeland – so that they create what he refers to as 'a modern martyrology' (*Government* 38). To be sure, communist totalitarianism 'tested' them all, as they lived in important places and 'dangerous times.' Yet compiling their lives to form a 'modern martyrology' participates in a perilous type of romanticization. Whereas the 'record of courage and sacrifice' provided to us by Eastern European literature doubtless deserves 'our unstinted admiration' (38), this admiration may make use of a Romantic rhetoric that veers close to Messianic necromancy.

Whereas Heaney does not recognize this danger, his literary heroes do. Miłosz, in particular, speaks out against the Romantic glorification of martyrdom, which feeds into an abject view of the suffering nation and makes egregious demands on writers to serve as national(ist) bards. We cannot fault Heaney for lack of grounding in Eastern European literature – his knowledge of the English tradition is formidable enough, and picayune insistence that Heaney should have learned Polish, Russian, Czech, and Romanian to read Miłosz and Herbert, Mandelstam, Holub and Sorescu is mean-spirited. Insisting that he should know better than to slip into the discourse that his heroes oppose is more appropriate, though still rather fussy, given the difference between the type of Romanticism embodied in Heaney's beloved Wordsworth and the recalcitrant, reactionary Romanticism that haunts Eastern Europe in the twentieth century (for a fruitful complication of this issue, see Cavanagh, *Lyric Poetry* 260–5). All told, it is still dangerous to speak of 'martyrology.' Heaney is certainly not attempting to single-handedly create an international cult of martyrdom – his essays on Polish poets attend to their poetry more than to their lives – yet when he lists his 'heroic names,' he participates in a cult that is already present, albeit in shadow form. For Heaney, however, this cult of heroism takes on a specific resonance that is unique to him: it pits Romantic spiritual energy against modern scientism. The spirit temporarily vanquishes the machine.

Science versus Romanticism

Agata Bielik-Robson hypothesizes that Romanticism can possess a force that guards modernity against its own deformations. The title of her book (translated into English) – *Romanticism: An Unfinished Project* – tellingly alerts us to the metaphorical valence that Romanticism may possess, as a 'project' that can be viewed as a basic force, or constellation of forces, casting Habermas's analysis of modernity into an Eastern European mould. Both modernity and Romanticism can be viewed as unfinished projects, then, with one warring against the other in much the same way Miłosz views the quarrel between Naphta and Settembrini in Thomas Mann's *The Magic Mountain*. He assigns ethical and metaphysical terms to the same dichotomy, positing that the religious imagination has eroded under the impact of science; the effect is 'one of the essential problems of our time – the incapacity of contemporary man to think in religious terms' (Miłosz in Haven, *Czesław Miłosz* 153). Modernity represents the triumph of the scientific world view. Bielik-Robson, among others, posits Romanticism as its antithesis; being the most powerful movement prior to Modernism, this dichotomy makes sense. Romanticism can be understood in the twentieth century as a counter-pressure originating in one cultural pole of thought. Its opposite is not so much the work of M.H. Abrams's mirror as, here, irony and scientism. Against the Romantic lyric poet we may set the rationalist; against the mystical we may set the undeluded; against the nationalist we may set the poet without allegiances. Heaney himself knits together two strands of thought when he states that Yeats can be cast as a representative figure of the poet-mage in the age of science, immersing himself in 'secret disciplines,' 'a neo-Platonist still defiantly at his practices in the age of enlightenment,' and as such can also reveal 'the disjunction between the artistic and the scholarly disciplines' (of which rational science may, by implication, be considered the prototype) (*Articulations* 18). Heaney discerns a similar sympathy in Miłosz, although the Polish poet doubts the sort of 'practices' that Yeats so 'defiantly' engaged in: poetry must 'maintain instead its centuries-old hostility to reason, science, and a science-inspired philosophy,' a statement that Dillon Johnston notes 'sounds remarkably like Yeats, ... but with a Polish accent' (Johnston 196). This is slightly overstated: Yeats insists upon a differentiation of sciences, so that 'we must study a new science' in the modern age, one that admits that 'the mechanical theory has no reality, that the natural and supernatural are knit together,' and that will result in Europeans finding 'something attractive in a Christ posed against a background not of Judaism but of Druidism' (*Selected Criticism and Prose* 262–3). The science to which Miłosz objects is the one allied with Yeats's despised 'mechanical theory.'

In this dichotomous scheme, we can understand the Romantic as a locus of energy rather than a specific program. It can serve as a counter-pressure against modernity, as Bielik-Robson has it, or can, more simply, summon a different ethos. For Arent van Nieukerken, the scholar who most seriously considers the claims of Anglo-American Modernism upon Polish poetry, it provides an epistemology as well as an aesthetic, so that the relation of the poet to national identity is understood in the Romantic spirit by poets such as Herbert, Miłosz, and Yeats (van Nieukerken 226). This assemblage is only surprising at first glance: Ireland and Poland developed more politicized forms of Romanticism than countries where the survival of the nation and its culture was not at stake. We could widen the circle to include, perhaps, Scotland, and other countries of Eastern Europe that suffered imperial conquest. Joseph Brodsky affirms the importance of a politicized Romanticism for Russian culture despite the fact that Russia was, for much of its history, a colonizing power itself. The development of a Romanticism exalting the martyr and the bard had an enormous effect in Eastern Europe long after the Romantic age was thought to have ended, as a literary-historical period, in England. Its ethos continues well into the late twentieth century.[1] This ethos is at least implicitly nationalist, reliant on a notion of community, of group solidarity. Its motivating emotion is a desire for something lost but attainable in the future, after a necessary period of struggle. This is what van Nieukerken means when he posits that Yeats's understanding of the poet's relation to his people (as he understands them, a qualifying phrase that is always necessary when speaking of Yeats), which is avowedly Romantic, bears comparison with Herbert's and Miłosz's understanding, which, for both poets, is avowedly anti-Romantic.[2] This ethos also underpins Brodsky's assertion that 'ever since the Romantics we have this notion of a poet throwing down the glove to his tyrant' (*Less than One* 136), a situation that only slightly changes shape when the tyrant becomes a censor or an entire ideological apparatus.

This dichotomy between the Romantic and the rational(ist) or ironic mode will be vital to understanding Heaney's attitudes towards his favourite Eastern European poets. They are far from being unitary, even if he *speaks* of the unitary influence of Eastern European poetry, as do so many other scholars in the 1970s and 1980s. His view of Osip Mandelstam participates in the modern martyrology that he provocatively affirms, which is fundamentally Romantic; his casual mentions of Anna Akhmatova – her nobility, her sense of responsibility – are made in the same spirit. His view of Joseph Brodsky, though, is anything but Romantic. The fact that Heaney met Brodsky several times must be accounted for, but the substance of Heaney's comments on this second exiled Russian are different in character from those on the first, Mandelstam, and this difference has everything to do with the anti-Romantic ethos with which Heaney associates Brodsky. Miroslav Holub furnishes a still separate case: an immunologist by profession, he cannot very well be divorced from the scientific subject matter which infiltrates his verse, or from the irony that everywhere pervades his tone, yet he does not appear to challenge Heaney as much as Brodsky does. Brodsky represents a test; Holub, a fortuitous pleasure. These phenomena cannot be discussed without reference to the dichotomy just established. Without it we also cannot make sense of the various and sundry comparisons that critics have essayed between figures as disparate as Yeats and Adam Mickiewicz, Yeats and Miłosz, the 1960s generation in Poland and in Northern Ireland, and the possible influence of W.H. Auden upon Eastern European poets.

Osip Mandelstam's Gift to the Desperate

... I sometimes see a falling star.
If I could come on meteorite!
Instead I walk through damp leaves,
Husks, the spent flukes of autumn,

Imagining a hero
On some muddy compound,
His gift like a slingstone
Whirled for the desperate. (*North* 72–3)

In these lines from Heaney's 'Exposure,' Mandelstam is thought to be a ghost presence even more than the exiled Ovid, who comes to the poet's mind as he sits 'weighing and weighing' his 'responsible *tristia*.' Ovid may be Mandelstam's own poet of reference – let us not forget his definition of Acmeism as a nostalgia for world culture – but his modern-day *Tristia* are the product of Eastern European political

oppression. After his sixteen-line 'Stalin Epigram' gained quick notoriety in late 1933, Mandelstam was arrested and interrogated in May
1934, miraculously spared execution, and lived in exile from Russia's
major cities together with his wife Nadezhda. Exactly four years later
he was arrested again, was sentenced to five years in a labour camp
near Vladivostok in the far north, and perished that winter, buried
anonymously. Nadezhda outlived him by forty-two years, constantly
reciting her husband's poems to herself so that she might remember
them for the future, in order to pass them on to a greater public.

These are the skeletal details of the heroic biography that Heaney
was holding up as exemplary and inimitable as early as *North* (1975).
There is more, of course, to Mandelstam's life, such as his high position
in the world of Russian letters as one of the foremost Acmeists, the intense lyricism of the poems themselves, his literary and cultural essays,
and the career of his poetry in Russia and beyond. Yet this is not all
equally accessible to Heaney, who must read in translation, and who is
not a scholar of Russian literature but a poet who – as poets inevitably
do – reads in order to steal. What is most important to him is Mandelstam's biography, and in particular, his *example*. Heaney does not
take poetic influence from Mandelstam. He reviews a translated book
of poems and expresses his admiration for them, but he does not write
extensively of the poetry (he wishes to hear Hopkins in Mandelstam,
but this wish is formed more by reading Mandelstam's eccentric and
ebullient essay on Dante than by examining his poems). He does not
try to write *like* Mandelstam.

He does, however, write *of* Mandelstam. His tragic life seems pre-
destined for hagiography, and Heaney is not alone in this belief – even
in his native Russia, Mandelstam is seen in martyrological terms, as
one whose 'instinct for self-preservation had long since yielded to his
aesthetics,' and whose aesthetics ultimately subserved his ethics (Mandelstam tried his hand at socialist realism, but the poems in this style
proved laughably unsuccessful). Brodsky notably connects Mandelstam's heroism and lyricism by positing that 'lyricism is the ethics of
language and the superiority of this lyricism to anything that could
be achieved within human interplay ... is what makes for a work of
art' (*Less than One* 137). This is coming close to Heaney's reaction to
Mandelstam's jubilant expository tone, but goes farther in asserting the
way we must understand the lyrical voice.[3] Mandelstam's singular suffering justifies Brodsky's deduction that 'lyricism' constitutes a higher
sphere of value than mundane action, a view he enjoys propounding in

various ways throughout his expository oeuvre. Mandelstam serves as a touchstone for argument. He serves as an icon.

The 'hero' on his 'muddy compound' is summoned as a counter-weight, as a possibility for tragic heroism. In Heaney's self-reflective 'Exposure,' the atmosphere of 'let-downs' and damp husks that surrounds the speaker is no excuse for quietism: Mandelstam's heroic example proves to this speaker that the gift of art – art as address, redress, and pure challenge – may be practised in the most unpropitious circumstances. More than that, it *should* be practised – 'the desperate' are in need of it, even while a whirled slingstone is a purposefully ludicrous weapon (nor does it serve as an objective correlative for Mandelstam's poetry). Significantly, the speaker sinks down to his psychological nadir after this evocation: 'How did I end up like this?' he wails. The answer lies in the metaphorical language of the poem itself: by associating a missed comet ('those million tons of light / Like a glimmer of haws and rose-hips') with his friends' 'beautiful prismatic counselling' recalling 'the diamond absolutes,' and by *opposing* this imagistic cluster to the muddy 'let-down' landscape of speaker and hero, the poet demarcates the landscapes of 'responsible *tristia*' from visions of transcendence. This corresponds to a separation of monocular from 'prismatic' vision. The latter word is etymologically linked to the action of cutting a substance asunder, as an optical prism refracts (cuts up) light into its component colours. The speaker of 'Exposure,' however, is mired in singularity. The hero cannot help him achieve prismatic vision.

When he is viewed as a hero whose gift is 'whirled for the desperate,' the *futility* of Mandelstam's imagined heroism, its incapacity to serve as adequate redress or as a vision of splendour, comes clear. When associated with 'responsible *tristia*,' he becomes associated with the self-punishing responsibility that Heaney frequently sets apart from the self-pleasuring goal of poetry: *tristia* (sorrows) against pleasures, 'let-downs and erosions' against 'million tons of light.' Yet Mandelstam believes that obedience to the poetic impulse approximates obedience to conscience. Why cannot this master lyricist be associated with the jubilation that other poets call forth in Heaney? In his 1974 review of Mandelstam's *Selected Poems* (1973), Heaney calls the early poetry 'fastidious and formal,' while the later work imparts a 'bare authority' (*Preoccupations* 218). Neither phrase communicates the celebratory quality that he *wants* to commemorate in his later essay 'Osip and Nadezhda Mandelstam' – Heaney cannot find the note he longs to hear. The reason is that the poetics of commemorating heroic martyrdom are separate from those of celebration; in 'Exposure,' the poet's chosen register occludes his view of the 'comet's pulsing rose.' Whereas Yeats's responsibilities were incorporated into a rich, gorgeous music to which Heaney cannot help but respond, he cannot quite hear Mandelstam's lyricism: 'In the case of Mandelstam, my joy there is all that he says *about* poetry. I cannot *hear* Mandelstam. I cannot hear the jubilation. I *suspect* it's Hopkinsian' (Heaney, 'Poets' Round Table' 46, my emphasis). He needs to associate the hero with the music of Hopkins, one of Heaney's earliest loves, in order to counter his own bleak image in 'Exposure' (these comments are made twelve years after 'Exposure' is published in *North*). His 1989 remarks emphasize expository writing '*about* poetry,' but only there can Heaney 'hear' Mandelstam: 'But everything that he has written in those rhapsodies that pass for critical writing is so liberating and world-extending, it extends the world of poetry. It goes beyond our rather crimped lingo in English for talking about poetry. It takes the roof off, it raises the roof a bit ... [,] and that's my relish' (46). This is the Heaney we are used to, the reader who eagerly seeks out purveyors of liberation and rapture. He takes a bit of perverse pleasure in noting the 'crimped' state of Anglo-American criticism, though this is secondary to his enjoyment of 'raising the roof' – even if taking it off altogether is, he realizes, not quite metaphorically apposite.

What allows Heaney to hear a 'world-extending' strain in Mandelstam's work is, then, his critical writing, especially his substantial essay on Dante. The Italian poet also informs 'Exposure,' travelling through Eliot, as Dante's beatific vision of the Holy Trinity becomes the fiery rose knotting together the imagistic strands of Eliot's *Four Quartets* at the choral conclusion of 'Little Gidding.' In 'Exposure,' it becomes a once-lost comet that 'should be visible' but is missed, a 'once-in-a-lifetime' portent and not an eternal image. Whereas Eliot's poem thinks through the relation of temporality to transcendence ('only through time is time conquered') in a manner that aims for synthesis as salvation, Heaney's insists on the heaviness of loss without redemption. Dante is here a vexing presence, not a jubilating voice. Paradoxically, Heaney needs Mandelstam at this point – the 'roof-raising' Mandelstam, not the martyr – in order to counter the 'erosion' of salvational vision into dull penitence. By his example, Heaney can counter the 'stern, didactic' Dante of Eliot with the Mandelstamian Dante, who is 'the apotheosis of free, natural, biological process,' a 'focus for all the impulsive, instinctive, nonutilitarian elements in the creative life.' This is also a situated Dante who responds to local politics and history while he crafts images of transcendence (Heaney, 'Envies and Identifi-cations'). It is also, importantly, a Dante whose trust and conviction in a higher authority Mandelstam stresses (much to the dismay, apparently, of Nadezhda, who had had quite enough 'authority' in the early Stalin-ist Russia of the 1930s).

Heaney chooses to highlight one particular aspect of Mandelstam's Dante, although he does not elaborate the possible emotional paradox of celebrating what is impulsive, free, and natural while honouring religious authority. Granted that this paradox may tell us more about Mandelstam than Heaney, it is notable as something Heaney does not *wish* to stress in his project of counterpoising Mandelstam's Dante to Eliot's. The two readers do not differ as much as Heaney wishes them to, however, and his dichotomization of Eliot and Mandelstam's views of Dante primarily reveals Heaney's need to stress the difference of Eastern poets' views, even while both essays discuss Dante's pan-Europeanism. Dante is, for both the American and the Russian, a child of Europe with a remarkably universal voice. Yet Heaney focuses on the opposition between Eliot's didactic Dante, who 'writes on official paper,' and Mandelstam's jubilant, at times child-like, physical poet (he 'bring[s] him from the pantheon back to the palate'). The difference can be schematically understood by their circumstances of encounter – Eliot's study of Dante at a university versus Mandelstam's delight in Dante as a poet-exile in his thirties. Heaney draws conclusions from these circumstances, underscoring his own need for jubilant Hopkin-sian cadences at a time when he, like Mandelstam and Dante of *The Inferno*, is in the responsible middle of his life, shouldering his commu-nity's *tristia* and compiling a martyrology while seeking to glimpse the comet's pulsing rose.

Joseph Brodsky

Joseph Brodsky, above and beyond any other Eastern European figure, focalizes Heaney's discussions of poetry and politics. Heaney does not, of course, *need* Brodsky to debate a subject of such long-lasting personal importance for him, but the acerbic Russian dissident is in-evitably summoned by him in order to discuss poetry's power to press back against political exigencies, to refuse subsumption in them, and to serve as a figure of tough-minded intelligence and integrity. Al-though Heaney is the elder by one year, he looks up to the Russian as an exemplar. The drama of Brodsky's life, as of Mandelstam's, affects this posture: the infant Joseph suffered from the siege of Leningrad, an effective starvation campaign with massive civilian casualties, in a way that the infant Heaney did not suffer from the Second World War. Meanwhile, Brodsky's minoritarian position as a Russian Jew may remind Heaney of his own minoritarian position as a Roman Catholic in Northern Ireland, though he does not make much of this possible similarity. Anna Akhmatova's championship of Brodsky, her affectionate and ironic attitude towards him, would be of interest to Heaney, but not necessarily influential. Most important for Heaney is Brodsky's arrest in 1963 and famous trial in 1964, which shows the poet defending his vocation in a way that Heaney never, fortunately, had to: accused of social parasitism, he was brought into court and questioned about matters that Heaney would call the mysteries: vocation, inspiration, and poetic authority. Asked for his profession, Brodsky replied, 'I write poems, I translate.' Asked again if he had 'a permanent job,' he countered, 'I thought that I had permanent work,' and then, 'I wrote poems. I thought that they would be published.' This did not satisfy the judge. More provocatively, when further queried as to who 'recognized' him as a poet, and 'enrolled [him] in the ranks of poets,' Brodsky retorted, 'And who put me in the ranks of mankind?' Most provocatively of all, when asked how he had acquired his poetic skill, he replied, 'I thought it came from God' (Shtern 141–2).

A note on Heaney's paraphrase of this transcript is here necessary. A good forty years after the trial transcripts (secretly scribbled down by the journalist Frida Vigdorova, then translated by various hands) were leaked to the West, Heaney retells Brodsky's story with relish, unabashedly revelling in his own fascination with the circumstances of life in the Soviet Union. He envisages Brodsky's arrogance at his trial, at which he asserts 'I think it came from God' when asked about the basis of his poetic authority (*Articulations* 17). Yet the translated transcripts place an ellipsis, a repetition ('I thought ... well [perplexed], I thought,' Shtern 142), and a marker of indeterminacy ('well, ...') within Brodsky's response; when asked who enrolled him in the ranks of the poets, he is parenthetically described as indifferent or unchallenging. These slight authorial emendations are made in order to communicate compliance and nerves, if not indecision; 'extravagance and arrogance,' two of Brodsky's qualities that Heaney singles out (*Articulations* 17), do not seem to be present, unless the ellipses signal an actor's pregnant pauses and not a nervous man's awkward stutters. Heaney's view of Brodsky obviously colours his retelling, and shows the extent to which he *enjoys* viewing his Russian coeval as a provocateur. What is made evident by Heaney's anecdote is his desire to view Brodsky as a personal icon, a larger-than-life figure. Neil Corcoran's gently ironic view of Heaney's tendency towards sacerdotal worship of his exemplars is relevant here (Corcoran, 'Seamus Heaney' 120); yet his posture towards Brodsky is less that of a worshipper than that of a pupil, notwithstanding the fact that he is the elder. Brodsky shows us how we *may* behave in threatening situations. At the same time, he bears the pathetic aura of 'a man who has suffered, has been exiled, has been treated as a social parasite,' Heaney recounts in a 1984 interview (Beisch 167).

The third-hand retelling of Brodsky's trial highlights certain traits that are tentatively and somewhat fearfully admired by Heaney – his determination to be nobody's fool, to speak out against stupidity and wrongness whenever it presented itself to him. Brodsky is not an easeful, comforting presence. He unsettles others and does not shy away from argument. Heaney's short later essay, written after Brodsky's death, intensifies this quality until a near-caricature is created (*Finders Keepers* 437–40). Interestingly, however, Miłosz also responds to Brodsky's personality, noting, 'For me, the value of Brodsky was his sobering effect, and his enormous feeling of hierarchy. He had a great feeling of hierarchy of value in works of art.' His poems, however, are deemed untranslatable and less influential in the West than his essays, many of which are written in English (see Miłosz's remarks in Haven, 'A Sacred Vision' 303–14). This 'feeling of hierarchy' is noteworthy for the anti-relativist, who may well have influenced this very trait of Brodsky's: Miłosz, his elder by twenty-nine years, was one of the younger man's favourite poets. Even in the well-tempered Nobel acceptance speech, Brodsky asserts that literature should not speak the language of the people; it is the people, instead, who should speak the language of literature. Here he also expounds his influential belief that 'aesthetics is the mother of ethics'; the aesthetic dichotomy of good and bad anthropologically precedes that of moral good and evil, and the more 'substantial' a man's aesthetic experience, the sharper his moral focus will be and the more complete his freedom (though not necessarily, he is quick to add, his happiness) (Brodsky in Frängsmyr and Allén 106–14).

This unapologetic sense of hierarchy was important for Heaney as well, who viewed Brodsky with a modicum of fear and awe. He associates Brodsky with his phrases as well as his social persona, stealing them where he sees fit, such as the notion of a 'plane of regard': one creates such a plane by attaining a certain pitch of expression. Brodsky himself creates this plane of regard through his work. He 'would have life live up to the demands of art and not vice versa,' Heaney writes, and such a position has obvious merit for Heaney, who writes almost with envy of this quality (Heaney, 'Brodsky's Nobel' 7, 63). Heaney consistently affirms the ability of art to possess a degree of autonomy, as realized through an obligatory fidelity to its own demands above and beyond topical, occasional demands, yet feels a concomitant need to address 'our predicament' and speak with a 'social voice' that does not always mesh as happily with the former fidelity as he would like. Heaney's own insistence on the exigencies of poetic vision testifies to an uncertainty that is less than defensiveness but more than fleeting doubt. He feels the need *to* defend art, to assert its agency and demands. Brodsky baffles him. His belief that 'the surest defense against Evil is extreme individualism, ... even ... eccentricity' (Brodsky, *Less than One* 385) does not easily mesh with the communal focus of the other poets Heaney admires, though it is not necessarily opposed to community altogether. 'Extreme individualism' does not strike Heaney's note; the imagined shade of James Joyce needs to remind him that he *may* strike out on his own in 'Station Island.' Brodsky's faith in the poet's freedom and singularity is curiously allied with Romanticism by Heaney, but it contains an aggression that cannot be explained by this alliance, and a toughness that can turn inward. Brodsky refuses to glamorize the dire circumstances that led to his exile; he refuses to concede that poetry may incorporate the prosaic; he refuses to compromise the strenuous vigilance with which he deals with the world. He educates himself by reading 'the greats' (Heaney's phrase) and establishing a high bench-mark for his own achievement.

Heaney uses the phrase to help him construct his own defence of art, which offers a 'plane of regard' when a person or culture finds itself *in extremis*. It affords us a point from which to establish a sense of perspective (Heaney, 'A Poet's Europe' 160). This echoes Brodsky's faith in the capacity of art to condition the way we understand life. His 'total conviction about poetry as a force for good' (*Finders Keepers* 438) raises the threshold for Heaney, whose own belief in the force of art works itself out through the troubled musings and self-interrogations that begin the first essay of *The Government of the Tongue* ('The Interesting Case of Nero, Chekhov's Cognac and a Knocker'). Heaney cannot stop being haunted by the notion that art exists at some distance from life, and that its efficacy as a causal agent is compromised, if not obliterated, by this distance. Brodsky's favourite English-language poet, Auden, is a salutary example of one who stubbornly believed that art *does* make things happen – however often his elegy for Yeats, who yoked the life and the work to a much greater degree than *his* 'Choice' would think possible, is quoted as evidence to the contrary. Brodsky's Polish mentor Miłosz affirms that poetry may be written *for*, not just *to*, a community of people. The Russian must be seen within this matrix of influences in order to clarify how he fits into the literary landscape of which Heaney is so acutely conscious.

The literary landscape uncomfortably coexists with the political one. Brodsky not only helps Heaney to focalize his thoughts about politics and poetry, but himself exists as an example of both literary fame and dissident glamour. The fact that Brodsky won the Nobel Prize in 1987 has not dissipated the morbidly compelling aura of martyrdom that hangs about his life. He is still known as one who suffered – first in his infancy during the siege of Leningrad, and then in his twenties, after the trial, when he was convicted of social parasitism (a communist moniker used to damn artists and intellectuals as 'antisocial elements') and sent to a labour camp near Arkhangelsk. The extraordinary circum- stances surrounding the almost-immediate translation and publication of the Brodsky transcript in German, Polish, and English publications are powerfully compelling (for one, Frida Vigdorova, the intrepid jour- nalist who circulated the trial transcripts and agitated on the poet's behalf, died a month after the trial, of cancer – unrelated, obviously, to Brodsky's circumstances, but tragically fascinating). Protests of the sentence began right away – Brodsky's connections with the Russian intelligentsia were numerous and deep – and already in the summer of 1964, information on the trial was being published in German, Polish, American, and English periodicals, and Radio Free Europe carried the news. Brodsky gained international celebrity on a very particular basis – as a political victim who came to be associated with moral authority by virtue of his suffering for the sake of poetry. When he was officially exiled from Russia in 1972, he came to the United States as a poet with a powerful aura and with powerful friends (Sartre, Shostakovich, and Akhmatova had rallied in his support), though his dry sense of hu- mour prevented him from being typecast as an abject victim, as did the numerous awards to follow. It is curious, then, that Heaney follows Brodsky in refraining from glamorizing these circumstances. Miłosz's later 'Notes about Brodsky' take the path not chosen by Heaney: 'life as a moral fable. The poet imprisoned and condemned by the state, then sent into exile by the state, and after his death, the head of that state kneeling beside his coffin. A fairy tale, yet it did happen like that, in our hardly fairy-tale-like century' (*To Begin Where I Am* 423). To be sure, not all the notes take such an awestruck tone. Miłosz justifies this excerpt by later stating that 'the greatness of a poet was inseparable from the poet's greatness as a human being' for Brodsky. Most important for him is Brodsky's affirmation of a hierarchy of value, of the ethical force of art, and his absolute devotion to the formal lyric.

This biography would have proved fascinating to Heaney in the 1970s and 1980s: just as he was searching for symbols adequate to his country's predicament, another man was being exiled for crafting symbols of his own. Yet his view of Brodsky is very different from that of Mandelstam. The reason has much to do with real-life personality – he met Brodsky at various times and places, occasions providing Heaney with immediate impressions rather than second-hand tales – but even more so with romanticization. Mandelstam perished while Brodsky survived; Mandelstam's death nearly coincided with Heaney's birth thousands of miles to the west; Mandelstam's age at his death was exactly that of Heaney when composing *The Haw Lantern*. Whereas the former was available to Heaney to romanticize as he saw fit, Brodsky proved an intractable presence. He 'scrupulously' resisted glorifying his time in the labour camp (Heaney's word), and abjured easy sentiment in favour of 'concentrated vigilance,' setting the reader's comfort below the poem's necessities ('Brodsky's Nobel' 63). At the same time, his staunch belief in singularity is, to Heaney, an 'old Romantic faith.' So is his belief in the poet's freedom. What we have here is a complex set of attributes that call forth atypical reactions from both Miłosz and Heaney.

The aspect of Brodsky's legacy that calls forth the broadest reverberations in Heaney's work remains his insistence on the absolute differentiation of politics and poetry. The only lesson we can generalize out of art, Brodsky holds, is one teaching the privacy of the human condition. Art is polyphonic and fastidious, whereas politics rely upon univocality and resolute action. As 'the highest form of locution,' poetry, in effect, is the goal of our species (Brodsky in Frängsmyr and Allén 107, 109). It compels a 'flight from the common denominator' and into the particular numerator, into autonomy and privacy. The experience of reading is that of a face-to-face meeting; neither the author nor the reader encounters the other in a collective form.[4] Heaney, however, speaks with a voice firmly rooted in its community, and insists upon differentiating the human collective from politics. As counter-voices to Brodsky, his friends and compatriots Michael Longley and Derek Mahon both state that the form of a good poem can serve as a paradigm of good politics. The ethical care with which poetry is shaped can serve as a counter-weight, perhaps, to the dishonesty, simplification, and ugliness of political language. This view is close to Brodsky's own, but the Russian poet fiercely disclaims any obligation on the poet's part. In a 1985 conversation between Heaney and Brodsky, the latter insists upon the priority of poetry, while the former attempts the role of interlocutor and mediator simultaneously. He offers as an example of the 'poetry and politics' dilemma his own commission for a poem on human rights from Amnesty International, which he instinctively steered away from, even writing a letter of refusal; then, 'freed, having created that space of freedom,' he did write the poem, entitled 'From the Republic of Conscience.' He insists, however, that 'it's not political, it's a fiction' (Heaney, 'Poetry and Politics' 42). Yet he is still clearly more accommodating of political obligation than his interlocutor, who insists that art is not at the *service* of any reality even if it can lend itself to application. It is 'more ancient and much more inevitable' than the state (42), a grand pronouncement of a sort that Heaney does not allow himself. His sense of responsibility clearly prevents him from agreeing with Brodsky; he feels that the 'spirit of the age' pushes one to identify with the oppressed, that the free poet is haunted by the sense that he may betray 'the beggar at the gate,' and that he does, and would, have a 'feeling of betrayal' if he did not engage his times (43). His touchstone during the conversation is Miłosz. The Polish poet, it seems, serves as a virtual third party in the discussion. Brodsky ends the conversation, though, by considering the West, and reminding Heaney that protest can also become oppressive when sustained for too long: critics who fetishize art coming from the oppressed Eastern countries create their own ideology (48). This is Brodsky's constant point: unanimity is dangerous. Politicians value unanimity; poets value eccentricity. This is why readers of poetry are less likely to fall prey to demagoguery than those who are impervious to poetry. Establishing uniformity of language, and prescribing poetry's aims, is a dangerous act.

The attractiveness of these views exerts an effect on Heaney. He cannot, however, push away the spectre of communal responsibility, which partakes of the political, and is responsible for his attraction to Eastern Europe in the first place. Brodsky, then, will remain a light upon his moral horizon but not a close fraternal presence. To concur with Brodsky too readily would be to invalidate the complications of *Station*

Island, The Haw Lantern, and the essays of *The Government of the Tongue.* He cannot utter opinions with Brodskian flamboyance because his work is enriched by the very hesitation and reconsideration that characterizes his thinking on the pressure of politics upon poetry. His poems must be complicated by reappraisals, contradictions, and the grounded recalcitrance of autobiography. He admires Brodsky's 'trust in poetry and ... unashamedness about it that was ... not a little dismaying to the ironists and dandies of Anglophonia' (Heaney in O'Driscoll, *Stepping Stones* 376), but when he searches for 'precepts to live by,' he turns to Miłosz as his support, since the elder Pole was 'a sage as well as an artist' (377). Whereas Brodsky serves as a whetstone for Heaney's intellect, he neither serves as the same sort of Romantic exemplar as the heroic Mandelstam nor elicits the same feeling of closeness as does Miłosz, or inspire the same compulsion to measure himself against this great master's achievement and to accept his soothsaying authority. This position belongs to Miłosz alone, though he is curiously matched by an earlier Irish exemplar who is, for obvious reasons, favoured by Heaney's Anglo-American critics.

Yeats versus Miłosz: Art and Life

The poems of Heaney's middle period are often said to focus on what Bernard O'Donoghue calls 'the Yeatsian concern with art and life' (O'Donoghue 15). Why Yeatsian? One might just as readily say Miłoszian. Even while he gently rebukes Neil Corcoran for thinking 'The Master' is about Yeats and not Miłosz, as Heaney has himself stated, O'Donoghue still persists in seeing Yeats as the Pole Star guiding Heaney's poetry, towards which he must turn when assessing Heaney's achievement. 'The influences from Wordsworth and Yeats are given centrality' in the volume of essays he edits, as he implies they should be, being 'the guides of whom Heaney is most aware' (O'Donoghue 16). What happened to 'my hero, Miłosz' (Heaney in Leith, n.p.)? He is given short shrift in Heaney criticism. Even when a sensitive and cosmopolitan reader such as Derek Walcott assesses *The Haw Lantern,* his discussion of influences upon the volume focuses on Yeats's *different* use of the abstract noun (*Conversations with Derek Walcott* 147) without mentioning whether the more fitting exemplar for these abstract poems is Miłosz. Miłosz's name invariably comes up in reference to *The Government of the Tongue,* where he is accorded several pages of direct commentary; it is rarely mentioned in reference to Heaney's poetry, and if so, only in terms of the poems in which Miłosz is explicitly mentioned ('Away from It All,' the recent 'Out of This World'). Yet he is the strongest contemporary influence upon Heaney in the late 1970s and 1980s.

The concern with art and life, then, cannot be readily labelled as Yeatsian. The terms in which Yeats treats these concerns are important to Heaney, but not a great deal more than they are to other Irish poets. What is unique to Heaney in his middle period, however, is his turn to Miłosz as a rival voice. The Polish poet writes eloquently of the constant tension that the artist must maintain between his desire to tell the truth of life – particularly when that truth is routinely silenced – and his desire to defend the rights of art (*Eseje* 121). Although Miłosz cannot believe in art for art's sake, he holds that the artist must fight for art's autonomy. This is a key position to place beside Yeats's mid-career responsibilities and his topical concerns. Yeats is as aware of the self-delighting, self-appeasing nature of art as Heaney, but the latter views him as a poet engaged with society in life as well as in verse, though this view is tempered and balanced in his later introduction to Yeats's selected poems (Faber, 2000; 2004). Heaney in the 1970s and 1980s was viewing Yeats as a poet chiefly concerned with art's place in the world, and hence compatible with Eastern European poets in general. Importantly, both Yeats and Miłosz connect the practical world with the visionary, though Miłosz's metaphysical thought is suffused with theology rather than theosophy. In fact, their spiritualities have little in common, but their interest in linking actual events with metaphysics is shared and is important. They are both, in a sense, philosopher-mages (though Miłosz's speaker swears he possesses no 'wizardry' over words).

John Desmond attempts to show that Heaney's aesthetic is likewise based upon a belief in 'a transcendent metaphysical order that is the ultimate source of meaning in his work' (2–3), and thus partakes of this strain in Yeats and Miłosz. Desmond's thesis has much to commend it, though Heaney keeps his feet firmly on the ground in his expository work and never allows himself to write the philosophically discursive essays that Miłosz does or to construct an elaborate system in the manner of Yeats. The metaphysical is, however, an important realm for Heaney, one that must be recognized in order for poetry to get off the ground. Contrary to received opinion, the gulf between *The Haw Lantern* and *Seeing Things* is not as vast as most critics believe. The immateriality at the heart of *The Haw Lantern* has partly to do with literal absence (the death of Heaney's mother motivating 'Clearances') but more to do with immaterial orders of thought – the metaphysical – and value – the ethical. The latter category is directly applicable to the social order, but that is not the main effort of *The Haw Lantern*. (As a side note, it is curious that Eastern European critics are much more comfortable with the term 'metaphysics' and its corollaries than English-language critics, who view it more suspiciously than their Eastern counterparts. This may have something to do with the corrosive preponderance of irony in the modern West that is lamented by Herbert and Miłosz.) Desmond uses Miłosz's essay 'Speaking of a Mammal' to underscore the Polish poet's insistence that man cannot be reduced to a cog in the historical machine, even if the view of man as a metaphysical being has generally given way, in Western culture, to a view of man as a histori-cal being (Desmond 6; 'Cosmic perspective has been completely lost' – Miłosz, *To Begin Where I Am* 208). This view is fundamentally amoral, even if historical philosophers fail to see it as such; 'History is unable to produce a moral judgment unless we ascribe magic qualities to it' (Miłosz 215); Marxist necessity has a paradoxically providential cast. He must situate a force above history, which he allies with amoral rela-tivism, and believe – against all odds – in 'a single true content': 'Con-trary to all those powerful slogans of historicism, which denies that there are immutable, constant elements, I believe that one such element does exist ... I am searching for a reliable foundation apart from any faith and ... I see that foundation in the ethical instinct' (Miłosz 197–8; this is from an impassioned letter to the writer Jerzy Andrzejewski). This instinct, however, can guide people to abhorrent acts, and Miłosz suffers from his inability to find a fixed higher system that could not justify such acts (his native Christianity bears with it a chequered past – he is acutely aware of the wrongs perpetrated in the name of the Chris-tian church). The ethical instinct, then, holds its own as an immutable element above historical process, but it cannot be trusted to choose justly and humanely, which leads us back to a dangerous, untenable relativism that makes Miłosz put his head in his hands, realizing both the impossibility of his task *and* the fact that he has 'tendencies, which prod me toward a greater zealousness than I desire. It is enough for me to loosen the reins a bit, and I begin to pontificate in the manner of a prophet or preacher ... I have very few qualifications to be a bard. So let us quickly extinguish exaltation with renewed doubt; let us return to bitter, scathing questions' (191).

Yeats does not fear such zealousness, happily investing himself with bardic authority and making use of the old bellows full of angry wind that he worried had destroyed the soul of his dear Maud Gonne. In later

life, though, his early zeal tempers itself considerably. The metaphysical system of *A Vision* occupies his energy just as the search for a fixed
system does Miłosz's, but Yeats creates his own system out of different
mythologies and belief structures, idiosyncratic as it may be. It is a historical system, not a system of ethics, and is different from the 'reliable
foundation' sought by Miłosz. This is one of the deepest differences
between the two poets. Heaney is at least subliminally aware of it, associating Miłosz with ethics and Yeats with politics. Yet Miłosz is also the
author of *The Captive Mind*, which is about politics first and foremost,
and briefly held political posts (as a cultural attaché) in Washington and
Paris. Here we find a surprising connection between the two poets in
their later years. Yeats, after his six years in the Irish Senate had ended,
thus admonishes his friend in a letter: 'Do not try to make a politician
out of me, even in Ireland I shall never I think be that again – as my
sense of reality deepens, ... my horror at the cruelty of governments
grows greater ... Communist, Fascist, nationalist, clerical, anti-clerical
are all responsible according to the number of their victims. I have not
been silent, I have used the only vehicle I possess – verse' (unpublished
letter, 7 April 1936, in Ellmann, *The Man and the Masks* 278). Granted,
these are the words of an elderly man, frightened by the current state
of Europe, yet they sound similar to words that Miłosz might utter as
one who had seen the rise and fall of many ideologies. Had Yeats lived
into his nineties, the similarity of his sentiments to those of the elder
Miłosz may have grown more apparent. The current issues occupying
them, however, are obviously different, just as the national politics to
which they respond differ. For the young Yeats, folk culture could serve
a political purpose; not so for Miłosz. Yet this is due to a difference
of cultural period – fin-de-siècle Poland rediscovered folk culture in
a manner roughly analogous to Ireland (see Merchant). This temporal
difference troubles a comparison of the two poets and an assessment
of their national positions: both viewed as bards, to be sure, but what
it means to be a bard in the context of the Irish Literary Revival is not
what it means in the so-called postmodern period (a term that signals,
in this context, the development of literature *through* the modernism of
Eliot, for example, to Auden, two important Anglo-American figures
in contemporary Polish verse). This affects the way in which each poet
writes about nationality.

Yeats, like Miłosz, writes out of, and of, his belonging to the nation,
with the important qualifier that 'a writer is not less National because
he shows the influence of other countries and of the great writers of

the world' (Yeats 144). Even more than does Yeats, however, Miłosz frequently escapes from the first-person singular altogether. Despite the cultural significance of his biography – which, as Heaney points out, serves as an image of civilizational change (not necessarily progress, to be sure) from medieval to contemporary periods – the voice of his poetry often escapes our grasp. We have considered the communal consciousness that is common to many Eastern European poets; Miłosz is no exception, and his occasional escape from singularity is a type of self-effacement: the first-person singular is sweet, but 'I am, however, immersed in humanity, given up to it, created by it anew everyday, so that my barely-perceived essence escapes from me' (*Eseje* 10, my translation). This surprisingly fluid notion of identity is not readily associated with Miłosz, but it represents an important conception of selfhood to put beside Yeats's resonant first-person plural ('We were the last Romantics'). The Polish poet would not consider himself a Romantic for choosing traditional sanctity as a theme. Yeats's sense of belonging to a guild is shared by Miłosz, but the latter tends to expand his circle considerably when he meditates on selfhood: 'I am brave and undaunted in the certainty of having something important to say to the world, something no one else will be called to say. Then the feeling of individuality and a unique role begins to weaken and the thought of all the people who ever were, are, and ever will be[,] … people superior to me in strength of feeling and depth of mind, robs me of confidence in what I call my "I"' (*Visions from San Francisco Bay* 4–5). This is a note that Yeats never strikes.

For Miłosz, then, the self is cowed by grandeur, though the ambition to write is not. It is a matter of will versus identity, or of *daimonion* versus self. The great effect of Miłosz's writing is often exactly that of Yeats's as assessed by Eliot: Yeats exemplifies the 'poet who, out of intense and personal experience, is able to express a general truth; retaining all the particularity of his experience, to make of it a general symbol' (Eliot in Unterecker 57). Similarly, as Yeats grows more Irish he grows more universal, Eliot claims, learning to master Irish myths for his own purposes (58). These points are not lost on Heaney and they may condition his reading of Miłosz: universality is dangerous only when it is a condition yoked to ideology (the 'universal, beautiful ideas' of future dictators, for example); when truth is arrived at through the local rather than imposed from on high in the form of abstraction – such as the tempting abstraction of Marxist egalitarianism – then it can become a general truth. Eliot's focus is upon aesthetics but for Miłosz the point is ethical. Similarly, the real man's experience serves as the basis for his symbols, and this is true of both Miłosz and Yeats after their early poems.

Yeats and Mickiewicz (An Odd Affinity)

Adam Czerniawski sees Yeats as 'the Irish answer to ... Adam Mickiewicz': he straddles the worlds of poetry and public affairs, is unapologetically hieratical, visionary, 'somewhat insane,' and a champion of folk culture (Czerniawski 7). At first glance it appears an off-handed comparison, perhaps not worth taking seriously; Czerniawski's humour, though, belies the more serious task of establishing a deep basis for aligning contemporary Irish and Polish literature so that we may make sense of Heaney's attraction to Miłosz and Herbert. The obvious comparison, which is made much more frequently (including, albeit indirectly, by Heaney), is between Miłosz and Yeats, yet this is generationally incorrect. Here is where Adam Mickiewicz, Poland's foremost Romantic, becomes relevant. Temporally, the comparison is still off-kilter: Mickiewicz lived in the nineteenth century, born in 1798 to an impoverished noble family (a lineage Yeats would have gladly embraced), and died from illness prematurely in 1855, living in poverty despite his great fame. Culturally, the two poets share certain important traits: both are serious mystics – Yeats would say theosophists – and, at similar ages, seek to expound mystical systems that bring together history and literature. Simultaneously, they involve themselves in public affairs, calling for the independence of their colonized countries (although they admire the influential literature created by those colonizing powers England and Russia) and taking direct part in politics. Most importantly, they believe that folk culture can serve as the cornerstone for a national cultural resurgence. This quintessentially Romantic idea subtends the work of both, and both are seen as nationalist poets. Their mysticism befuddles future commentators, but is nonetheless an important facet of their views, chiefly because it underpins their hieratical and bardic roles vis-à-vis their people. It is also, to them, an essential part of poetic composition: the artistic impulse is a sacred one, dependent upon a sense of man's immortality according to Yeats, and the sacral quality of creative work helps to justify a view of poet as *vates*. It also equips him with a system defiantly (Ellmann would say enthusiastically) at odds with conventional beliefs.

The bardic status assumed by Mickiewicz and Yeats is exactly the quality against which Heaney, Miłosz, and Herbert all rebel. None of these contemporary poets wants to wear the prophet's mantle, though it is offered to them all. Heaney's precise essays on Yeats – essays that highlight Yeats's concrete circumstances, such as the disciplined 'slog-work' that writing must entail – looks beneath this mantle. He constantly affirms the centrality of influences other than Yeats upon his own poems. Yet Heaney – similarly to the Poles – cannot ignore the looming presence of the great national bard. Miłosz and Herbert expend a considerable amount of energy speaking out against Romanticism and, even more crucially, its legacy in the twentieth century. This legacy encompasses both thematics (nationalism, heroic martyrdom, politicized folk culture, and nostalgia for the past) and style (Yeats's grandiosity; Mickiewicz's vatic timbre). Heaney does not speak out against Romanticism in this way. His Ireland is, of course, not occupied in the same way that Poland is, and that renders the fight for liberation slightly anachronistic, though not wholly so, as his angry statements about life in Belfast make clear. This is what Arent van Nieukerken gets wrong in his otherwise penetrating passages on Irish and Polish literature: when he speaks of Yeats's sense of responsibility towards the problems of a backward nation, his need to unmask 'tribal' stereotypes and ironize the culture's sacred cows, he speaks not of Yeats but of contemporary culture (233), and forgets that Yeats was actually responsible for *creating* many of the terms against which post-independence writers rebel. This is why a comparison of Yeats and Mickiewicz, as two founding fathers, makes sense.

Perhaps the most obvious link between the two poets is one that highlights their centrality in determining twentieth-century poets' affinities. Just as every modern and contemporary Irish poet must, to some extent, struggle with the shadow of Yeats, so must every Polish poet struggle with Polish Romanticism, of which by far the most influential exponent is Mickiewicz. The latter poet's writings are ur-texts, posits Marek Zaleski, and Miłosz cannot help but echo his predecessor, especially as a poet in political exile, for which Mickiewicz is (again) the prototype (Zaleski 250, 254). As we study the influence of Mickiewicz, we see how biography becomes text, and how a text becomes the biography of an idea, posits Ryszard Nycz (Nycz in Zaleski 251). Heaney makes a similar point in reference to Yeats. What happens here is that the poet becomes a cultural metonym and a historical sign; his life becomes public cultural property. This brings us back, however unwillingly, to the figure of the bard. Just as the Romantic bard offers his whole self to the nation, so do Mickiewicz and Yeats ... and, despite their anti-Romanticism, so do Miłosz and Herbert, whose virtual canonization will be discussed in greater detail in the following three chapters. These two Romantics, Yeats and Mickiewicz, set forth a template that exerts a powerful influence.

A disclaimer is necessary at this stage of the comparison: although it is important to establish Heaney's connections to Eastern Europe in relation to the complementary pairings of Yeats and Mickiewicz, and Yeats and Miłosz, Heaney does not form his literary alliances with exclusion in mind.[5] The problematic nature of the Yeats-Miłosz comparison does not hinder him from conflating the two in 'The Master'; his stated preference for Patrick Kavanagh does not prevent him from referring frequently to Yeats; his delight in Mandelstam's 'rapturous' Dante does not preclude him from invoking Dante in dark circumstances (as in the nightmare vision of 'Ugolino'). Heaney's masters, in short, do not cancel each other out in necessary patterns of exclusion. They cannot be unified, however, and any search for a ground common to all of them will prove strained and possibly distract from the depth of their achievement. It is fair to say that Heaney is not afraid to be contradictory. Neither is Miłosz, though Heaney finds this quality hard to recognize in him. Moreover, the substance of his writing, as with Yeats, is not always consonant with his reputation: for example, Miłosz's constant return to the landscapes of his youth renders his woodland Lithuania as memorable as Yeats's Sligo, even while both poets are frequently read as poets of ideas and not landscapes, of heroic deeds instead of autobiography.

In Poland, Miłosz's autobiography is matter for extraliterary debate as well as literary reference, but in the context of Anglo-American 'Slavic chic,' and particularly in relation to Heaney's use of him, Miłosz is seen in terms of politics and symbols (*pace* Alvarez's 'Witness') rather than as a model for recounting one's life. Yet his writings are, to an extraordinary degree, connected as facets of a massive autobiography. He could easily serve as a counter-influence to the Wordsworth of *The Prelude*. Heaney, however, does not need to replace Wordsworth. During his time at Glanmore Cottage in the early 1970s, he reads Wordsworth avidly; this reading momentarily displaces, perhaps, his reading of Eastern European literature, but does not cancel it out or impel him to form a compound ghost out of, let us say, Dante, Wordsworth, and

Miłosz. Reading more poets means taking on more influences. *The Prelude* will always be a sacred book for Heaney, and consequently, he does not *need* to associate contemporary Eastern European poets with Romanticism: his English and Irish Romantic models are well established and he need not look abroad to Mickiewicz. This means, however, that Heaney compartmentalizes his influences in a somewhat schematic fashion: Wordsworth on the one hand, as the greatest poet of Romantic communion with nature, as the poet of echoes and reverberations, the poetry of divination, and, on the other hand, the 'hard-bitten' Slavic poets. Never mind that Miłosz's philosophically autobiographical poems (which are very much about the growth of a poet's mind) could be placed side by side with Wordsworth's *Prelude*: a complex task, to be sure, but one that would be entirely relevant and perhaps even germinal for Heaney's work. Yeats stands as the middle term between Wordsworth and Miłosz. Heaney attempts to draw quick parallels between the two in his introduction to Wordsworth's selected poems (1988), yet they are unconvincing – his enumeration of Wordsworth's influential qualities brings him farther from Yeats than ever. Hazard Adams draws a schematic yet effective opposition between Wordsworth's lesson of 'wise passiveness and mesmerized self-consciousness' ('Personal Helicon' and 'Widgeon,' curiously not mentioned by Adams, may serve as examples of this tendency) and Yeats's 'implacable artistic drive' that aims to discipline his materials. Yeats, to Adams, dramatizes and seeks to overcome difficulties – we may add that he consciously seeks them out, fascinated by what is difficult, arguing about the relative values of abstraction and embodiment on his very deathbed. This is a fundamentally different artistic temperament from Wordsworth's, and this difference helps to explain why the distance between him and Milosz is so very long. Heaney's favourite Eastern Europeans, meanwhile, do not respond to Wordsworth with special passion (the polyglot Miłosz is more concerned with Whitman's influence, with Eliot's catastrophism, and with Shapiro's *Essay on Rime* as ars poetica). Instead, two particular Anglo-American poets, whose work travelled east with noteworthy results, must be mentioned to conclude this series of exemplary comparisons: T.S. Eliot and W.H. Auden.

Eliot, Auden, and the 1960s Generations

Arent van Nieukerken views Miłosz as the figure linking Anglo-American modernism with contemporary Polish poetry written under the aegis of Auden; the poets who debuted their work in the 1960s owed much to Auden, and found complementary echoes on the other side of Europe (*Ironiczny konceptyzm* 118). His bold thesis is worth elucidating, since it offers useful comparative background. Miłosz's tie to Eliot is clear and powerful: having made his name as a prophetic Catastrophist poet in the 1930s – very far indeed from J. Alfred Prufrock – Miłosz turned to Eliot during the Second World War, carrying a copy of *The Waste Land* around the ruins of Warsaw. This was the time when he famously realized that poetry needed to be adequate to a world where people die and cities are razed. He opposes Eliot to Yeats in this context: 'In contrast to Yeats, [Eliot] sailed to no Byzantium of perfectly frozen forms. He wanted to be a poet-interpreter' (*To Begin Where I Am* 390). The form of *The Waste Land* responded to the civilizational exhaustion that Miłosz felt in 1940s Poland. Yet in post-war Stalinist Poland, Eliot was one of the foremost authors blacklisted by communist authorities, bizarrely accused of bourgeois decadence. The counter-effect was that Eliot's popularity grew immensely. After the cultural thaw of 1956, he was the first modern poet writing in English to be published, in a bilingual *Selected Poems* (1960).

At first glance there is little to link Eliot with Poland. His apocalyptic landscapes have widespread relevance to a region that had experienced catastrophe, but Eliot's voice is distinctly different from the voices of Miłosz or Herbert or, for that matter, any of the poets whom Heaney admires, and he seems an unlikely link for Heaney in particular. Yet one of the most important characteristics of Miłosz's work is his use of personae, and this quality is difficult for Heaney to discern – his interpretation of 'Incantation' will be discussed in chapter 4, alongside a closer consideration of Eliot's structural influence upon Miłosz. Eliot is a master (along with Pound, a far lesser influence to the poets under consideration) of the disembodied voice. Behind Eliot's multiple voices, however, lie embodied myths. Their moral landscapes both jar against and are consonant with the landscapes of catastrophe that *The Waste Land* juxtaposes. They are linked by a despair that does not smack of nihilism, which Miłosz rejects, and are vivified by a 'compactness and energy' in which Eliot 'had no rival in the English language' (*To Begin Where I Am* 391). For Miłosz, Eliot evinces a nostalgia for the age of Dante, 'when the religious imagination shaped the cosmos without stumbling over obstacles placed there by discursive thought' (398), even if – maybe because – the American scholar was capable of discursively interpreting the religious structure for which he longed. We can now draw a line from Dante to Eliot, Miłosz, and Heaney, who responds to Miłosz's longing for the sacred as against the discursive, but who does not trace this lineage. Eliot's intellectualism stands for a defence of eternal, non-contingent values, and Miłosz's use of ironic quotation marks is telling: 'He was "intellectual"; that is, he proposed certain values which will not cease to be such even if they are considered as something other than components of a given artistic whole' (390). There is defensive emotion behind this redefinition of an often-maligned term as an ethical position – that is, concerned with the proposition of values, as opposed to a moral position, concerned with adherence to a value system. His view is not incompatible with Eliot's attempt to learn how the imagination might regain its once-vaunted privileges (398). Eliot is the English-language modernist most important to the young Miłosz. The Pole does not, however, dip into demotic speech, even when writing in different voices; the Miłoszian voice is unmistakable, while the impossibility of discerning a singular voice in *The Waste Land* is a foregone conclusion. Miłosz does not *sound* like Eliot; neither do many Polish poets of his generation, even if they read him avidly. Van Nieukerken puts forth the thesis that Miłosz uses Anglo-Saxon modernism to mediate his lingering Romanticism, which still remains a central facet of his work (van Nieukerken, 'Czesław Miłosz ...' 52). Despite his claims that Wallace Stevens serves as a shadow adversary in Miłosz's work, Eliot is the one poet who truly fits into this scheme.[6]

The second late modernist who frequently obtrudes upon discussions of contemporary Polish poetry is Auden, though it is more tempting to see Auden and Miłosz as simultaneous and separate influences upon their contemporaries rather than as linked ones. Miłosz was impressed by Auden's 'New Year Letter,' but Auden's strongest influence was on the generation younger than Miłosz. Joseph Brodsky admires both, proclaiming each one as his favourite poet on separate occasions. Auden's receptivity to the political issues of his day is the most obvious, but not the most interesting, connection to make. Van Nieukerken points out Auden's attractiveness to the so-called ironic moralists, among whom he counts Herbert and younger poets such as Stanisław Barańczak and the early Adam Zagajewski (118); Miłosz is the link between them. To complicate matters further, Miłosz writes eloquently *against* irony, as does the younger Zagajewski, viewing it as cowardice and as the first step towards a destructive nihilism, yet some of Miłosz's most important work is ironic (he reads his 'Incantation' and 'The World' as ironic poems, a reading at odds with Heaney's, resulting in a different view of poetry's relation to values and history). Echoes of Auden are present in the work of Polish poets, but cannot be ordered in a neat pattern of influence.

Zbigniew Herbert, the second major Polish influence upon Heaney, uses a poetic speaker – often a moralist and mentor, using a tone suffused with irony but reaching towards unironic moral conclusions and commands – who bears some similarity to Auden's (particularly Auden until the mid-forties; late Auden is different altogether). Van Nieukerken holds that Auden and Herbert both think it possible for man to rise above his own corporeality (the 'blood and soil' of his embodiment) and evaluate himself, society, and civilization from a transcendent perspective; this shared trait helps to define each poet's perspective from those of his contemporaries. There is always, however, a tension between the author and the subject in their work, since the former is always 'on the side of the sacred,' which he allies with good and truth; this ever-present 'vertical hierarchy' can make their poems appear, van Nieukerken posits, to be moralities (143–4, my translation and paraphrase). In other words, the conflicts within them lose drama when they gain moral resonance; yet is this actually true for a poem such as 'Apollo and Marsyas'? Van Nieukerken's parallel is bold and brave. When he uses it as a basis for criticism, however, it loses its specific applicability; it may be better to use the Auden-Herbert comparison to discern a possible crossover between West and East rather than as a critical tool.

How, then, do such parallels relate to Heaney? First, they reveal the cultural crossings that were taking place during his early years that influenced the way in which Polish poetry was written. Second, they reveal the importance of Polish poetry in particular. Because Miłosz is by far the strongest Eastern European influence on Heaney's work *and* a pre-eminent bridge figure, the intersections of Polish and Anglo-American poetry are especially relevant to understanding his centrality. We must also remember that Barańczak – poet, critic, translator, and professor of Polish poetry – was Heaney's colleague, friend, and co-translator at Harvard. Third, these literary borrowings and parallels complicate the task of the following three chapters of this study, which will trace the precise poetic influences at work upon Heaney, those of Herbert and of Miłosz. It is important, therefore, to know that whereas Heaney and Herbert do not take poetic influence from Eliot, Miłosz does, and his desire to transgress the boundaries of traditional lyric structure and discourse may usefully be compared to his Anglo-American predecessor's. The complexity of his irony may help to explain Heaney's difficulty in assimilating Eliot's influence, since it brings Heaney to a poetic road not taken. We have come to a much more subtle and multifaceted vision of Miłosz in particular, and Polish poetry in general, by working through these pathways of influence. This is a potentially immense topic, yet such glancing comparisons allow us to see how careful the tracing of Heaney's particular poetic connections must be. His Eastern European reading list, which we may surmise from his comments, essays, and allusions, does not furnish the entire picture of his encounter with this poetry from the late 1960s onward: we must supplement it with an awareness of crossings and borrowings between predecessors and contemporaries too often bypassed in discussions of Heaney's work.

3 Zbigniew Herbert and the Moral Imperative

Comparative Conditions, Critical Terms

'Twenty years ago, Herbert's writing was treated as a directive. His texts were deciphered in search of guidelines regarding key matters – who one is, what is reasonable, what is valuable, and what is worthwhile to do with one's life,' writes Piotr Śliwiński in 2007. Zbigniew Herbert, he believes, possessed an authority surpassing that of any other poet at the time, even Czesław Miłosz (Czapliński and Śliwiński 129, my translation). Śliwiński, in his end-of-the-century assessment of contemporary verse, assumes a Polish audience who may read such a statement polemically. The post-communist era is a great one for reassessments, and by means of his slight hyperbole, this major literary critic encourages us to view Herbert's authority with amused bemusement. It is, however, entirely of a piece with Heaney's view of Herbert, proving that authority travels across continents and oceans remarkably well.[1] Heaney feels no need to compare Herbert and Miłosz's gifts, but instead focuses upon defining the complex nature of each – complex because, in Herbert's case, we are faced with plain, even minimalist verse, animated by a prodigious and subtle moral sense that is constantly plumbing its own depths and judging itself not subtle enough.

Herbert writes starkly and commandingly of the moral imperative that poetry must bear, but Heaney insists upon Herbert's essential, if hidden, 'mellowness.' This is one of the seeming paradoxes around which Heaney's view of Herbert pivots; Herbert's example and Heaney's description of Herbert's work are not always aligned. This is partly explained by a generic split: Herbert represents, first and foremost, the sternness of Eastern European communist-era verse, in which moral pronouncements have the force of immediate utility as well as general applicability. Yet Heaney prefers to ally him with the Mediterranean sun and cultural bounty honoured in his essays entitled *The Barbarian in the Garden*, and not with the altogether different imagistic field of Herbert's poems. Herbert is a writer who loves order and beauty: *The Barbarian in the Garden* (first published in Polish in 1962, one year after his poetry volume *A Study of the Object*) eloquently chronicles his travels in the countries of the Mediterranean. The poetry is something different. It refuses the consolations of sensuality with a self-punishment that also refuses the consolation of self-flagellation.

In his expository response to Herbert, Heaney manifests a compulsion to blur the foreignness of his idiom, rendering it amenable to his own vision. In his verse, however, he summons a different example, adapting Herbert's study of objects as moral barometers to his own metonymic practice, though with important modifications of tone and situation. Herbert's 'reism' (most famously manifested in 'The Pebble') and his *artes poeticae* ('The Knocker,' 'Apollo and Marsyas') provide disquieting inspiration to Heaney. The descriptive critical terms themselves, though frequently used by Polish scholars, are contestable. Reism, the study of objects, is a neutral term, but Herbert's object studies are not neutral, but motivated by admiration – at times, nearly nostalgia, or idealization – of objects. We speak here of physical objects – stones, chairs and tables, pen and lamp – and not of objective correlatives or objectified humans. The more humble, the better. These things allow him to write about perception and judgment, and especially about their motivation of reflexive judgment. The term 'reism,' then, begs to be read with a touch of irony. The category of *ars poetica* may be similarly ironized. A poem that calls for a new art – 'let us say, concrete' – and offers as its first masterwork a nightingale turned to stone is no traditional *ars poetica* ('Apollo and Marsyas'). Rather, it shows us the conditions under which certain forms of art, such as the art of witness (Philomela's song) or traditional lyric (Keats's full-throated warbler) are rendered impossible. As the poem signals the existence of submerged content, so it becomes an *anti–ars poetica*. Its ethics depend upon the troubling of our descriptive terminology for it. In spite of such difficulties, Herbert is often discussed in terms of the 'messages' carried by his poems; as we will see, this conditions his posthumous legacy to a great extent (perhaps, too great an extent). Although it is de rigeur to mention his formal minimalism, he is most readily viewed as an ethicist who 'dehumanizes' art by showing its independence from the human subject (see Rudman, 'A Calm and Clear Eye'), which is constantly displaced from the possibility of egocentrism.

Another brief terminological clarification is in order. The terms 'ethics' and 'morality,' and their correspondent adjectives, are often used interchangeably. 'Morality,' however, is associated with the *systematization* of behavioural rules, so that we speak of 'moral principles'; moral psychology questions whether people are free to act as moral agents, thereby setting their own behavioural guidelines (Deigh in Audi 248–9). Simon Blackburn notes that one *usage* of 'morality' restricts the term to 'systems such as that of Kant, based on notions such as duty, obligation, and principles of conduct.' Ethics, by contrast, is seen by Blackburn as 'the study of concepts involved in practical reasoning,' involving exactly the Kantian notions enumerated above (Blackburn 121, 241). Ethics is associated with *study* (and is synonymous with 'moral philosophy'), a definition also upheld by John Deigh, who defines ethics as the philosophical study of morality (Deigh in Audi 244). There is a basic etymological distinction between the two terms – 'ethos' signifies 'character,' whereas 'mores' are customs and habits. Julia Annas holds that recent theoretical arguments support a view of ethics as a broader field than morality, lacking the narrowness of *mores* and the concomitant narrowness of twentieth-century definitions of morality.[2] One of the cornerstones of morality is responsibility and, concomitantly, obligation; Annas provocatively holds that ethical theories inevitably incorporate concern for the good of others even if they are founded on a care for the self and, thus, most ethical theories are *also* moral (Annas in Becker and Becker 485–6).

Zbigniew Herbert is primarily concerned with morality. Whereas Miłosz plays the role of ethicist in his verse, Herbert is more ready than he to postulate moral principles, hence his famous starkness. He exposes differences between systems that uphold different conceptions of the good and their relation to aesthetic modes ('Apollo and Marsyas'). In 'The Knocker,' a choice of artistic materials is simultaneously a choice of moral principles. Geoffrey Warnock's attention to morality's effort to counteract the damaging limitations of human sympathies is especially relevant for examining Herbert's reism. He is a moral poet because of his belief that values can and should be systematized, and that purity of language is one such value. His early poems are dramatic, bringing moral systems to life in precise situations. Herbert's conception of the self is, correspondingly, marked by the deliberateness of his choice of values.

It is difficult, however, to neatly encapsulate his influence upon Heaney; it does not announce itself in the same way as that of Wordsworth, Hughes, or even Dante. Despite Herbert's popularity in the English-speaking world, Heaney does not often quote him in poems, essays, or interviews, as opposed to his continual quotation of Miłosz. He is often subsumed into the mass of 'Eastern European poets' by Heaney and his critics alike, even though no poet stands as emblematically as Herbert does in relation to the Polish people suffering Soviet rule; no poet is so fully associated with the moral perspective of his poems. This phenomenon is common to English and Polish readerships, though they make two slightly different figures out of Herbert. His reputation at home was coloured by his participation in the anti-Nazi Home Army (Polish 'AK') during the Second World War, when Herbert was a very young man, his impoverished living conditions, and the many odd jobs – several of them strikingly humble, such as selling his own blood – that he held in his life. Herbert was a staunch lifelong opponent of communism, again unlike Miłosz, who worked as a cultural attaché after the war until his disgust with the regime reached a point of no return. Although such oppositions can be simplistic and even unfair (Miłosz, too, lived in poverty for several years, if this is to serve as any proof of moral authority), they undergird these poets' reputations, which depend so greatly upon their historical experiences, life conditions, and reputations as moralists. These individual biographical factors, however, were less important to English-language readers than the larger socio-political circumstances in which they situated him. Even an unabashedly formalist reader such as Heaney could not ignore their consequences.

A Brief History of Encounter

The conditions of Herbert's Anglo-American reception are different from that of Mandelstam, Brodsky, or Miłosz: his effect is immediate and dramatic. The slight irony is that Herbert is known as a 'late debut' in Poland, publishing his first volume during the so-called thaw of 1956 in his early thirties for reasons of internal censorship. Several volumes appeared in Polish thereafter and, fast on their heels, his first translations into English. He was introduced to the English-speaking world by his friend and compatriot Czesław Miłosz, who included a significant selection of Herbert's work in his 1965 *Postwar Polish Poetry* and then, together with Peter Dale Scott, created the *Selected Poems* published in 1968. Containing an introduction by Alvarez and published by Penguin in their new Modern Poetry in Translation series, it was a popular and accessible volume. Both books were available to Heaney when he was seeking to write a newly interventionary poetry.

Herbert was, therefore, better known to English-speaking audiences than Miłosz in the 1960s, in spite of his younger age and the fact that he did not live in an English-speaking country for longer than a few months' visit (again, as opposed to Miłosz). In their correspondence, we hear Miłosz begging the younger poet to hold poetry readings in English, despite Herbert's imperfect command of the language. He did not need to be reminded: in the same year as *Selected Poems* came out, Herbert undertook a coast-to-coast reading tour of the United States, followed two years later by a semester-long teaching appointment in California.[3] Bogdana Carpenter distinguishes Miłosz's emigration-turned-exile from Herbert's long-term trips abroad, calling Miłosz the 'poet of exile' and Herbert the 'poet of return' (Carpenter, 'Czesław Miłosz'). Herbert's years abroad in Europe cannot be called 'exile' or even truly emigration, since Herbert kept, as Carpenter points out, returning to Poland. He describes the quality of life under martial law to his friend Stanisław Barańczak when the latter accepts a post at Harvard University, and warns him not to forget his homeland, to 'denationalize' himself ('Proszę tylko – nie daj się wynarodowić,' in Toruńczyk, ed., *Zbigniew Herbert* 10). He keeps a close eye on national politics, discussing them in his correspondence with a good deal of fervour.[4] Herbert is clearly not a person who wishes to 'denationalize' *himself*. Perversely, perhaps, this helps to make him influential and even, to a certain extent, fetishized, in the English-speaking world: he is the poet-moralist par excellence.

The matter of Herbert's reception, succinctly summarized by Carpenter in her Polish-language article on Herbert in the Anglo-Saxon world (2000), reveals some surprising divisions among readers. Whereas Mark Rudman finds it surprising and praiseworthy that Herbert does not rely on his real historical experiences to furnish spectacles for poems, other readers, such as John Bayley, wish that there were more human emotion in his verse, which he finds *too* impersonal. Others believe his voice to be panhuman and intersubjective, not devoid of subjectivity altogether (Bell). Helen Vendler opines that post-war American poets searching for a new social consciousness in verse found this in Herbert's work, which Carpenter connects to the wave of student protests in 1960s Europe, occurring exactly as Herbert's *Selected Poems* were being published, and echoed somewhat earlier by protests against the Vietnam War in the United States. Herbert's work would have represented a type of social consciousness that was comprehensible for readers abroad, for whom dissidence was a noble posture, but we must not smooth over the discrepancy between conscientious objection to battles waged elsewhere and outrage at wrong perpetrated at home, affecting one's own health and safety. Bearing this caveat in mind, the category of 'protest poetry' could, possibly, be stretched to include Eastern European work. The matter of voice and impersonality may, however, trouble the efficacy of protest, which relies upon strength and distinctiveness of voice. Herbert's parable poems, which infrequently feature a highly individualized voice, do not fit comfortably into this category as a whole, though there are strong exceptions.

Alvarez's championship of Herbert runs along a very different track, and his voice is pervasive and strong. For him, Herbert's socio-political conditions are a central part of his poetic appeal, and their strength cannot be diluted by drawing too many parallels to writers under other regimes. The singularity of Herbert's experience commands our attention. This is a different attitude towards Herbert's poetry than that of Rudman or Bell, focusing upon what may *not* be highlighted by Herbert but is nevertheless, he believes, central to Herbert's appeal. Although Herbert does not write reportage, but uses Greek and Roman material to form allegories that can be read politically (though they are never merely topical), Alvarez calls his poetry 'unremittingly political' and, furthermore, asserts that 'it could never have been otherwise' (Introduction, *Selected Poems* 9). There is some geopolitical determinism about this view, though he qualifies himself by establishing Herbert as a 'party of one' sceptical of all dogma, and by pointing to Herbert's irony (10–11). Qualifications and disclaimers notwithstanding, Alvarez's introduction casts Herbert as a political poet concerned with survival (11), at odds with prevailing Western modes of writing (9), whose classicist restraint must be understood as a coping strategy (15). It can be read as a rather romantic preamble.

Alvarez makes himself into a champion of Eastern European poetry and, surprisingly, a critic of Seamus Heaney, lambasting the Irishman for his unjustly earned early fame – which, he believes, is due largely to the championship of Karl Miller and Christopher Ricks. He wishes Heaney shared Herbert's engagement with 'deep politics' as well as locally specific issues (Alvarez in Sommer, *Zapisy* 32–3, 38–9). This is hardly a fair criticism after *North*, and at this point Heaney does not need championing – if anything, he is too much in the limelight. He also does not need advice to read Herbert, whom he had been reading assiduously. Yet it took some time for Heaney's reading to percolate into his poetry, and this is why we confront a temporal gap between his exposure to Eastern European poets and evidence of their influence: as he recollects, 'It takes a while for new work to enter you deeply enough so that you can talk and be convincing to yourself about it. That historically aware, hard-bitten eastern European aesthetic meant more to me in the 1980s [than the 1970s], as a precaution against the ahistorical, hedonistic aesthetic that I was encountering in America.' The influence of Eastern Europe, curiously, is seen to work backward so that its aesthetic is precautionary, helping him to resist the seduction of ahistoricism (Heaney in O'Driscoll, *Stepping Stones* 281–3). The same point comes up in his reading of Miłosz. The salubrious preventative medicine of this aesthetic, then, was at work well before Heaney took on its influence directly.

An overall portrait, sketched by English and American hands, is emerging. Herbert is unremitting, uncompromising, stark, ascetic, impersonal. The *Selected Poems* contains a brief back-cover text that severely informs its reader, 'No country has suffered more of the brutalities of Communism and Fascism than Poland. Yet Zbigniew Herbert, the most classical of its poets, is neither nationalist or Catholic.[5] He speaks for no party.' That such language exerted an impact on Heaney's thinking is indubitable. Holding himself warily apart from (political) nationalism, embracing yet critiquing his childhood Catholicism, Heaney also wishes to 'speak for no party' in Northern Ireland. Major figures such as J.M. Coetzee contribute to this view, derogating readers who wish to equate Herbert with a party line – even if it be a noble party – and opining that Herbert's irony is itself an ethical value. We must not play censor ourselves by narrowing his range to fit our own biases (Coetzee 147–62).

The severity of these views may surprise readers of Herbert's epistolary correspondence, which was published after his death and is only available in Polish: the young Herbert, who would meet Miłosz for long evenings of wine and conversation, is no ascetic. When we consider Herbert's reflected image, we see a very sharp-edged figure, and this has much to do with the time during which Herbert's popularity among English readers was strongest. The dates of Heaney's encounter with Herbert are especially salient: for one, the poems that he initially read were those of Herbert's early and middle period, from 1956 until the mid-1960s, by which time he had published four volumes. These poems are marked by moral engagement with particular manifestations of cruelty and by a special interest in the physical object as instrument of judgment. They are animated by moral injunctions, sometimes latent and sometimes patently incorporated into the poem itself. In addition, these poems are written during the early years of communist rule, and are read by Heaney precisely during the escalation of the Irish Troubles.[6] By the 1980s, certain of Herbert's anthologized poems were 'as familiar as anything in Hughes or Larkin' (Heaney in O'Driscoll, *Stepping Stones* 114–15). Both poets work through myth and through attention to physical objects, even while the linguistic surfaces of their poems are strikingly different. Herbert's poems are marked by a questioning of the individual's historical role and an outward-directed focus towards reader and historical co-participant rather than an inward gaze; this is, we may recall, something Heaney wishes to emulate. Herbert's poems, like Heaney's, are spoken by an individual, yet unlike Heaney's, they often take individuality as a problem to be thought through rather than as a natural, given condition (see Heaney in Curtis 104–5, and Brearton in Campbell, 94–112). Although Herbert consistently addresses the moral capacities of the self, his orientation towards the self is not psychological. The self is a solid and yet faceless entity; it presents an ontological conundrum as well as a moral testing ground. The way in which Heaney brings the lyrical 'I' into existence is based on a radically different relation to the self than that underpinning Herbert's work. This is made manifest not just by its origins but by how the self comes into being and, as a voice, engages with the world outside of the self.

The Self as Individual

Arent van Nieukerken, one of the only scholars to undertake a deep comparison of Heaney and Herbert, posits that the difference between the poets' lyrical personae hinges on the individual's relation to nature and its psychological correlate, instinct. In his search for an adequate metaphorical persona for the Polish poet, Heaney does not choose Antaeus, his own mythological alter ego who is strengthened by contact with the earth, behaves instinctually,[7] and represents 'the pieties of illiterate fidelity' (Heaney in Deane 67). Instead, he chooses Atlas, a titan who, according to van Nieukerken, 'chooses his duty and field of struggle consciously.' He continues, 'This choice is no longer a straightforward act of identification with certain oppressed social or national groups. It results from the conscious selection of a transpersonal system of values' (261, my translation throughout). By associating Herbert

with 'transpersonal' rather than local values, Heaney additionally justifies his choice of Herbert as moral guide urging him to distance himself from cultural specificity (whether he does so is another question).
Van Nieukerken holds that the difference between Antaeus and Atlas
replicates itself in the poets' choices of alter egos – King Sweeney on
Heaney's part, Mr Cogito on Herbert's. Herbert's '*porte-parole*' evinces
none of the primal 'spontaneity that poets often associate with ... nature' (263), whereas Heaney's transmogrified avian king feels the same
sort of ecstatic communion with nature as the real Heaney when he
writes autobiographically. Herbert is 'a true poet of culture,' not of nature, whether in its benign or malevolent guises (260, 263). The choice
of Herbert as an exemplar, then, represents a decisive turn away from
Wordsworth, Hughes, and Kavanagh, poets for whom the 'I' defines
itself in intimate relation with – and agonistic struggle against – the
natural world.

At the heart of Heaney's ideational engagement with Herbert is the
question of individuality: does the lyric 'I' subsume itself into collective
endeavour ('Our pioneers keep striking / Inwards and downwards'
in 'Bogland'), does it subsume its particularity of thought into simple
decision (Herbert's 'yes – yes,' 'no – no'), or does it simply evade our
attempts to give it what we call personality? These represent three op-
tions for escaping the overly subjectivized 'I,' yet in *The Government of
the Tongue*, Heaney discusses several of Herbert's most famous poems
in a grand attempt to *personalize* the poet. This seems perverse. Heaney
appears ambivalent towards the notion of impersonality, which he
understands partly in accordance with Eliot's distinction between the
man who feels and the mind that creates and partly in view of an implicit correlation of personality with expression of character – in other
words, not just with individuality. 'Personality' is the presence of a feeling psychology in one's work and the establishment – through voice
and technique – of a particular character for the speaker. Herbert's poetry is almost always spoken by an individual. It is not voiced by a
collective. Yet it is not, most of the time, personal. The essay in which
Heaney most directly addresses this matter is 'Atlas of Civilization.'
It focuses on Herbert's volume *Report from the Besieged City* (1985); in
particular, Heaney mentions those poems ventriloquized by the persona of 'Mr Cogito,' who, he explains, serves as 'the poet's alibi/alias/
persona/ventriloquist's doll/permissive correlative' (60), and lightens
the 'possible portentousness' of Herbert's poetry 'because [its events
are] happening not to "humanity" or "mankind" but to Mr Cogito'

(60). The claim is, frankly, puzzling: when does a courageous, 'historically aware' poetry become dispiritingly 'portentous'? Heaney makes
a concerted attempt to personalize Herbert, and once the lyric speaker
is named, albeit with a generic denotative marker, the possible 'portentousness' that clings to general collectives ('humanity') dissipates.

Heaney's comment reveals his roots in a twentieth-century tradition
of embodied, concrete writing well situated in time, place, and psychology. Yet he consciously turns away from this tradition when he
immerses himself in Polish poetry. His derogation of 'portentousness'
reminds us that Heaney's early 'Personal Helicon' dramatizes an opposite sort of portentousness: 'I rhyme to see myself, / To set the darkness echoing,' he writes, and such lines, in which ominously echoing
darkness merges with the self-recognized narcissism of the young poet,
reveal that absorption in the 'I' can be as portentous as absorption in
'humanity' (see also Hobsbaum in Curtis 11–25). Heaney is wary of
speech too broadly disseminated among the constituents of 'humanity'
and speech that gathers humanity into the singular quantity of 'mankind.' The assumption motivating this notion – that the self is something to be celebrated – points up the difference between Heaney and
Herbert's degrees of personality.[8]

Herbert cannot celebrate the self because of his constant longing to
break through contingency into the absolute. He, like Miłosz, takes a
strong stand against the necessary contingency of morality. Although
he waxes cynical over the limitation of art's autonomy by its time and
place, and the manner in which time and place determine its relative
importance in the eyes of others, Herbert also believes in 'almost-
unreachable truths' (in Bożena Shallcross's useful collocation). We
can reach the absolute because our capacities are not absolutely limited. Shallcross posits epiphany as a state in which they are reached:
in such moments the artwork is pulled out of its historical and social
background, and we glimpse truths that lie beyond the material realm
(Shallcross 19–78). These epiphanic flashes beyond the contextual are
motivated at least partially by the poet's inability to *directly* engage his
context. Indirection not only finds directions out, but it allows the mind
to engage an immaterial realm of knowledge; allegory allows for engagement with superstructural ideas, '*almost*-unreachable truths.'

With a characteristic dash of irony, Herbert juxtaposes the high value
of allegorical verse written in unfree conditions with the implicitly
lower value of verse written 'freely,' in mimetic mode: 'It is unfortunate
that there is no censorship in Poland now [after 1989] ... since I shaped

my style in order to evade the censor. I used to write serious, tragic poems, and now I write about my body, my illnesses' (Czapliński and Śliwiński 321–2). The censorship bureau, then, plays an authorial role itself, shaping the country's literary production. Herbert's comment is purposefully provocative. In the late years of his life, which coincided with the entrance of Poland into the so-called First World, he gained notoriety for lamenting, rather than celebrating, the state of the country. In the above-cited interview, he makes socio-political change poetically relevant by daring the listener to disclaim a connection between politics and thematics. Changes in context impel changes in content; yet even the most ideologically minded critic would protest such a simplistic statement. We infer, instead, that Herbert criticizes his own late style, and its decreased sense of tragedy (the sufferings of the body, presumably, are not the proper stuff of tragedy). In 'Atlas of Civilization,' however, Heaney professes admiration of precisely those poems that strike an 'unusually intimate and elegiac note' (61),[9] praising the bits and scraps of the personal to be found in Herbert's early work. Heaney is naturally alive to personal expressivity. It gains him entry into the poem and affirms its own value, which can be counterpoised with the impersonal machinery of the totalitarian state (see 'The Interesting Case of Nero, Chekhov's Cognac and a Knocker' in *The Government of the Tongue*). Yet the 'intimate ... note' is typical neither of Herbert nor of the tradition in which he writes. Despite his anti-Romanticism, Herbert's use of a public-oriented voice hearkens back to the Polish Romantic mode;[10] it is not quite the individuated, personalized voice that Heaney wishes it to be.

Heaney, however, is an astute critic of his own thought processes, and habitually rethinks his first impressions. He quotes Herbert's own introduction to *Report from the Besieged City*: 'I wanted to bestow a broader dimension on the specific, individual, experienced situation, or rather, to show its deeper, general human perspectives' (*Government* 62). The individual is a *terminus a quo*, not a *terminus ad quem*. Specificity is not a value in itself; 'general human perspectives' are implied to be deeper than those of the individual. This phrase signals Herbert's particular brand of idealism, which is founded upon the belief that general perspectives *are* indeed accessible to the individual, and are best suited to attaining almost-unreachable truths. The inevitable specificity of experiential knowledge, however, cannot be disavowed; neither can the reality of experience: literature must be based on 'the description of objects, and not dreams. Out from the "I" of the artist there stretches a heavy, dark, but real world. One cannot stop believing that this world can be grasped in language' (Herbert in Bandrowska-Wróblewska 142, my translation). The 'I,' then, looks *out* from itself to the real; yet ethically responsible poetry must also depend on the inward gaze. Herbert's inward gaze has no interest in oneiric exploration or in confessionalism. Herein lies the central paradox of Herbert's lyrical persona: although Herbert is a public poet, speaking *to* the people, he is always a party of one, answerable to his individual conscience. The discrepancy between the speaker's solitariness and his publically pitched voice complicates Heaney's sense of 'unusual intimacy' with figures that are bereft of biography and spatio-temporal coordinates, figures who speak their piece in supra-temporal space (see Dettlaff 17).

It becomes clear that Herbert's own statement of intent points in an altogether different direction from the one in which Heaney points. It may be fallacious to base interpretation upon intent, but it is not fallacious to credit intent as the fuel which propels the poem into its own atmosphere, away from its intentionally constructed foundation. Mr Cogito is not fashioned with the intent of imparting intimacies. Tom Paulin views him as a 'Cartesian spectre called Mr Cogito whose thought processes never lead to the consoling infinite I AM. To call Mr Cogito Herbert's poetic persona is to clothe him in the myth of the individual' (*Minotaur* 204). Our search for poems revealing Mr Cogito's personality will bear little fruit. The poems in which he fulfils his function as generic thinking man are not only more numerous but, Heaney concedes, 'more brilliant as intellectual reconnaissance and more deadly as political resistance,' and to read them 'is to put oneself through the mill of Herbert's own personal selection process, to be tested for one's comprehension of the necessity of refusal, one's ultimate gumption and awareness' (61). An interesting dichotomy is thus created between intimacy and intellect, and between emotional efficacy, as it were, and political efficacy. The poems, however, go beyond the category of dissident poetry to become testing grounds for the deep ethics of writer and reader. They impel Heaney to consider 'ultimate' qualities and necessities; they prompt him to consider the limits of moral clarity.

Poems as Testing Grounds: 'The Haw Lantern' and 'The Pebble'

Heaney carries this concept of the poem as testing ground into the eponymous centrepiece of his volume *The Haw Lantern*. The burning hawthorn branch provides a small amount of light for a 'small people,'

who are judged in advance as unable to withstand the full truth of illumination. The core of the poem, though, occurs after its first quintet,
when it turns to consider the individual, who is summoned in an accu-
satory second-person pronoun. 'Your' breath forms the image of 'your'
own accuser, the Greek ascetic Diogenes, who turns the safely small
light into an instrument of judgment:

> and you flinch before its bonded pith and stone,
> its blood-prick that you wish would test and clear you,
> its pecked-at ripeness that scans you, then moves on. (*The Haw Lantern* 7)

The poem calls attention to its own inability to be a Petrarchan or a
Shakespearean sonnet: it contains a quintet and octave in a rough pentameter that is never quite iambic, its lines not quite isometric, and its
line endings not quite rhymed.[11] The poem's formal qualities ultimately
signal its own imperfection – the speaker has failed Diogenes's test. The
poem refers to form but does not embody it.

The second person is deictic, which confers immediacy on the poem's test – 'you' are (now) being accused – but functions generically,
much like Mr Cogito. This is rare in Heaney's work, which usually relies on a highly individuated first-person speaker. Here, though, the
subject's existence as *object* of moral testing is central to the poem. The
Anglo-Saxon monosyllables beat the gravity of the test into the reader,
while its anapests ('and you *flinch*') intrude an alternate influence into
the rhythm of the poem: this is Juvenilian satire. 'The Haw Lantern' is
at once utterly sincere, ending with a deep silence, and gently satiric of
the would-be moralist, who fails the very test that he has imagined. It is
not a poem of grand 'illumination' but one in which the small flame of
self-respect sputters a bit as it is lifted, perhaps, too high, and invested
with too much solemnity for the speaker to formally match. This is a
common thread in the poems summoning Herbert's moral tests and
ethical resolutions: the speaker finds himself unequal to the situation
that he has imaginatively created, and invests the poem with a tonal
complexity that undermines the affirmation he desires. This is what
Heaney means when he says that 'The Haw Lantern' is written in a tone
rather than a voice (Brandes 18). Whereas 'voice' is built upon selfhood
and personality, tone is a subtler entity to pin down. Heaney's early
poems have a strong voice. It is inescapable. After he internalizes Herbert's work, he begins to adapt his strategies. It would be fallacious to
claim that 'The Haw Lantern' replicates a Herbert poem. This would be

straightforward yet implausible – strained at best – and would depend upon dry clause-for-clause matching that would tax the most patient close reader. Yet it would also be fallacious to pretend that Herbert's influence does not inspire such poems. Heaney's *voice* will never sound like Herbert's, but the tone and the test are strikingly Herbertian.

This is how Herbert's influence is naturalized. 'The Haw Lantern' does not leave Heaney's beloved home ground for exotic provinces, it foregrounds the local haw and its seasonal life, and its linguistic home is Anglo-Saxon. Heaney's volume *North* definitively associated Northern European culture with brutality and 'behind-back' violence, and in *The Haw Lantern* and *Station Island*, he measures his lyric speakers by means of representatives from Continental, often southern European, cultures. Greek and Latin figures and terms are brought to scrutinize the hyperboreans; the south judges and satirizes the north. Helen Vendler, in contrast, offers an English genealogy for the poem, stating that '[its] mode is, surprisingly, that of the metaphysical emblem,' so that the burning haw owes a symbolic debt to George Herbert's rose 'whose hue, angry and brave, / Bids the rash gazer wipe his eye' (Vendler, 'On Three Poems' 68–9). Yet the generic 'you' scrutinized by the haw is not rash but unjust; the emblem is wintry and bare, 'pith and stone,' not bright, not angry, and befitting a 'small people.' William Scammell believes that 'the preacher mounts the lectern' in this poem, implying that the humble haw is miscast in its emblematic role: 'When symbol usurps fact, or fails to mesh with the literal, disbelief raises a basilisk eye' (Scammell 42–4). This is a technique learned from Eastern European parable poems, in which symbol *must* usurp 'fact' to take effect. The problem inheres in how we conceive of the poem's linkage of symbol, tone, and predominant 'mode.' Whereas Vendler opposes parabolic and emblematic forms on the basis of their sensory specificity, Heaney's haw partakes of both. The former quality inheres predominantly in tone, the latter in literary-historical mode.

'The Haw Lantern' satirizes the speaker's desire to rise above his 'small people' (a desire also critiqued in 'Exposure' and 'Holly,' which echo some of the poem's imagery) and maintains the unstated, unproved yet deeply understood importance – even, perhaps, necessity – of being 'scanned' as a necessary trial of conscience. This is a constant motif in Herbert's work. His central figures are constantly gazed upon, scanned, judged. The most influential poem of this kind must be 'The Pebble.' This object is perfect because 'mindful of its limits,' simply itself through and through, bearing 'a scent that does not remind one of anything' or cause emotion; it is, thus, 'just and full of dignity,' qualities put up against those of the speaker:

> I feel a heavy remorse
> when I hold it in my hand
> and its noble body
> is permeated by false warmth
>
> – Pebbles cannot be tamed
> to the end they will look at us
> with a calm and very clear eye

Heaney cites the poem in full within 'Atlas of Civilization' without mentioning the indentation of its last stanza. Both Herbert's original and Miłosz's translation bear an indent (see Herbert, *Selected Poems* 38–9 for a facing-page translation). The final three lines, therefore, appear to be spoken by a second voice, one which quashes the speaker's attempt – remorseful yet insistent – to 'tame' the pebble by imbuing it with the 'false warmth' of a tightly closed hand. The Polish verb 'to tame' is 'oswoić,' which has at its roots the adjective 'swój,' or 'one's own.' The pebble, thus, refuses to be humanized, to be made our own, in our image. Moreover, the passive construction ('cannot be tamed') is active. Here are the last three lines of the original: 'Kamyki nie dają sie oswoić / do końca będą na nas patrzeć / okiem spokojnym bardzo jasnym.' Polish allows Herbert to invest the pebble with more power to refuse likeness, to choose alterity, at the same time as it is perversely viewed in terms of human qualities, both corporeal and ethical, which leads Jerzy Jarniewicz to opine that 'Herbert does not so much allow objects to speak as he speaks through an object'; this is a sort of 'anthropomorphism *à rebours*' (Jarniewicz, 'Reizm pozorowany' 39, my translation). Jarosław Anders goes further, claiming that the poet ostensibly speaks of an object in this 'existential parable' but actually speaks of himself, his sense of entrapment within subjectivity and his unresolved internal oppositions (Anders 83–4). Herbert does not trust his senses enough to allow the pebble its individuality, but must subsume it – and all of his objects, Jarniewicz holds – into a historico-philosophical or an ethical discourse (39). Barańczak believes that the poem seeks to conceal the speaker's submerged horror at the pebble's indifference to experience (Barańczak 48–9). Viewed from this angle, Heaney's 'object poems' humanize their physical objects *by* turning them into emblems ('The Haw Lantern') or viewing them as partners or antagonists within the speaker's ethical project ('Sandstone Keepsake' and the 'Shelf Life' series). This horror at true objectivity is not fully engaged by Heaney. The question underlying Herbert's 'object poems' must be whether he does feel horror or rather its psychological antipode, envy.

'The Pebble' intrigues Miłosz as well, yet his reaction differs importantly. Herbert's object poems, he maintains, react to a spectre that frightens both poets, the spectre of moral relativism.[12] Its threat becomes acute when we consider the machinations of the communist regime. Herbert's poems obliquely convey the socio-political – not simply personal – experience of watching the powers-that-be manipulate language. This view of the poem roots it in the experience of life under totalitarianism. Herbert's socio-political experience informs a search for apposite moral terms and, correspondingly, for fitting poetic imagery. An object, to Miłosz, is precious 'simply because it is free of human attributes and, for that reason, deserving of envy.' He goes deeper: Herbert's historical experience has forced him to realize that the 'human domain' has 'shaky foundations,' both physically and ethically. Objects have the value of 'simply existing' (with the connotation of 'existing simply'). They reify what is absent: 'History is present in an object as an absence: it reminds us of itself by a minus sign, by the object's indifference to it.' Herbert's focus on objects is a provocation, then, to affirm the centrality of human coordinates – historical, psychological, moral – when faced with their denial. This interpretive strategy fundamentally differs from Heaney's, which focuses directly on those human coordinates.

Miłosz holds that Herbert's poem encodes a political statement: 'Pebbles cannot be tamed, but people can[;] tamed people are full of anxiety because of their hidden remorse; they do not look us straight in the face' ('Ruins and Poetry,' *To Begin Where I Am* 363–5). The pebble refuses to be a witness of history. Corollary to its disengagement is its clarity beyond innocence. As a representative of perfect clarity and untameable solidity, the pebble represents a moral absolute. Its qualities are non-human, and for that reason the human speaker of the poem must recognize it as an emblem of what he cannot, but must strive to, attain. Herbert explains his 'objective turn' in the oppositional framework clarified by his compatriot: 'At a time when everything went mad, transformed itself, I turned to objects in order to fashion a sort of private ontology ... I am on the side of values. They have to be lasting [*stałe*]; one cannot say 'Ah, we're living in a different epoch, now everything has changed.' Something must be lasting' (Herbert in Gorczyńska 165, my translation). The 'private ontology' takes its creative impetus from the spectre of public madness – that is, the Second World War and Soviet oppression, which changed its contours throughout the 1950s and 1960s. In other words, the pebble's solidity is correlated to its function as guardian of lasting values.

Heaney, in contrast, reads 'The Pebble' as a poem gesturing towards – if not enacting – a process of personalization: 'The poem's force certainly resides in its impersonality, yet its tone is almost ready to play itself on through into the altogether more lenient weather of personality itself' (*Government* 64–5). Yet the poem shifts in the last tercet into an entirely disembodied and impersonal voice. If personality is inextricable from humanness, then it is also personality, by extension, that the poem seeks to decry as a quality 'false' to the pebble, whose absolute alterity is necessary to its moral function. Miłosz insists upon the pebble's inhumanity as a precondition for the tacit, yet deep, critique of human beings underlying the poem. A focus upon play and eventual lenience has the opposite effect. Heaney's words are coloured by a profound desire to humanize Herbert, which is part of his own ability to write morally engaged yet humane verse. Neither poet accepts himself as a judge in these 'object poems' – the force of which resides in the objective judgment passed by lantern, pebble, or, we shall see, sandstone or granite – yet the quality of the judgment they propose differs. Heaney must reckon with the impersonal coldness of the pebble's moral compass, and he does so by searching for metaphors with which to personalize this foreign exemplar.

The distinction between force and play is not elaborated by Heaney, yet it is central to his reading of Polish poetry. The poem's 'force' resides in a quality alien to him, yet the 'altogether more lenient weather' associated with the play of voice is clearly what gains his sympathy. What emerges from Heaney's reading of the poem is almost opposite to its ostensible intent. This is also where interpretations vary: Miłosz does not note any lenience in the poem, but insists upon its 'polemical' stance as a philosophical piece and not a lyrical evocation. Its subtext reaches into the realm of political ethics, not into the lenience of individual personality. Polish poet Julia Hartwig sets her own distinction between poetry of intellect and of instinct, and posits Herbert as a representative of the former (Hartwig 47). Nicole Krauss draws her distinction between the exact and the inexact with reference to 'The Pebble': 'The acute precision normally reserved for the realm of biology, geometry, or some other unflinching science becomes, in Herbert's hands, a tool for investigating the imagination, the soul, suffering; in short, everything inexact' (Krauss 13). Joseph Brodsky likewise allies Herbert with science: 'Herbert's poems unusually remind one of mathematical proofs or, if you prefer, fables, because of their concision and rawness' (Brodsky in Toruńczyk, 'Dukt pisma' 176). In his offhanded alliance of fable with mathematical proof, Brodsky points towards a specifically Eastern European correlation, one between word and ontological function: Herbert's 'private ontology' is reliant upon a faith in the word's ability to take on the hard contours of a scientific instrument used for the purpose of moral investigation – in which there is, indeed, a clear 'objective' perspective towards which one reaches. This is the 'absolute' clarity of the pebble.

To Heaney, Herbert is a poet who begins with a 'hard pure ... tartness' and eventually, by the early 1980s, mellows into a more palatable ripeness (*Government* 65). He even, surprisingly, allies the Herbert of 'The Pebble' with the forces adding to 'the world's anxiety' and not with conscience-clearing revolt: by 1985, Heaney writes, 'he has eased his own grimness, as if realizing that the stern brows he turns upon the world merely contribute to the weight of the world's anxiety instead of lightening it' (66). The criticism is surprising and surprisingly sharp. Herbert is not a poet who seeks 'lightening' as his stated intent, nor is he the poet to whom one would turn for such an effect. Heaney admires the hard-edged tone of such poetry, yet reveals his temperamental inclination to seek lightening over toughness; looking forward, this statement also reveals why Heaney will turn to Miłosz rather than Herbert when he seeks attunement with clearances and lightenings in his own work. In spite of this wide-ranging criticism, however, Heaney takes on the burden of influence: his 'object poems' debate the relative weight or levity with which the speaker's situation should be metaphorized.

Transmogrifying Herbert's Pebble

'Sandstone Keepsake' transmogrifies Herbert's pebble by placing it in uneasy territory, outside the Magilligan internment camp in Northern Ireland, where it is immediately politicized in a manner impossible for Herbert in his time and place. What we see, then, is a rather objective parable of a pebble turned into an act of local rebellion against specific socio-political practices; the calm and clear eye of the pebble becomes muddied and sullied. Although these qualities are initially seen as innocent (the stone is 'a kind of chalky russet / solidified gourd'), he later wonders if it is '[a] stone from Phlegethon,' 'bloodied' in the hot river of hell. Moving through a Herbertian questioning of the speaker's potential for historical action, the poem starts and ends by underplaying the moral and political weight of both stone and speaker:

> Anyhow, there I was with the wet red stone
> in my hand, staring across at the watch-towers
> from my free state of image and allusion,
> swooped on, then dropped by trained binoculars:
>
> a silhouette not worth bothering about,
> out for the evening in scarf and waders
> and not about to set times wrong or right,
> stooping along, one of the venerators. (*Station Island* 20)

This poem begins, as all of Heaney's 'object poems' do, with an evocative, personalized portrait, focused upon the 'kind of solidified gourd' held in the speaker's restless hands, then swerving into the free state of ambivalent engagement. Jerzy Jarniewicz, who believes 'Sandstone Keepsake' is a direct response to 'The Pebble,' notes that Heaney pays attention to the physical characteristics of objects, whereas Herbert treats them symbolically (*The Bottomless Centre* 116–17). This hearkens back to Miłosz's statement that Herbert is a calligraphic poet (Toruńczyk, 'Dukt pisma' 176). The physicality of Heaney's keepsake, alternatively, correlates to its capacity to 'actualize history' by providing material – rather than symbolic – links to a biographical past. It is different, however, from the archaic cultural objects in *North*, which are contemplated but not questioned as participants in ethical exploration.

The 'objective' relation to history in *Station Island*'s poems, such as the sequence following 'Sandstone Keepsake,' entitled 'Shelf Life,' is far less objective, in fact, than that vivified by Herbert's poems.[13] Herbert's pebble 'does not remind one of anything,' whereas a 'keepsake' is kept explicitly to summon the past, and bears a sentimental weight. Sentiment eventually joins with political history: likening the wet red stone to the heart of Henry of Almain, who had been killed by his cousin Guy de Montfort for political *and* personal motives, the speaker allows the world of politics and revenge to obtrude upon the seemingly private domestic realm.[14] It is, therefore, not quite Herbert's pebble that 'does not remind one of anything.' Although Herbert does not always avoid historical details, he habitually points away from those events to a sphere of universal values (Stala in Franaszek 206–7); although Heaney is tempted by this sphere and admires Herbert's ability to enter it responsibly, he shies away from taking this step himself, preferring to couch his explorations of values in specific cultural terms. These terms are certainly not always universal or neutral.

The difference between the poets and poems, though, runs deeper than this. Heaney's relation to language is different from Herbert's. His language is full of colloquial turns of phrase ('a kind of,' 'not worth bothering about'), words mimicking actions ('swooped on, then dropped'), particularities ('chalky russet,' 'hint of contusion,' 'sedimentary'), and colloquialisms. Donald Davie calls the meter 'licentiously variable' (Davie, 'Responsibilities' 60); Mary Kinzie thinks its 'conversational ease ... [amounts] at times to impudence' (Kinzie 36). This style personalizes the poem, marking it culturally and temperamentally ('Anyhow, there I was'). It also imbues the moral question at the centre of the poem – that is, whether the speaker should try 'to set times right,' to match the reliable weight of the stone with weighty judgment, to cast the stone of judgment at the keepers (abusers?) of power – with tonal levity, and even, at times, slight awkwardness (present in the stumble of 'about,' 'out,' and 'about'). This man is neither Herbert's moralist nor Yeats's emblematic fisherman; although Heaney customarily allows Latinate words to add gravitas, his 'venerators' are quietist non-participants in the historical drama. The comical rhyme with 'waders' is deflationary, and the speaker absolves himself of responsibility by affirming his insignificance. If Herbert is a master of a certain style degree zero, then Heaney is his opposite, the master of baroquely individuated utterance.

The eponymous objects to which Herbert and Heaney's poems are dedicated are obviously similar. The stones are dense, impermeable, and definitively other to the humans who clasp them. Both speakers impart 'false warmth' through physical touch and psychological extension. The object is made into a witness. It is necessary to do so because of the radical unreliability of human judgment. Herbert, however, vivifies the troubling nature of this unreliability, and builds his contrasts around the speaker's vexation. The speaker of 'The Pebble' longs to recognize a moral absolute, yet the poem refuses the elegiac consolations that an expression of longing would make manifest. Heaney's speaker, in contrast, does not long for absolutes but announces his unfitness to stand guard over this philosophical territory in 'Sandstone Keepsake' and 'The Haw Lantern.' He does not allow himself to make the choice that Herbert's speaker makes, but either deflects the choice (in the verbal swerve of 'Anyhow' in 'Sandstone Keepsake') or concludes that he cannot make it ('The Haw Lantern'). The stone does not bear the clear eye of inhuman judgment but represents a challenge to opaque fidelity, which is politically tested – the poem's central question is whether the speaker will redress injustice with an act of grand anger – and fails the test. Neither Herbert nor Heaney, then, allows his lyric personae the satisfaction of achieved heroism or perfect clarity.

Such a comparison, though, brings us back to where we started, to the issue of personality and readerly sympathy. Heaney's metaphors invite sympathy in their modesty – the stone is 'a kind of ... solidified gourd.' They enable, therefore, a different readerly act to take place: by grounding the poem so firmly in humility and concreteness, its poetic arc – from earth to air, from stone to 'free state of image and allusion,' from humility to imagined heroism – is put in relief. The poem undertakes an imaginative journey. Herbert's procedure is different: 'The Pebble' is an extended act of evaluation. Its short, compressed lines carry the mind along its length, but not the imagination: 'the pebble / is a perfect creature,' not needing metaphor. Neither pebble nor human observer gain much in readerly sympathy; Herbert does not situate his speaker, clothe him, or allow him colloquial turns of phrase. We do not need to speak of 'mankind' or 'humanity' to render abstract the human contours of Herbert's speaker. Such a comparison delineates each poet's relation to personality all the more clearly. The keepsake is not enough to summon the moral weather of Herbert's pebble. By keeping the surface of 'Sandstone Keepsake' local and, in Heaney's term, 'mellow,' the poet cannot summon the impersonal force that he wishes to emulate. In 'Granite Chip,' he will try to do otherwise.

Returning from Words to Things: 'Granite Chip'

Smoothness and mellowness may be counterpoised with dissonance and also depth; as we work through Heaney's attempt to create a Herbertian 'object poem,' our question must be how Heaney 'break[s] up the crust of surface realities' by reaching into 'the deeper levels of mind and culture' in his poems (Boss in Westarp, Boss, and Caudery 135), given that his *reluctance* to break up the personable surface of his poetry, in order to go beneath personality, is continually made manifest. Heaney openly cherishes the beauty of appearance and states his preference for a mellowness that does not add to the weight of the world. The issue subtending our question, though, is one of faith – not of the religious kind, but in the stable relation of words and things. Heaney has been faulted for his adherence to this faith, yet his irony and self-consciousness opens up a space of doubt. In this regard he is ably matched. Herbert takes the next step beyond irony, describing the experiences that provoke his suspicion of the surface realities themselves:

> I lived through ... more than one compromise of ideology, the shattering of a falsely created picture of reality, the capitulation of faith in front of facts. And then the domain of things, the domain of nature seemed to me like a point of stability, but also a point of departure making possible the creation of a picture of the world that would accord with our experience. After the false prophets departed, things, if you will, revealed their innocent face, unstained by lies. This is connected to the poets' old dream ... of paradise ... But poets don't have dominion over the world. Their only kingdom is language ... [Yet language is] every day tortured, made banal, and surrendered to nefarious courses of treatment. So the poets' dream is to ... give fitting words to things. (*Poezje wybrane*, 15–16, my translation)

Although his experience is obviously different from Heaney's, Herbert's need for a 'point of stability' to counter the vagaries of ideologically motivated behaviour would be well understood by the Northern Irishman. National history deeply permeates individual psychology. In Herbert's case, poetry is not used as a vehicle to explicate individual psychology but to gesture towards – if not to reach – the 'old dream' of paradise in an almost grotesquely simplified form. Only the innocent simplicity of objects can hold its own against the teachings of 'false prophets.' Objects, therefore, will represent the ideal in a more trustworthy manner than abstract theories. But they will also, Herbert implies, guarantee a certain noble accuracy of language, in contrast to the tortured, ignobly manipulated words used by the powers-that-be. Because the pebble is equal to itself and mindful of its limits, the language used to lyricize it must also bear these virtues.

Language is a value in and of itself. Its guiding ideals must, however, be clarified: every writer over the age of thirty must, Herbert states, ask himself why he writes, in defence of which values, and in opposition to which wrongs ('w obronie jakich wartości, przeciwko jakiej krzywdzie?' *Poezje wybrane* 14). A poet's character consists of 'a conscious moral posture toward reality' and an uncompromising sense of a boundary between good and bad. Herbert himself, in turn, espouses the value of linguistic accuracy, as against obliquity and Romantic 'inspiration' ('I don't like these so-called "inspired artists" ... making oneself into someone extraordinary is Romantic, and alien to me'). An author's intention must be as clear and disciplined as his language. Herbert consciously chooses rhetorical modesty in the interest of transparency: 'I don't attempt to astound the reader with a richness of metaphors, unusual language or remarkable rhythms and images. I would like the words of my poems, and their order, to be transparent ... not to have them hold the reader's attention, not to cause him to cry out "Oh, what a master," in order that they communicate reality in a clean and transparent manner' (*Poezje wybrane* 6, 12–13). A 'clean' manner contrasts with the sullied and tortured language the poet must refuse, and works in tacit reference to Apollo's shudder of disgust at his own instruments in 'Apollo and Marsyas.' This view of language justifies the critical commonplace that Herbert is a classicist poet, using chaste diction and spare language, avoiding Romantic excess and unfettered emotion.[15]

John Carey points to Heaney's need to 'warn against the imperialism of language [,] ... to return us from words to things,' which is close to Herbert's project. Heaney is, however, unlike Herbert, drawn to sophisticated rhythms – his poetic beginnings owe a great debt to Hopkins – and idiosyncratic language (sometimes unfairly derogated as 'Heaneyspeak'). He does not aim for transparency. Yet Heaney governs his tongue and disciplines his words, however much he may wish to remain 'untrammeled' and free, because he too realizes, together with Herbert (and Miłosz, and Yeats) that poetic discipline is linked to representational accuracy and ethical carefulness. He, too, wishes to recuperate the value of physical objects, not so much to discover their radical innocence as to uncover an ambiguity at their impersonal core.

His 'Granite Chip' cuts the speaker's hand, 'brilliant' and uncompromising in its inhumanness, its inability or (he implies) unwillingness to offer comfort or respite from worry:

Granite is jaggy, salty, punitive

and exacting. *Come to me*, it says
all you who labour and are burdened, I
will not refresh you ... (*Station Island* 21)

Whereas the surface features of the poem remain harmonious, the speaker's failure to find personal sustenance is emphasized. The object cannot always subserve his desire and intent. It cannot enter the lenient weather he longs for in his essays. Heaney's sandstone could not compel action, but could be domesticated as a 'keepsake'; the granite chip refuses to enter the world of personality. It also refuses to bear a singular meaning, which would enable its domestication. It leaves behind its initial cultural referentiality to become pure matter: 'Granite is jaggy, salty, punitive // and exacting.' The chip leaves its local habitation behind to become the bearer of wisdom, however unconsoling ('*I / will not refresh you*'). Unlike the inhumanly clear eye of Herbert's pebble, this stone belongs to one particular complex of values – it is a 'Calvin edge' hacked off a Martello tower – associated with a 'punitive' brand of northern Protestantism (stunningly metaphorized in Tom Paulin's 'Desertmartin,' published one year earlier). It bears a complex genealogy. The Martello fortifications were erected to repel foreign invasion, yet Heaney's terms of reference for his physical objects are, frequently, foreign, non-Irish. Is the tower chip repelling southern influence, and thus becoming repulsed itself after it tauntingly reminds the poet, 'You can take me or leave me'?[16] Its 'northernness' recalls Heaney's forays in *North*, the project of which was to *disclaim* foreignness by providing a cultural genealogy for contemporary Northern Irish violence. Yet here its 'Calvin edge' cuts through the speaker's 'complaisant pith' and, from its different cultural field, judges the speaker's lack of hard-edged determination in the same way as the bloodied sandstone recalls the unchristian act of revenge of which the speaker is incapable in 'Sandstone Keepsake.' We cannot so easily read the poem as a battle between Protestant north and Catholic south. Herbert is Heaney's paragon of minimalism and of classical geometric order, and the poem self-consciously pares itself down to approximate – in some guise – the bare perceptual conditions of Herbert's poems. In doing so, it begins to reconsider the object's claim upon the speaker: *is* it imperative to confront this ascetic object-judge?

The question is real, and derives from the split within Heaney's own assessment of Herbert between awed admiration for the 'tough-minded' writer of 'anti-poetry' and attunement to the 'tender-minded' celebrant of culture. Wishing for attunement with the former – despite his championship of the latter – he reminds himself that Herbert's 'impassiveness, the perspective, the impersonality, the tranquillity, all derive from his unblindable stare at the facts of pain' as well as his love for beauty (*Government* 58). This stare has to accept lack of consolation as well as uplift. It also has to accept banality (as opposed to the glamour of *North*'s treasures) and the lack of moral guidance: '*I / will not refresh you.*'

In a series of telling echoes from 'Sweeney Redivivus,' the speaker's home community is 'pious and *exacting* and demeaned' (my emphasis; *Station Island* 101), while 'The Scribes' are 'petulant / and jaggy,' scratching their myopic and angry way through 'texts of praise' (*Station Island* 111). Taken together, these lines stake out a fundamentally different relation to a certain complex of values – 'exacting,' 'jagged,' and ultimately 'punitive' – than Herbert's 'Pebble' does, which concentrates upon positive 'ardour and coldness,' which are 'just and full of dignity.' The speakers operate under divergent associative principles. A culture of moral exactitude may arise in response to demeaning conditions – minoritarian stature, socio-cultural oppression, and so on. Should we view its 'exacting' nature as a triumph over such circumstances or a dispiriting, self-defensive, and ultimately powerless reaction? The answers will differ according to historical context: 'jaggy' anger, moral exactitude, and hope for a better political future can spur successful rebellions. Each poet establishes his matrix of values in response to different cultural referents. Heaney reacts to the division between 'punitive' Protestants and 'exacting and demeaned' Catholics, and although he would surely object to such a negative dichotomy, it emerges from *Station Island* and conditions his response to the moral imperative.

Anti-Aestheticism and Asceticism: 'Apollo and Marsyas,' 'The Knocker'

How to stare unflinchingly, to write a meditative rather than a reactive poem: this is one lesson Heaney wishes to learn from Herbert. Heaney does not, however, wish to write too abstractly of moral choices, which would imply 'culpable detachment' (*Government* 58). His knowledge must be embodied. Its embodiment is physical and cultural. This is why Heaney is so frequently tempted to re-open local wounds. Herbert, however, is a master of what we may call abstract embodiment – the use of parables, classical myths, or adapted stories from antiquity to vivify ethics, to shape the moral system we must craft in answer to such situations. He is not, after all, a professional ethicist but a professional metaphorist, a poet. His defence of humanism – not, to Herbert or to Heaney, an obsolete or culpable term – and his study of pain are undertaken impassively. We watch through a pane of ice, to use Heaney's own metaphor, and this 'iciness' can only be observed from afar, not emulated. When Heaney quotes one of Herbert's darkest poems, 'Apollo and Marsyas,' he takes it as exemplary of an anti-aestheticism that he cannot embrace himself. This poem, together with 'The Knocker,' is a work of extremity in which the 'supra-individual principle' exacts strict obeisance. Its substance, though, would seem to banish the possibility of impersonality, and this is both the most affronting and affecting trait of the poem.

The 'real duel' between god and satyr is taking place after Marsyas won their musical contest, and is gratuitous. The poem carefully describes the flaying of Marsyas as the empirical basis for what may be 'a new ... art.' Apollo is focused upon the meticulous performance of his gruesome task while his victim howls an undifferentiated note of pain, yet the god is periodically 'shaken by a shudder of disgust,' reaching the limits of his endurance. Marsyas, by contrast, proves his artistic range by transforming the organic basis of art altogether, leading to an ultimate question:

> whether out of Marsyas' howling
> there will not some day arise
> a new kind
> of art – let us say – concrete
>
> suddenly
> at his feet
> falls a petrified nightingale
>
> ... the hair of the tree to which Marsyas was fastened
> is white
>
> completely (*Selected Poems* 26–9)

The poem contemplates the possibility of art in the face of conditions that silence lyricism, extending Adorno's dictum affirming the simultaneous impossibility and necessity of writing lyric poetry after Auschwitz – with the 'calm and absolutely clear eye' of the pebble. Yet the pebble is inactive and unreactive, while Apollo shudders twice in the course of the poem, can hardly endure Marsyas's howl, and only hypothesizes the foundation of 'concrete' art after he is no longer visually violated by his own act. Barańczak holds that Apollo's disgust is purely aesthetic, as manifested by his compulsion to clean his 'instrument' and by the unsettling aside – 'let us say' – which bespeaks cold indifference (*Fugitive from Utopia* 58). While his reading is canonical, it is doubtful whether the poem opposes ethics and aesthetics so neatly, if at all. Might not Apollo's shudder be both aesthetic and moral, encompassing the ambiguity of our own reaction to the abject body? Apollo imagines an art that moves out of the world of emotion altogether into concreteness, and is thereby divorced from the possibility of manifesting opposition or acquiescence. While Barańczak believes that 'the world of nature ultimately proves to be more sensitive than the god' in its reactive petrification, in shedding its organicism it also sheds its capacity for sympathy. The petrified bird cannot raise its voice any more than the pebble can take active part in human history. Herbert does not associate stone with heightened sensitivity or with cultural representation at all, unlike Heaney. Herbert's stones refuse to stand as objective correlatives but maintain a stoic inadequacy to the human situation, and here, emotional adequacy *is* a moral value. The poem's affective surplus becomes internalized by the reader. Barańczak's reading associates the emotion attendant upon interpretation with the materials of the poem itself. The poem, however, is unflinching, despite the note of surprise we hear when 'completely' is pulled apart to stand on its own, as a conclusion. This is its only hint of judgment, its only indication that the observer may be moved by the scene to remark upon the extraordinariness of the poem's procedure.[17]

Why 'concrete' art? The petrification that follows Marsyas's flaying mutes the voice mythologically associated with testimony, that of Philomela. In her comparison of Herbert's poem to its Ovidian exemplar, Joanna Niżyńska posits that Apollo's speculations on aesthetics represent the amorality of an art that *feeds* on suffering. The 'concrete' art associated with petrification formalizes pain and, thereby, deadens it; this type of art is associated with José Ortega y Gasset's theory of modernist dehumanization (Niżyńska, 'Marsyas's Howl' 162–5). Dehumanization encompasses de-personalization. The step away from personality is also a step away from pathos, and hence from tragic catharsis. Niżyńska, then, views the poem as the dramatization of a repellent aesthetic, not simply of indifference, thus provocatively – and dangerously – conflating stylization with deadening petrification. A similar view is expressed and supported in a different manner by Małgorzata Mikołajczak, who usefully compares the poem with Herbert's 'To Apollo' ('Do Apollina'), in which the god is portrayed as a walking stone, and associated with the pure beauty exemplified by the pebble's clear eye. She opines that this conception of art reveals

Herbert's disillusionment with 'pure' aesthetics, which he associates with unfeeling *levity*, and she counterpoises this unbearable lightness with sympathy, endurance, and effort. Yet Mikołajczak differentiates stoniness ('kamienność') from petrification ('skamieniałość'), which contains within it a tragic narrative. Herbert eschews an art that contemplates 'the small, sick soul'; for him, 'to survive ... *is* to petrify' (Mikołajczak 210, my translation and emphasis).

Such readings critically review the basis of classicism. They suggest that too much formalization deadens lyric material; that it is possible to formalize away the affect at the bottom of a poem. This view, however, is ultimately unsupportable if we allow that formal patterning may *itself* carry affective weight. Arent van Nieukerken claims that the author is a critical participant in this poem's event, tacitly accepting that the humanistic ideals involved in creating dispassionate art may be inadequate in the face of a 'dirty reality' (van Nieukerken 248–9). Apollo himself may be ambivalently dispassionate: his repeated shudder, necessitating a sort of psychological self-petrification, allies him with the guilt-haunted Lady Macbeth rather than the hypothetically dehumanized modern artist.

Heaney's own poetic force resides in a pathos that usually leads to cathartic realization. It could not be further from the force of 'Apollo and Marsyas.' This is why he insists upon the dry objectivity of the poem, which, as we see, is not an uncontested point. Herbert would no doubt encourage our ambivalence: he defines a humanist as one who tries to assimilate the broadest possible spectrum of realities – not a singular reality, or one modelled on selective reading of the classics – and who wishes to create an image of the world to adequately match human experience (Herbert in Bandrowska-Wróblewska 18–19). Van Nieukerken appositely notes that Herbert seeks to identify with the maximal number of perspectives in his poems (249). Although Herbert has come to be known as Poland's arch-moralist, poems such as 'Apollo and Marsyas' should be viewed as interrogative rather than declaratory: as the author reminds us, he had 'words in abundance' to write tendentiously, to endorse one perspective, and yet eschewed tendentiousness in order to reveal the 'deeper, general human perspectives' that are consonant with his vision of humanism (Herbert in *Government* 61–2).

The amount of disagreement permissible in discussions of Herbert's poems could itself be the subject of a book-length study. His role as national moralist has much to do with his readers' desire to view poems as strict moral commands rather than to credit their ambivalence.

Nowhere is this clearer than in the poem that towers over all Herbert's poems of self-abnegation, 'The Knocker.' This is an *ars poetica* though, as Heaney realizes in his commentary, it refuses the indulgence of poetic self-fashioning: the imaginative poets who, in the poem, grow imaginary gardens, travel to sunny imaginary cities, and compose spontaneously when they *close* their eyes and allow 'schools of images' to swim around them, are antithetical to the speaker. His imagination is a wooden board and a stick. The 'green bell' of nature exists for those others, who give themselves up to evocative images and natural communion; the 'moralist,' concerned with judgment, has an unmusical instrument that, like the pebble, is not evocative:

> I thump on the board
> and it prompts me
> with the moralist's dry poem
> yes – yes
> no – no

Heaney discusses this poem in 'The Government of the Tongue,' wondering whether poetry 'should ... go as far in self-denial' as this poem wants it to go (99–100). The poem's central assertion, however, depends for its force upon the imagery that it rejects: the imagistic surfeit of gardens, sunny cities, and, especially, 'schools of images' elicits its own affective response. It is, however, a mixed response. Heaney asserts that the poem's imagery 'carries truth alive into the heart – exactly as the Romantics said it should' (100), but this 'truth' is more ambivalent than he implies. Affect is also truth, yet there are two incompatible affective responses made possible: one accepts the moralist's stick and board and one does not. The first reacts against spontaneous evocation, 'schools of images' that both clog a poem and dilute its force, and welcome the 'dry poem' as a clean alternative. This reaction encompasses both the excesses of Romanticism, with its reliance upon image and self, and of Modernist experiment and avant-garde aestheticism. The second response longs for sunny cities and gardens, the 'green bell' of nature, and is let down by a poet who proclaims his imagination is a piece of board, his 'sole instrument' a wooden stick. Both responses are affective truths, but is there a *singular* truth that the poem forces home?

The echoing bell of the imaginative poet's mind summons a Romantic orientation in which nature echoes the poet: he strikes the bell, and it responds (Polish 'odpowiada,' replies) to him; the reverberations are

crafted into verse. The knocker, however, makes no answering call. Instead, it dictates, and prompts (Polish 'podpowiada') the poem. The
moralist-poet does not choose his materials. He is reacting to the imperative of his calling to produce 'the moralist's dry poem.' Rather than
running the risk of solipsism, he runs the risk of materialism, of total
subsumption in external realities rather than his own states of mind.
This subsumption is, though, effected in order to uphold ideals of moral
conduct – what should and should not be done. This is a different truth
carried 'alive into the heart' from that of communion and spontaneous
overflow – the truth of spontaneous *judgment*, of stark moral reaction to
one's conditions, 'yes' or 'no.' This sort of truth does not need irony, one
of Herbert's most pervasive yet difficult qualities.[18] As in 'The Pebble,'
his classicist restraint leads to a curious clairvoyance: the lyric speaker
sees so clearly that there is 'little room for the customary decorations of
art' (Weissbort 18). The poem's apparent simplicity contains a clairvoy-
ant knowledge that is barely made manifest in the text.

The issue, then, is one of finding befitting emblems of adversity, of art
being suited to the exigencies of its times. Heaney's question whether
art *'should'* go this far in self-denial is a moral question, and at times it
must be paraphrased: *must* it go to this length? Not if the poet closes
his eyes, but perhaps it must if he keeps them painfully open: vigilance
comes at a price that Herbert implies to be necessary. The poem's ontological and ethical irony is summarized by Heaney when he states
that it is 'a lyric about a knocker which claims that lyric is inadmissi-
ble' (*Government* 100), operating by means of affective response – what
Heaney terms 'absorption' in its process – while another type of absorption (solipsistic, self-pleasuring) is decried.[19]

The poem's imperative runs contrary to nature, including Herbert's
own human nature, if we apply his comments in an interview to the
poems (always a tricky procedure when considering a habitual ironist):
'I am fond of things. I am almost sensually attracted to them ... When I
was a boy I used to look out of the window at the street outside. I saw
people passing by, a brick wall and the setting sun. And in my mind's
eye, I was the people in the street and also the wall that was soaking up
the sun' (Oramus 11). By understanding how Herbert severs his sensual fondness for things from his compositional technique, we understand the necessity of keeping separate the man who feels and the mind
that creates. The *natural* feeling of the poet is not what carries over into
the composition of the poem, which prioritizes *moral* feeling; the poet
rejects the 'false warmth' of nature. The material of natural life may be

kept separate from artistic composition, at the cost of spontaneity and even pleasure. Poetic form is again affirmed as an integral facet of the 'moralist's poem.'

The desire to blur this division is a natural part of our feeling for a poet; feeling for and feeling with, or feeling against, though, are different emotive positions to take vis-à-vis the poem. When Heaney reads Herbert, we hear Heaney's feeling *for* the poet fighting against his need to feel *with* the poet in the way that the poem demands. As a result, his strategies for approaching the text war against each other: Heaney's feeling for Herbert's essays (*The Barbarian in the Garden*) fights his disciplined attempt to feel with the poems ('The Pebble,' 'The Knocker'). Heaney is one of the poets least likely to narrow and reify his imaginations into board and stick. In his expository assessments of Herbert, Heaney is caught between accuracy and desire, between attunement to the demands of the poem – given that these poems *do* constantly make demands upon us – and desire to naturalize Herbert, in the many possible meanings of that word, so that he can assimilate his influence. The material he confronts is not consonant with his own poetic imagination, and he struggles to bring the two into harmony (a struggle also evident in his often-criticized reading of Hardy's 'Darkling Thrush'). The otherness of Herbert's aesthetic, which derives largely from his disavowal of Romanticism, is a sticking point for Heaney. It points up the deep differences between their relations to the Western literary tradition.

Revising Herbert: Heaney's Hyperborean

Heaney's later poetry takes a striking turn: the Herbert with whom he grapples in the 1980s appears entirely different from the Herbert memorialized in the elegiac volume *Electric Light* (2001). In many ways *Electric Light* reads as a return to the Heaney of the sixties and seventies, and as a volume of farewells to those who have trained his eye and ear. The aspects of Herbert's poetic that Heaney finds so difficult are smoothed over; Herbert's role as stern moralist is replaced by a new role, as, surprisingly enough, disciple of Apollo, 'one of those' from the far reaches of the north who were 'favoured' by the god. Apollo would return to such as he in winter, establishing the mortal poet as his music-giving representative, one who offers life-affirming music when summer is long gone:

... among your people you
Remained his herald ...

You learnt the lyre from him and kept it tuned.
('To the Shade of Zbigniew Herbert,' *Electric Light* 81)

This is obviously not the same Apollo we have seen in 'Apollo and Marsyas,' but a lyricist who brings the warm music of summer to the Hyperboreans. This poet is gifted with a musicality that 'The Knocker' ostensibly denies. These are subtle counterpoints to Herbert's major poems, and carry with them the certitude of summary. The poem's sestet comfortably encloses itself in the antithesis rhyme of 'wind' and 'tuned,' and it is absolutely un-Herbertian. Even if we apply van Nieukerken's point that Heaney began attending to dichotomies present within mythical figures or stories after his reading of Herbert (van Nieukerken 232), the poem lacks the ethical focus of Heaney's previous poetic responses to Herbert. It is, in short, an unlikely elegy.

It was not always so. The poem's first version, entitled 'A Hyperborean,' contains an initial eight lines that turn the poem into a Petrarchan sonnet.

Ruined temples. Poetry. Zbigniew Herbert,
The inside of your head was a littered Delphi
Where satellites and eagles sailed in orbit ... (56)

The 'uncensored' oracle dwells atop a hill reached by a path that is both sacred and 'untransfigured' stone. There is, indeed, far less transfiguration at work here, and the rhetoric of choppy nouns differs substantially from the formal tones of its later version. Herbert the antiquarian, whose mind is littered with the ruins of classical culture, takes precedence over Herbert the Apollonian disciple, so that the hyperborean curiously takes on Eliotic qualities. Yet Herbert does not shore fragments against ruin but re-views classical wholes: the flaying of Marsyas is seen at a contemporary slant, so that questions of art and pain, testimony and petrified silence, receive a new layer of meaning. 'A Hyperborean' attempts to do too much: ruins and poetry, litter and oracles, satellites (Soviet?) and sanctuaries, transfigured and actual locality, come together in the strewn landscape of the poem with the awkward rhyme of 'Herbert' and 'orbit' and odd description of the Delphic oracle as 'the one thing still uncensored.' By contrast, 'To the Shade of Zbigniew Herbert' is consistent in tone, convincing in melody, and compelling in imagery.

The second-person address of the later version is significant in its newfound directness – Heaney's relationship with Herbert is finally unmediated, and the poet he has found so forbidding can be named, typified ('one of those'), and his gift summarized. It memorializes him through the grandeur of amplified pathetic fallacy ('the land was silent,' 'summer's promise thwarted'), grammatical precision, and largely end-stopped, self-contained lines of classically sonorous hexameters. This new Herbert brings music to a silent land. He is an artist of the beautiful, a lyricist in the literal sense, and not a board-and-stick moralist. He is a 'favourite' and a 'herald.' Mythical Hyperboreans inhabited a land beyond the north wind, with a temperate climate, which drew Apollo to spend the winter months with them. The Hyperborean, then, inhabits the 'lenient weather' that Heaney wished to associate with Herbert in his 1980s essays, upon a silent land, not one riven by war and rebellion, with a host of vocal and celebrated poets. It is a curious reworking of Herbert's legacy.[20]

This turn to a new image of Herbert signals that Heaney has decided to resolve his conflicted view of the Polish poet into a synthesis that is amenable to his own type of lyricism. Herbert is granted his northern nature and yet represents the works of sun and lyre. Heaney is, here, resolving the dichotomy – borrowed from Alvarez – of 'tough-minded' and 'tender-minded' by which he had understood Herbert (*Government* 57). His treatment of the object emphasizes the exigency motivating the poet when his surroundings call for 'a new sort of art.' Herbert is, according to Heaney, painfully caught between the call of art (which Heaney allies with vision) and of suffering. The visionary strain in Herbert's poetry is a matter of potential, though, not of actuality (in this he differs from Miłosz). The capacity for redemptive vision should be recognized, though, much as the small people of Heaney's 'Haw Lantern' recognize (and flinch before) Diogenes's flame. This recognition is not incompatible with tough-minded observation and thinking. Heaney desperately wishes to affirm Herbert as a celebrant of the aesthetic, and this comes to the fore in his surprising elegy.

Heaney's change in view can also be understood as a part of his project in *Electric Light*, which not only elegizes fellow poets (Brodsky, Herbert, Hughes) but, perhaps, un-elegizes the young Heaney by forcibly reviving the early material of his poetry. The elegy for Herbert is usually passed over by critics and reviewers. This oversight is, however, only partial, because the substance of the elegy is part of a volume-wide retrenchment: '[*Electric Light*] restates all Heaney's themes and approaches to date,' writes Robert Potts for *The Guardian*. The images of the volume are comforting, whereas Heaney's earlier poems trouble and displace our sense of readerly pleasure ('The Haw Lantern' is exemplary in this regard). In this context, it is not surprising that sun and lyre would replace stone, and that Apollo would regain his typically radiant countenance. We must remember that both Heaney and Herbert are public poets who trouble considerably over the role(s) that poetry must play in the world. The self-conscious schematization of 'The Knocker' represents an extreme attempt on Herbert's part to reconcile himself to his public voice. It is a poem pitched towards the community (who listens to the 'yes' and 'no' of the moralist), yet it is anti-bardic, spoken as it is by a voice that seeks to silence itself. It is a poem that can be contextualized in terms of its 'work' against communist totalitarianism – a poem that says no – but it is simultaneously a poem in which locality is absent, a poem that pitches itself into what Jahan Ramazani calls 'intergeographic space' ('Travelling Poetry' 291). This duality – not quite paradox – is one of the main facets of Herbert's work that prevents him from being easily categorized, and that lends credence to Heaney's abrupt change of assessment.

Poland's Public Herbert; Heaney's Private Herbert

Heaney's response to Herbert is strikingly formal: he reads Herbert as a poet first and foremost. The large themes upon which we have focused – judgment, moral clarity, art's response to cruelty, art's relationship to nature and to ethical idea – are always, in our and in Heaney's discussions, grounded in the work of the poems. Heaney does acknowledge Herbert's worth on the so-called home front, but does not elaborate – it is not his design to do so – how this worth is assessed. The sad fact of Herbert's later life is that it was unhappy and psychologically unstable, *and yet* his reputation remained strong, perhaps stronger than the man himself. Herbert is, indeed, a quintessential moralist-poet. Although Carpenter sets apart Herbert's reputation as political dissident, earned early in his life, from that as a moralist, which came to dominate his image in the English-speaking world, her distinction is illusory. The glamour of dissidence *is* moral, based on the belief that moral conviction can be carried forward into the political realm by acts of principled resistance. The idolization of dissidence is utopianism. On the other hand, a shrug of the debilitated shoulders, as Heaney would put it, smacks of an even more dangerous apathy – politically safe, to be sure, but creatively and spiritually dangerous. Luckily, Herbert does not elicit apathetic responses. Although his raw, sharp minimalism takes

Heaney aback, these qualities contribute to the cultural myth of Herbert in Poland, according to Halina Filipowicz:

> The reverence surrounding any great writer can be more conducive to canonization than to critical inquiry. With Herbert, ... the need to afford him only a narrow range of personae and to create his ennobling portrait is particularly strong. There is, then, Herbert the classicist whose poems are not radical fragments but classically compressed wholes; Herbert the fine cultural historian who has a sharp eye for European high culture; Herbert the moralist who, not unlike T. S. Eliot, is dismayed by what he perceives as the spiritual devastation of the modern world ... But the enormous prestige that surrounds Herbert depends primarily on his reputation as the conscience of the Polish people under communist rule and an inspirational figure whose work offered his readers a blueprint for moral and civic responsibility. (Filipowicz 521)

According to this account, Herbert may have been lifted *above* exemplary status: a 'blueprint' is not always 'inspirational,' and Filipowicz's terms reveal the difficulty of reconciling the power of Herbert as a heroic figure exemplifying 'moral and civic responsibility' with his power to *creatively* inspire. Heaney's remarks about Herbert as 'a finished poet' are apposite. The possible gulf between heroic moral action and poetic inspiration is at stake. Inspiration to do good is not necessarily compatible, in any organic way, with inspiration to write. Filipowicz usefully pries apart 'canonization' from 'critical inquiry,' and her terms imply that 'classically compressed wholes' resist the sort of inquiry that would pull out fragments that could serve as seeds. Heaney comes closest to doing this when he transmogrifies Herbert's stone of judgment.

Heaney creates a dichotomy between Herbert the cultural historian and Herbert the moralist, yet precisely when he tries to smooth over the dichotomy by personalizing the voice of Herbert's most depersonalized poems, his appraisal becomes problematic. It is equally important to allow for a writer to embody different personae – even if they may seem irreconcilable – as it is to allow for a broad spectrum of expression that encompasses infinite variation. The poet must be allowed his masks. The author of *Barbarian in the Garden* may well speak with a different voice than the author of 'The Knocker.' The difference between these voices may be generic; it may be thematic; or it may be a matter of conscious creative purpose. Critics such as Filipowicz, Carpenter, and Niżyńska seek to place Herbert's work in relief for an English-speaking public who may need to be apprised – as a Polish audience would not – of Herbert's reputation as 'the conscience of the Polish people under communist rule.' Heaney, by contrast, carefully situates himself on the socio-political margin when he writes of Herbert. Jarniewicz decries Heaney's role in forming Herbert's reputation as public conscience, however, stating that Heaney reinforces 'the lasting image of Herbert – a poet of ethical obligations and patriotic zeal,' which is also created by English-language commentators (*The Bottomless Centre* 33), to the detriment, Jarniewicz implies, of our *poetic* appreciation of Herbert. It is certainly true that a cult of Herbert is present in Poland, and equally true that the canonization of great poets is a frequent and obvious phenomenon that is less interesting per se than the particular manner in which the canonization is effected. In the case of Herbert, he becomes a symbol of social conscience and a paragon of moral responsibility. This distinction conditions the way in which a poem such as 'The Knocker' may be read: if taken as an *ars poetica* proclaiming the poet's choice of stick and board, of yes and no, over the echoing bell of artistry, then the view of Herbert as national conscience lies only a short step away. If read as a gently ironic denial of the stick and board as the only materials available for art, as Heaney reads it, underlain by the knowledge that 'the moralist's dry poem' may be elicited in particular – but not all – circumstances, then a view of Herbert as public conscience becomes implausible.

We must also grapple with a (possibly superficial) contradiction between Herbert's public voice and his solitariness. He is alone *and* he is a public poet, a solitary who concerns himself with the values guiding society, who is seen as the people's conscience. He does not seek moral uniformity but an integrative code of values (see Herbert in Bandrowska-Wróblewska 150). He does not greatly approve of his popularity in the West. Even as Herbert keeps his voice solitary, so he is repeatedly amalgamated into a collective, even – or perhaps especially – by his admirers: so the dissident journalist Adam Michnik declares that Herbert wrote 'the most magnificent pages in the book of Polish honor' (Michnik in Grudzińska Gross, 13). Irena Grudzińska Gross points to the important fact that as the anti-communist Solidarity movement gained strength in Poland, Herbert's poems began to be widely read by people who did not normally read poetry; Michnik's widely circulated statement that Herbert's poems helped him to sustain his spirit while he was imprisoned (14) did much to popularize the image of Herbert as national conscience. The result was, in the words of Stanisław Stabro, that an intellectual, refined poet was turned into a political poet of the masses thanks to strict yet facile readings of his work (Stabro 48). He sketches out the central 'myths' of Herbert in a recent retrospective; most relevant for Anglo-American readers is the myth of Herbert as a consummate rebel. Stabro does not, curiously, speak of Alvarez's part in propagating it, but does point to Barańczak's seminal *A Fugitive from Utopia: The Poetry of Zbigniew Herbert* (1987) as a book reinforcing the view of Herbert as rebellious 'party of one' (Stabro 46).

What does such canonization mean for Heaney's very different view of Herbert? The strictness that Heaney finds so difficult to assimilate with his own poetic is responsible for Herbert's reputation as a moralist. Both perspectives rest upon a basically emotional response to poems that are, strangely enough, characterized by emotional stoicism rather than effusion. These divergent types of interpretation bespeak various culturally mediated needs. The need for spiritual sustenance in the face of oppression, as we see from Michnik's example, will result in a view of poetry as succour, as moral ballast. Herbert serves as a rich test case for considering the way in which a poetic oeuvre may be homogenized in the interest of fulfilling such a socio-cultural need. Yet the significance of Herbert for Heaney is different from this. Heaney is held back from a narrowly political view of Herbert by his distance from Herbert's home ground and by his own culturally mediated considerations of poetry's connection to politics and its unfortunate co-optation by particular socio-political interests. Instead, he chooses to 'elaborate' on the Polish poet's significance in response to his own aesthetic mandate.

As Heaney's oeuvre continues to develop, the manner in which he summons Herbert changes in inverse proportion to the direction in which Herbert is canonized. This may simply be a result of further reading, of continued imaginative companionship that results in a different relation between poets, or it may be a counter-reaction to the establishment of Herbert as symbol. Although there is little evidence that Heaney was intimately aware of Herbert's image in Poland, there is overwhelming evidence that Heaney was aware of English and American reactions. 'To the Shade of Zbigniew Herbert' represents a new internalization of Herbert's legacy: Heaney has stopped struggling against a type of poetry whose voice is not amenable to his own. The poet is showing his readers the way in which his exemplar may be celebrated. He is not 'coming to terms' with his legacy so much as he is showing us the terms by which these poets enter his affective mind. Herbert furnishes us with a remarkable example of a poet who is used to satisfy various needs. The needs of Polish readers are not the needs of English-language readers even when there is a surprising overlap between the two. Heaney, meanwhile, is not motivated by need, but by desire. Despite his calls for freedom and signatures on his *own* frequency, he desires a foreign poet, an 'other' voice, to let him hear a radically different frequency from what he had heard before. Heaney will never sound like Herbert. Herbert is a minimalist; Heaney is not (although *Human Chain* contains poems composed of poetic minima, they do not recall the Polish poet). Herbert, however, is a necessary guide through the uncompromising moral territory that Heaney feels compelled to traverse in *Station Island* and, to a certain extent, in *The Haw Lantern*. Where Heaney worries if his personae should attempt to 'set times wrong or right,' Herbert is guided by an imperative, a resounding 'yes.'

4 Approaching the Master

Miłosz in America

Although Herbert's work took on life in English before that of Miłosz, the latter poet eventually became Heaney's source of wisdom, heroic father figure, and perpetual touchstone. As with the work of Wordsworth and Dante, once encountered, it is never dismissed – we cannot say that their influence ever truly ceases. In the early 1970s, Heaney initiates a lifelong relationship with his Polish master, and his influence proves to be broader and deeper than that of any other Eastern European writer. He is sometimes bewildered by Miłosz, as in the ludicrously comical 'Away from it All,' but cannot escape the Polish poet's presence in his written and aural utterances: the amount of times Heaney quotes from or refers to Miłosz is prodigious. The reason Heaney's critics allow their search for influence to be thwarted before it is seriously undertaken, though, is that direct references to Miłosz's poems or person are tricky to locate. He is not immediately present in the same way as Hughes in the early poetry, or in the same way as Dante is directly summoned in Heaney's middle-stage work (*Field Work*, *Station Island*), or, alternatively, the same way as the formal mode of Vergil (in the Eclogues) or the voice of the *Beowulf* poet directly, unquestionably, enter Heaney's poetry. No, Miłosz's influence upon Heaney's poetry is questionable. It is not direct and, of course, it is mediated by translation from a language whose structures are fundamentally different from those of English. Because it is questionable, it is questioned.

Aside from a few choice prose quotations, Miłosz's work is never put side by side with Heaney's. Are scholars put off by the unlikeness of biography, or of cultural context, or of language? The question is not entirely rhetorical. The following two chapters will consider these unlikenesses in the interest of discovering why Heaney himself looks past them. The Polish poet's inspiration is both poetic and intellectual: Heaney's remarks on the abstract language of Miłosz's poems, and its surprising difference from the poetic language with which he was raised, exist side by side with remarks on Miłosz's prose, most notably the autobiographical *Native Realm*. Yet Heaney's scholars tend to couch their refusals to engage this material in fatalistic ways: we *cannot* pin down Miłosz's influence and, therefore, it cannot be pervasive.[1] The only reason we cannot pin it down, however, is that we fear the convolutions such a search for precision would entail.

The first step in determining this influence must be a brief reconnaissance. Miłosz's complicated life took him from Lithuania to France, wartime Poland, Washington, and France yet again as a cultural attaché, eventually ending in Berkeley, where he took up a professorial post in the Slavic Department of the University of California, Berkeley. Like Heaney, he did not come as a career academic, but as a writer (Heaney would gently deprecate his own arrival through the 'back door' of creative writing); in fact, neither poet obtained a doctorate, although both took up academic posts. When Miłosz emigrated to Berkeley in 1960, he came as a defector from the communist regime – not quite a refugee, though his passport was revoked and his condition was one of de facto exile. The distinction between emigration (voluntary) and exile (forced) must be borne in mind while considering the relationships of Miłosz and of Heaney to the United States, despite Heaney's frequent mention of 'exile' in a loose sense (as in his 'exile' from home to board at St Columb's College as an adolescent). So must the distinction between English and Polish:

> There are moments when it seems to me I have squandered my life.
> For you are a tongue of the debased ...
> ...
> But without you, who am I?
> Only a scholar in a distant country,
> a success, without fears and humiliations.
> Yes, who am I without you?
> Just a philosopher, like everyone else. (*New and Collected Poems* 245)

Read autobiographically, as one poem that is *not* voiced through a mask, 'My Faithful Mother Tongue' thinks through the poet's scorn of his own exilic position, which compels a change not just of place but of calling. This lattermost term, which Heaney uses in reference to his poetic vocation, designates the role – or rather, the purpose – of which Miłosz considers himself denied.[2] The calling of poetry is musical, rhythmic, and finds its expression in the response of readers and listeners, which is predicated upon their participation in the linguistic event; 'without you,' the poem's speaker asks his language, 'who am I?' Better to have the ballast of belonging to a 'debased' nation, perhaps to conclude that 'I have squandered my life' in service to this language, than to be deprived of the 'I' altogether. The former carries the possibility of repentance, if we follow the original Polish text's concealed allusion ('zmarnowałem życie') to the prodigal son, who was lost in a distant land but is found when he returns to his father begging for work. Here, he returns to his mother tongue, whom he had never truly abandoned, and which dispenses ambivalent rewards. His prodigality would inhere in his 'success,' as measured materially, and the untranslated English phrase – 'a success' – sarcastically punctuates the original Polish poem.

This small phrase, within these lines, delivers a capsule commentary on the Polish poet's domicile, while the essays of *Visions from San Francisco Bay* enrich and expand on the topic. It is loaded with disappointment (at himself), anger (at the temptation to enter spiritual bankruptcy), and sarcasm (regarding his cultural environment), spoken in the tongue of those voicing the temptation. In its utterance, the speaker steps out of his individuality, away from his mother tongue, in order to take his part in a culture of reward: '[I am] *a* success.' Reward for what? Because it has been bought at the price of exile, a reward for embracing the furthest extremity of abandonment, that of language as well as of land. A change of language entails a change of life, of identity. Without the mother tongue, the poet becomes 'just a philosopher' like every thinking man, yet divested of the humiliation attending his membership in a nation of 'the debased,' and lacking the fear that accompanies pursuit of a vocation clearly allied (by both Miłosz and Heaney) with the sacred.

Miłosz does not always strike this same tone when writing of his new American home, nor does he abandon his faithful mother tongue. He insists that native readers are the most important judges of a poet's work ('Notes on Exile'), although he takes great care to ensure the quality of his work in English, keeping a close eye on his English translators and taking a hand in the process himself.[3] He plays a major role in introducing English-speaking readers to Polish poetry, countering his outcry against the 'tongue of the debased' by educating the public about its finest fruits: *Postwar Polish Poetry* (1965) was published shortly after his arrival in the United States and his *History of Polish Literature* shortly thereafter (1969; reprinted 1983). *The Captive Mind* was published in English translation even earlier, in 1953, then reprinted (1981). Although he insists on being a poet, not a political scientist, *The Captive Mind* was read as a sort of primer on life under communism, and together with his anthology and history, helped to create a context for Miłosz himself. The problem is that this context was established in prose, not in poetry. Miłosz's high reputation as a poet in Poland was not yet complemented abroad, and the 'scholar in a distant country' suffers by not having his actual vocation – the service of language – recognized by others. He had translated Herbert but not himself.

Miłosz's anthology and history, however, contain sections of his own poetry (he refers to himself in the third person), and his translated poems appeared in several American periodicals such as *Ploughshares, Antaeus, Ironwood*, and *The Threepenny Review*. It was not until the 1970s, though, that his poetry became well known among English-language readers: *Selected Poems* (with a brief, laudatory introduction by Kenneth Rexroth) appeared in 1973, *Bells in Winter* in 1974 (subsequently reprinted), the Neustadt International Prize for Literature came in 1978, and then the Nobel Prize in 1980. The oddity of this list of names and dates is that it obscures the centrality of verse to Miłosz's writing career. In the year the Nobel was awarded, there were only two books of his poetry available in English. There was little reason for Heaney, or other English-language readers, to consider him a poetic 'Master' in 1970, and the eponymous poem was over a decade in the making, yet Heaney was already coming to see Miłosz as the single most important Eastern European poet for himself, for his own work. This has much to do with their complementary reactions to contemporary American culture.

Meetings and Choices: Heaney and 'The Master' at Berkeley

Although Heaney claims that 'by the middle eighties, Miłosz more or less counted as an American poet' (O'Driscoll, *Stepping Stones* 283), in the 1970s (if ever), this was emphatically not the case, and the 1968 translation of *Native Realm*, subtitled *A Search for Self-Definition*, proved it so. The cultural background of Heaney's academic appointments in the United States was the subject of chapter 1; how this background compares with that of Miłosz, and how we can understand their relation, is the subject here at hand. We can now appreciate the oddity of Heaney and Miłosz meeting in Berkeley, and can, perhaps, understand why Michael Parker, whose *Seamus Heaney: The Making of the Poet* (1993) remains his best biography, skips over Heaney's Berkeley year in two pages. This event does not fit into a logical picture of how influence should work: although Heaney *read* American poets with his usual avidity, he retained his preference for a tight weave and a spirituality rooted in Catholic imagery rather than the New Age mysticism prevalent in Berkeley at the time (1970–1). Exposure to a new poetic did not automatically lead to influence. He admits, 'I can *hear* a lot going on, but I don't let it into my own writing. There are only two or three references to the United States in all of my written work. It's not that I'm against it. It's just that I haven't found a way to get at it' (Heaney in Thomas 64). Miłosz, in contrast, did find a way to 'get at it' in the informal musings of *Visions from San Francisco Bay*, though the book was not published in English until 1982 (before Heaney's *Station Island* and *The Haw Lantern*, but after Heaney had left Berkeley). He 'got at it' by asserting his difference.

Language would seem to divide Heaney and Miłosz, but there is a kernel of similarity in their relation to language as homeland and as umbilical cord to the nation; it is complemented and offset by their belief in a sacral dimension to the poet's role, which will come clear in 'Sweeney Redivivus.' The faithful mother tongue loads the poet with 'fears and humiliations,' Miłosz writes. They are a result of language's historical burden and of the community it creates; language bears the weight of the people's experience. Immersion in a new linguistic medium, however, does not automatically integrate the émigré into the host country's history. Neither Miłosz nor Heaney wish to bury their heads in the sand and change their national allegiance – quite the opposite – but act in accordance with Miłosz's early account: 'I conserved my status as a person coming from outside' while in the West, he writes, 'not pretending that I wanted to align myself with its ways and mores. Just the opposite ... [;] a clear sign of this opposition was holding on to the Polish language in verse and in prose. Even when I made use of English ... [,] I dreamed my tale of [being] a spiritual inhabitant of lands exotic to people in the West' (Preface to *Prywatne obowiązki* 5, my translation).[4] Such a posture bespeaks pride more than humility. Yet 'dreamed' points out the self-styling at work here: exoticism is relative, and Miłosz consciously inhabits the concept in order to avoid being *only* 'a scholar in a distant country,' 'just a philosopher,' and especially 'a success, without fears and humiliations.' He proudly styles himself *so that* he may re-assume a posture of humility – a communal humility. There is something quite Yeatsian about Miłosz's insistence on self-conquest: 'He who does not constantly overcome himself ... disintegrates within' (*Native Realm* 273).

Heaney does not need such a strategy because his year in Berkeley was one of 'enrichment,' whereas Miłosz's is redolent of 'tragic destiny and fierce historical irony: he, whose sense of gravity is over-loaded with the tragic, ends up in the Bay Area, among the hippies and the flower people' (Heaney in Thomas 65). His implication is that this society, with its heady utopianism and New Age mysticism, does not possess the sense of history with which Miłosz is saturated; yet Heaney does not specify that Miłosz's historicism – that is, the historical sense which his persona embodies – is forced upon the poet by his circumstances. 'In Warsaw' is the best-known lament at the fate of one who 'swore never to be / A ritual mourner' but, in the ruins of Warsaw in 1945, cannot resist the demands that his historical situation places upon him, and cannot resist the 'dark love / Of a most unhappy land' enclosed in his heart (*New and Collected Poems* 75–6). Again, the poem cries out for a biographical reading as a sort of dialogue between historical self and creative soul:

> I did not want to love so.
> That was not my design.
> I did not want to pity so.
> That was not my design.
>
> ...
>
> I want to sing of festivities,
> The greenwood into which Shakespeare
> Often took me. Leave
> To poets a moment of happiness,
> Otherwise your world will perish.

Heaney's concept of gravity does not fully account for this sense of forced destiny that is so crucial to Miłosz both as a personality and as a poet. Heaney's programmatic early 'Gravities' metaphorizes the homing urge as a kite string, 'strict and invisible,' as the pull of love, as Joyce's astonishing memory of Dublin while abroad, and the nostalgia of Irish monk Colmcille (St Columba) while evangelizing on the island of Iona, in Scotland: 'And on Iona Colmcille sought ease / By wearing Irish mould next to his feet' (*Death of a Naturalist* 32). Gravity is involuntary yet positive, connected to a sense of mission or artistry, motivated by devotion more than compulsion, though the former could turn into the latter (as when Heaney states, 'I just couldn't leave the gravitational pull of the poetry field I knew,' O'Driscoll, *Stepping Stones* 145). The strict, end-stopped insistence of 'In Warsaw' does not correspond to the tone of 'Gravities.' These are different concepts. What links them, though, is the poets' sense of their absence in the United States: 'Six thousand miles away, / I imagine untroubled dust, / A loosening gravity,' writes Heaney in 'Westering' (subtitled 'In California'; *Wintering Out* 79–80). Whereas the poem imagines this situation as a surreal reversal of Good Friday's crucifixion (and a possible reversal of John Donne's 'Good Friday, 1613. Riding Westward'), the act is merely imagined – no 'nails dropped out' in the alien West, no trouble lessened, no gravity loosened. The cinematic poem provides an ambivalently utopian closure to *Wintering Out* (1972), though its Christian *volte-face* wreaks hypothetical havoc with Heaney's subliminal Catholicism – which seems to gain the upper hand, paradoxically enough, over the poem 'unreeling' from it – and the dominant image of California with which it leaves us is that of 'The empty amphitheatre / Of the west.'

The phrase would be of interest to Miłosz. The musings of *Visions from San Francisco Bay* circle around the subject of American emptiness, the 'something incomprehensible' that stymies a humanistic mind (8),[5] as manifested by 'the abstract city and the abstract theater of nature, something one drives past' (28). This, Miłosz insists, is the central metaphor for America, and in opposition we may place Heaney's bogland, governed by a vertical epistemology, as opposed to the horizontal knowledge quest of American manifest destiny. Miłosz takes the idea a step further, positing that the pacification of nature and prefabrication of perception that he sees at work in the United States impedes us from gaining knowledge and leads to 'ontological anemia,' characterized by a sense of 'nothingness sucking from the center in' (39). This condition is dangerous for the imagination. Heaney's poem considers the liberation attending the sense that one's spiritual gloom may evaporate in the sunny, secular West, but he recognizes that this redemptive vision is born of the hierarchical Catholic imagination; Heaney, like Miłosz, cannot write from *inside* the empty amphitheatre, but must juxtapose it with the geographical and spiritual landscapes of his childhood.

Heaney's critics insist on the American influence, however, with a tenacity that is surprising given the lack of evidence for many such claims. The search for echoes of Gary Snyder and Robert Bly does not yield much fruit; the mention of Louis Simpson in 'Making Strange' hardly invites one to an influence study; Heaney's great admiration for William Carlos Williams is certainly worth mentioning, yet Williams's short lines sound nothing like Heaney's drill-like stanzas of the 1970s.[6] Heaney feels more free to admit his separateness from American poetry, save for the long-term influence of Robert Lowell, after his ties with American academe loosened. It is only in 2002 that he openly states, 'There are only two or three references to the United States in all of my written work.' Dennis O'Driscoll's collection of interviews (*Stepping Stones*) contains invaluable reminiscences of prior decades. Heaney lets his interlocutor know that he had read *Postwar Polish Poetry* even before he came to Berkeley, that he 'was totally alive to the Miłosz anthology material' (in other words, to major Polish poets), that it took him 'a while' to be able to write about and to it, and (as we have mentioned in the previous chapter) that the 'eastern European aesthetic' served as a 'precaution' against an 'ahistorical, hedonistic' American aesthetic (114–15), demonstrating a sense of guardedness against a powerful, popular, and tempting American style ('I was susceptible' – 141). This characterization of the American aesthetic is clearly reminiscent of Miłosz's *Visions of San Francisco Bay*, even if Heaney never names the book. Likewise, the psychological effect of American exoticism upon him reminds one of Miłosz: 'What the Californian distance did was to lead me back into the Irish memory bank' (142), so that the fashion for Japanese and Chinese poetry 'encouraged me to trust the "nature" aspect of my own material' such that an interest in 'origin and the inward path' actually led back to *Ireland*, culminating in *Wintering Out* and then in the atavistic explorations of *North*. 'Westering' leads to a meditation on Good Friday and the poet's Irish Catholicism instead of taking what Heaney (quoting Larkin) calls '"a deliberate step backward"' and entering 'all that New Age stuff, the chant and the dance, whether as a rite in the commune or a style in the poem' (145). The aboriginal chant and dance in 'Station Island' are imagined as the speaker seeks reconciliation with his unquestionably Irish origins ('I hate where I was born, hate everything ...') and desperately clutches at an image of intervention in the organic process of life. Not only is his image devoid of New Age pseudo-mysticism, it announces its own self-gratifying self-enclosure: 'Then I thought of the tribe whose dances never fail / For they keep dancing till they sight the deer' (*Station Island* 85–6). This means that the dance continues until the sight of a deer appears to corroborate the tribe's belief in their spell, thus satisfying their spiritual need. Such a passage is ambiguous at best.

In the context of *Station Island*, we must wait until the poet has finished his pilgrimage and undertaken the self-examination of the 'Sweeney Redivivus' sequence before we see a deer again, not actual but incised into the wall of a Lascaux cave, and the speaker moves from being 'a panicked shadow / crossing the deerpath' to meditating upon its 'stone-faced vigil' until 'the long dumbfounded / spirit broke cover' ('On the Road,' 120–1). These examples show us how far Heaney is from dabbling in the sort of spirituality that he encountered in Berkeley and how anxious he is to come to terms with his own spiritual origins; the project of these poems is to justify the poet's voice. Interestingly, Miłosz struggles with the same issue in Berkeley. He, too, needs to defend his capacity to speak communally, even while he is permanently exiled from his audience, and to take on the subject of speaking from the margin of each society. Heaney, like Miłosz in 'My Faithful Mother Tongue,' takes a parable of a rich young man as his intertext, though his does not squander his goods but refuses to part with them; whereas Heaney's narrator mulls over Jesus's advice to 'Sell all you have,' using this parable to Christianize his itinerant Sweeney, what he actually does is to take the other piece of advice Jesus gives the man – to look within himself to find light, until his 'spirit broke cover.' Heaney is going back to Catholicism at the exact moment that we would expect him to, perhaps, break free from it. Just as he states Miłosz 'suffered for' his ability to encompass both California and Lithuania in his mind, contributing to his sense of alienation (Heaney in Thomas 64), so Heaney cannot exit his native gravitational field of Ireland. Daniel Tobin connects this poem to Zbigniew Herbert's 'Eschatological Forebodings of Mr Cogito,' a poem likewise driven by the request (of 'severe angels') that the speaker rid himself of earthly habits in order to reach Paradise. There is, however, a basic disjunction between the speakers' positions: the hopelessly sensuous Mr Cogito clings to sensation and to 'a few weathered images / on the bottom of the burnt-out eye,' whereas Heaney's speaker, ruminating upon Jesus's advice, wilfully takes himself back to what Herbert calls 'the cave of the beginning' in order to rejuvenate his spirit. Mr Cogito is not the same character as Heaney's speaker. Tobin goes on to metaphorize the desiccated source as a tribal centre from which Sweeney has fled to the 'justified margin,' as the 'font of the *omphalos*,' and as

St John's eternal fountain (Tobin 214), although Heaney summons these alternative metaphors under the umbrella of the Christian parable.

Their sojourns in the United States sharpen both Miłosz's and Heaney's already keen senses of coming from outside, of being 'au contraire.' The phrase is used by Samuel Beckett in answer to a French journalist who asks the writer, 'Vous êtes Anglais ...?' Heaney revels in the anecdote, taking it as an idiosyncratic 'definition of Irish,' in comical counterbalance to his statement that 'in artistic circles, the adjective "Irish" effects a deleterious chemical change on the noun to which it's applied' (Heaney in Kinahan 405). Miłosz makes similar statements about Polishness. Being 'au contraire' is a position that brings with it perverse gratification, and Heaney's thoughts on this topic are strongly influenced by the example of Miłosz's life as well as his art.

Biography as Destiny?

Miłosz's is no ordinary biography. 'The biographical *time* of this poet, more than that of others stricken by history, is also a mythical time,' explains Marek Zaleski (Zaleski 9). Biography becomes myth: this situation is obviously attractive for a poet such as Heaney, whose fascination with myths and local legends is patent throughout his career. Miłosz's life lends itself – ironically, given his attitude towards Romanticism – towards romanticization. Within Poland, its romance is also a function of its anachronistic setting and, paradoxically, its confusing national characteristics, given Miłosz's nomadic early youth and then his settled life in a largely pre-industrial Lithuania. An important cultural difference between Anglo-American and Eastern European audiences here comes into play: whereas Miłosz's Lithuania may appear vaguely anachronistic or picturesque to Western readers, it possesses a definite cultural significance for local readers, for whom the era of the Polish-Lithuanian Commonwealth represents the highest point in the regions' fortunes. Lasting for over two centuries, this union was ended once and for all by the 1795 partition of the area between Russia, Prussia, and Austria. Whether or not we choose to view the Commonwealth as a colonial entity, in which Poland was the dominant power, this historical era may be retrospectively gilded by the events that succeeded it, events that may also be viewed in colonial terms, so that Poland moves from being a dominant power to a subordinated, partitioned victim.

We may ask what this history has to do with twentieth-century poetry. As Alvarez noticed upon his travels in Eastern Europe, history is present to a high degree in the popular imagination. The destruction of the Commonwealth and the ensuing subjugation of Poland are events that correspond to the birth and triumph of Romanticism and a mythology of the nation that sustained it late into the twentieth century. Miłosz's Lithuania bears valuable cultural freight. This region – his 'native realm' – is not uncontested (see Venclova, 'Vilnius/Wilno/Vilna') or straightforward in its cultural identity (see Petković's call for postcolonial theoretical 'reclamation'), yet it serves a symbolic function in Polish culture that is relevant to the popularity of Miłosz's work within Poland. Here, it is viewed as a mythical Alma Mater of primeval forests, ancient pagan customs that persevere into the mechanical age, the cradle of Polish Romanticism, and a crucible for differing ethnicities and religions (central to the myth of the Polish-Lithuanian Commonwealth is its high degree of religious tolerance). When Miłosz, escaped from the massacre in wartime Warsaw, tried to reach 'the roots of that calamity,' he 'continually communed with the seventeenth century – the century before the disaster' (*Native Realm* 255).

Miłosz, then, serves as a link to a mythicized place and indirectly to a bygone golden age. This autobiographical currency affects his contemporaries' assessments of his biography: Andrzej Kijowski writes, 'Miłosz stands for consciousness of choice; a sense of poetry's standing; a designation of the nation's place in the historical and the divine plan; a quest for the central point of human consciousness; the consciousness of its indeterminacy and inexpressibility; meta-literature, that is, the word which does not [simply] communicate but which purifies' ('oczyszcza') (Kijowski 44, my translation). In culmination, he serves as a guarantor of his own work, as the living embodiment of its themes. It is not unusual to see a poet as a living symbol; it *is* unusual to enumerate the qualities for which a poet 'stands' merely by being. This critical approach lifts biography onto a symbolic plane that becomes ethical – in Kijowski's statement, Miłosz embodies ethical and cultural values which are also the subjects of his poetic meditations and arguments. The poet becomes, in a way, depersonalized, becoming the values that his biography and work are seen to embody. Unlike Herbert, he is not predominantly the conscience of his nation but a cultural amalgam whose very nationality is sometimes at issue.

This view is not, however, universal, and in the vast field of Miłosz scholarship there are voices who dissent from the mythical and symbolic approaches. Jan Błoński is a distinguished example: 'Miłosz's poetry is in the main anecdotal and autobiographical: it constantly refers itself to private and individual experiences, especially [his] readings and travels, *which compels* commentary more than poetry that reaches for historical costumes and stylization [does]' (Błoński, *Miłosz jak świat* 59, my translation and emphasis).[7] Such a remark indicates that we should be drawn to the biographical elements of Miłosz's oeuvre, since they compel commentary (the referent for 'compels' is clearly his auto-biographical and anecdotal poetry), both by the poet (in, for instance, *Native Realm* and *Beginning with My Streets*) and by readers. Miłosz's artistic aim, argues Błoński, is the reinstatement of mimesis. This simple (yet, Błoński adds, unfashionable) aim demands that we reckon with Miłosz's poems as descriptions, imitations, statements, and not as linguistic or aesthetic games dazzling the reader (217). Such a procedure would meet the approval of the poet himself, though while assessing Miłosz's impact upon English-speaking readers, we must reckon with the foreignness of his idiom and the frequent difficulty of pinning down the voice of his poems.

For Heaney, encountering Miłosz from a great cultural distance, the Pole does not stand for particular values as much as he embodies wisdom itself. For readers encountering Miłosz's work across a cultural divide, this difference between local (Polish) and non-local views of the symbolic heft of Miłosz's life should not be surprising. The Polish poet's alterity – which he insists upon, not downplays, in works such as *Visions from San Francisco Bay* – necessitates that non-local readers must try to situate his work anew outside of the cultural matrix within which local readers operate – in this case, within which the 'purifying' function of the lyrical word may be understood in Romantic-political terms as concomitant with its millenarian teleology, or in a Catholic framework – in which *logos* has the power to illuminate and to reveal the sacred, or simply as a view of poetry that is based on a high notion of the poet's bardic status, and would be viewed with far more scepticism in the secular culture of Anglo-American academe. Heaney does not often comment on Miłosz's particular cultural situation. He does query the values with which Miłosz's work can be correlated and, similarly to Miłosz's other critics, uses him as a constant dialogic presence in conversation and expository work. For him, this temporal sweep of Miłosz's autobiography is fascinatingly vast, and, naturally, not as *locally* resonant as it is for Poles: 'What Miłosz can do is to rhyme, if you like, his personal biography with the history of western civilization' (Heaney in Brandes 9). He has 'gone through' the major events of twentieth-century history, reckoned with his temporary seduction by Marxism, his decision not to join the Home Army during the Second World War, and assessed his reaction to post-war California 'so in a life-time he has moved from Medieval Catholicism, with a deep root back into early Christian time, right up into late twentieth century postmodernism.' Heaney, however, says the same of *his own* childhood: 'It was actually medieval almost ... You felt you were born, culturally speaking, 400 or 500 years ago, you know? The world I grew up in was romantic – lamplight, fires, horses, wells' (Heaney in Farndale, n.p.). These comments, however, are not made in the same interview, and Heaney does not explicitly connect their two biographies. To complicate the situation further, when asked by Rand Brandes in April of 1988 whether his life paralleled Miłosz's, Heaney merely identifies the 'background of Catholicism' (10) as a shared facet, understating the case considerably. Thirteen years later (in April of 2001), he tacitly gestures towards this similarity of cultural trajectory to Nigel Farndale. The reason has to do with authority and self-positioning: the Nobel Prize intervened between the two interviews. Heaney has moved from viewing Miłosz as an unapproachable master to seeing him as a fellow-craftsman. He has spent decades mulling over his influence, maintaining a sort of long-distance friendship with, and tutelage under, the legendary Polish master.

Miłosz's life confers an authority born of experience, 'and I find that authority irresistible,' says Heaney in 1988, 'because there is the weight of personal hurt and loss, and the weightlessness of impersonal despair for the humanist venture' (Brandes 10). The last part of this comment will be the subject of our future speculation in this chapter and the next (i.e., the extent to which the seemingly 'impersonal,' because general, can actually be viewed as 'weightless'). For now, Heaney's fascination with the *cultural* span of Miłosz's life is at issue, in part because it calls up the surprisingly pre-industrial surroundings in which he himself lived, and is, thus, reacting to a reflection of his own trajectory from farm to metropolis raised to a higher power, and partly because this very span is responsible for Miłosz's fascinating yet oddly exotic charisma in the West. The bare facts of his life are, to reinvigorate an overused term, almost incredible. Equally incredible is the need to reconcile these facts with his life in California, where he meets Heaney during the heyday of hippie culture and New Age spirituality. In Heaney's 'Sweeney Redivivus,' the itinerant hero finds himself back among his people, who are 'far too eager' to believe his tales: 'And there I was, incredible to myself, / among people far too eager to believe me / and my story, even if it happened to be true' (*Station Island* 98). What happens when we cast the speaker out from his role as cosmopolitan prodigal son, as a conventional reading would have it, and instead see him as a middle voice (as in the often-discussed 'Making Strange' in the same volume) playing two roles, cosmopolitan to his credulous people yet also filial apprentice to the seasoned master, as represented by Miłosz?

Miłosz Enters Ireland: 'Sweeney Redivivus,' Texts of Praise, and Books of Withholding

The title poem of Heaney's 'Sweeney Redivivus' invites readers to view the sequence as a tale of return quite different from the original 'Sweeney Astray,' and its accompanying endnote in *Station Island* asserts that these 'glosses' on the original can survive independently of the tale of the transmogrified Irish King Sweeney. The author's gently self-justifying statement that many poems in 'Sweeney Redivivus' are imagined in contexts 'far removed from early modern Ireland' (*Station Island* 123) is a tongue-in-cheek understatement matched by the trope – extended across two poems – of unwinding. Here, unwinding is unlearning in order to relearn, *reculer pour sauter*, a necessary distancing in order to travel farther, as Heaney's sequence plays with its own metaphor of movement as epistemology – travel, quest, exile, mastery of 'new rungs of air' (103). The avian poet's head is a ball of twine 'dense with soakage, but beginning / to unwind' (98).

At first glance, though, this seems an unfitting, even antithetical, trope with which to imagine knowledge and through which to summon a master such as Miłosz. A word on the difference of 'Sweeney Redivivus' from 'Sweeney Astray' is here necessary, since it may be salutary, if highly unusual in the context of Heaney scholarship, to view them as nearly *opposite* cultural and epistemological endeavours. 'Sweeney Astray' must be seen in a political and cultural light: King Sweeney is enraged by Bishop Ronan Finn and thus represents an anti-Christian impulse that Tobin provocatively associates with pre-Christian druidism of the sort also represented by the child poet of 'Oracle' (who is 'lobe and larynx / Of the leafy places,' *Wintering Out* 28; Tobin 79). Heaney's translation of the Irish legend was followed by a sequence of heavily autobiographical lyrics rather loosely based on the original, lending credence to Tobin's linkage. Real-world (i.e., non-legendary) events bookend the composition of the Sweeney poems: news of the civil rights movement in the United States, which Heaney came to see first-hand during his Berkeley year, reached Ireland as concerns about cultural identity and difference had become life-or-death matters. Poets who had traditionally sought to subsume divisive questions of origin into a general tolerance, or what Heaney refers to as a 'faults-on-both-sides tact' in 'An Afterwards' (*Field Work* 134), were called upon to align themselves with political positions, to situate themselves in socio-political as well as geographical and literary space. Heaney could not help but be sympathetic to the civil rights movement, but several months after his return to Belfast, voices a sense of having had enough: 'I am fatigued by a continuous adjudication between agony and injustice, swung at one moment by the long tail of race and resentment, at another by the more acceptable feelings of pity and terror' (*Preoccupations* 30). Heaney's 'race' must here be construed as tribalism, but the more common American meaning broadens the remark's resonance. Beneath these words is a clear exhaustion with identity politics and political correctness, flip sides of the same coin. The remarks precede the unabashed atavism of *North*.

Heaney, speaking in retrospect many years later, remembers a generalized sense of anxiety lest one manifest and thereby exacerbate the negative emotions inspiring aggression in the first place. Whether *North* actually exacerbated these emotions or whether critics simply feared that it may do so, it did not deter Heaney from taking on the explicitly political project of the 'Sweeney Astray' translations. 'I simply wanted to offer an indigenous text that would not threaten a Unionist ... and that would fortify a Nationalist (after all, this old tale tells us that we belonged here always and that we still remain unextirpated),' he writes, though 'belonged' and 'unextirpated' (not to mention 'we') allow for no ambiguity of intent. What happened was that Robert Lowell (an East Coast formalist, not a West Coast radical) stepped in, this time as a *translator*: Heaney decides to emulate 'his unabashed readiness to subdue the otherness of the original to his own autobiographical neediness. I began to ... make analogies between this early medieval Ulsterman who rocketed out of the north, as a result of vehement squabbles there ... , and this poet from County Derry who had also come south for purposes of retreat and composure' ('Earning a Rhyme' 97–8). Another wearisome adjudication is avoided: rather than balancing the claims of Sweeney with the claims of Heaney, Lowell teaches the poet to simply conflate both. The text was pressed into service 'to show me off' and, after another trip to the United States in order to take up a temporary professorial post at Harvard (1981), it was formalized into 'hard-edged' rhyming stanzas. An even greater change happened: Heaney 'got fed up with [his] own mournful bondings to the "matter of Ulster"' and, after the translation was finally finished, the story 'yielded itself over' and he speedily composed the 'Sweeney Redivivus' sequence, extend-ing and exaggerating the autobiographical elements that had crept into 'Sweeney Astray' ('Earning a Rhyme' 98–100). The experience was, in-deed, revivifying: he was writing 'at full tilt. Reckless and accurate and entirely Sweenified, as capable of muck-raking as of self-mockery ... I got a lot out of my system, for instance, in relation to the northern re-sponse to *North*' (Heaney in O'Driscoll, *Stepping Stones* 262).

Another change, this one virtually unaccounted for by Heaney's critics, happened: as 'Sweeney Redivivus' took flight from 'Sweeney Astray,' Heaney's long-time interest in Eastern European poetry began to affect the text. Now that race and resentment could be put by, and new rungs of air finally achieved, the influence of a different type of po-etry (neither indigenous nor Anglo-American) could enter, producing dramatic monologues that relieved the poet of himself (see O'Driscoll, *Stepping Stones* 261). When Heaney speaks of his lines containing 'a "bare wire" quality' (262), he uses a phrase of the same sort employed to describe Eastern European poetry. Its influence is far from buried; 'The Master' announces it with some pomp and circumstance:

> Deliberately he would unclasp
> his book of withholding
> a page at a time and it was nothing
> arcane, just the old rules
> we all had inscribed on our slates.
> Each character blocked on the parchment secure
> in its volume and measure.
> Each maxim given its space. (*Station Island* 110)

To reach the Master's 'unroofed tower,' the speaker climbs through an unpopulated land, over 'deserted ramparts.' There is a clear, dra-matic sense of hierarchy here; the poem maintains a dual perspective between 'him' and 'me' that corresponds to its shuttling between open and closed spaces: the 'unroofed tower' hints that the speaker's jour-ney is a quest, and the master is one on guard, separated by fortifica-tions from the outside world, withholding easy knowledge of himself and his words. Is this a fair portrayal of Miłosz, however? The meta-phorization of his exilic position as dwelling up and beyond the land, available only to the questing pupil, is not quite befitting a professor-poet who tirelessly anthologized, taught, and wrote about his native culture to render it accessible to his foreign audience. This is, of course, reading extremely literally. Heaney would, no doubt, not approve of this strategy himself. He speaks of the poem's composition as an act of transmogrification: '"The Master" ... is a transmogrified account of meeting Czesław Miłosz. A meal with him in a Berkeley restaurant, in the company of Bob Hass and Robert Pinsky, gets turned into an episode where Sweeney stops to consult a "master" in an old tower' (Heaney in O'Driscoll, *Stepping Stones* 262). Literary socializing becomes a lonely quest; Miłosz's high position in a group of translators and younger poets becomes sequestration in a 'coign of seclusion,' in a tower; sensuality (a meal) turns into asceticism (a climb up deserted ramparts). The difference between inspiration and finished product is striking.

The master's words are also transformed in the course of the poem, and another draft of 'The Master' shows Heaney effecting their subtle transformation. This slightly altered version (published in the small *Graham House Review*) has the third stanza ending in 'measure,' whereas the published version more fittingly ends with each maxim being 'given its space,' which matches the sense of opening that concludes the poem:

How flimsy I felt climbing down
the unrailed stairs on the wall,
hearing the purpose and venture
in a wingflap above me.

Closeness and openness, flimsiness and purpose: these are the dichotomies setting apart the master and the speaker. This ending, however, casts the master out of his tower into the open air, above the speaker but uncloistered, just as 'the old rules / we all had inscribed on our slates' relieve the poem of its previous hint of portentousness. There is no withholding, after all, but open communication of simple truths. The poem is marked by this dramatic turn, when the poet himself seems surprised at the lack of arcana in this erstwhile magician's book.

Our question is now *why* the speaker is surprised that Miłosz's words would be so accessible, even almost 'foretold,' to borrow a phrase. Heaney claims, 'My hero is Czesław Miłosz. When I hear that voice which is wise and full of wisdom-speak, I feel steadied' (Heaney in Gussow, n.p.). Hence the image, in the poem, of words as 'coping-stones.' Yet there is plenty of unsteadiness in the 'flimsy' speaker's perilous voyage to and from the tower, and a sense of inferiority that motivates the poet's metaphorization of himself as pupil. What has happened is, strangely enough, that Heaney's terms of reference for Miłosz and Yeats have crossed paths. We can hardly blame his critics for assuming that Yeats is the master here, given that Heaney so often speaks of Yeats's readiness to don 'the mantle of the wisdom-speaker' and criticizes him for an 'exorbitant identification of himself with the figure of the prophet' in later life (Heaney, 'Yeats' Nobility'). Of course, Yeats also lived in a tower.

Compositionally, Heaney allies Yeats with deliberation rather than Wordsworthian spontaneity and overflow. He makes clear his own preference for the latter, speaking with particular ease in interview ('Poetry doesn't quite have to do with industry or intention ... I always believed in poetry as a grace,' Heaney in Ni Anluain 87) and more guardedly in essays. A master of vatic deliberation, then, would bring Yeats to mind for Heaney's readers.[8] The compound ghost of Miłosz and Yeats would stand on the side of beauty born of difficulty, in spite of both poets' longing for visitations of grace. Miłosz's poetry is likewise characterized by solemnity and 'a peculiar visionary stance' (Venclova, *Forms of Hope* 120), but the man himself does not resemble a magus as much as the elderly Yeats. Even a Polish reader purposefully looking for Miłoszian echoes, Arent van Nieukerken, reaches for Yeats before Miłosz while discussing 'The Master,' even though the poem's Polish translation (done by Stanisław Barańczak) first appeared in a newspaper issue dedicated to Miłosz.[9] He cannot, however, reconcile the master with Yeats either, nor decide what rules and maxims Yeats might deliver; instead, van Nieukerken reaches for yet another draft of the poem, that published after *Station Island* had come out, published in *New and Selected Poems 1966–1987* and then again in *Opened Ground: Poems 1966–996*. This version adds two telling lines after 'Each maxim given its space': '*Tell the truth. Do not be afraid.* / Durable, obstinate notions' (*New and Selected Poems* 202). These lines startlingly echo the injunctions of Zbigniew Herbert's 'The Envoy of Mr Cogito' ('Do not be afraid ... ,' 'Be faithful Go'). Yet the poem continues to revise its last image: Helen Vendler believes that the maxims themselves 'miraculously change from prescription to refreshment' when they come to seem, in subsequent lines, 'Like coping stones where you rest / In the balm of the wellspring.' They are durable, but provide comfort and refreshment (unlike 'Granite Chip') after a wearisome quest. She sets these images against the 'unwinding' beginning 'Sweeney Redivivus,' which the speaker has thought was his only task; 'The Master' sets a higher goal, the ambition to tell the truth and not be afraid, and this growing confidence is further expressed in the next poem, 'The Scribes' (Vendler, 'Seamus Heaney's "Sweeney Redivivus"' 180–2). She does not, however, take up the Miłosz-Yeats-Herbert connection. The 'durable, obstinate' nature of the master's maxims fits well with Herbert's poem and with the public image of Herbert we have discussed previously. After an abortive attempt to attribute these sentiments to Yeats, by which the critic himself is unconvinced, van Nieukerken identifies the Herbertian echo and notes with some surprise that a very wide gulf indeed separates Yeats from Mr Cogito (264–8). There is little we can do to make the parallel work.

Instead, we must reckon with a compound, mutable poem that withholds perfect referentiality. An image of Miłosz shades into one of Yeats, uttering lines from Herbert. We obtain a composite *impression* (if not a convincing composite image) of stricture, seclusion, nobility, and loftiness coupled with surprising accessibility. The master's maxims are at the centre of the poem, but the mental acrobatics through which we must put ourselves in order to make them applicable to all three poets are discouraging; additionally, van Nieukerken soundly points out that the poems of 'Sweeney Redivivus' actually parody the strict constraints of religious, political, and domestic obligation (260). Their speaker does not shy away from sarcastic and scornful tones as he expresses his distance from everything that made him (in the words of 'Station Island') 'biddable and unforthcoming' (*Station Island* 85), and his people 'pious and exacting and demeaned' ('The First Kingdom,' *Station Island* 101). If we view 'Station Island' as a poetic exorcism allowing Heaney to distance himself from his early poetic masters (see Cuda 152), then the 'The Master' can work as a poem of realignment.

Michael Parker notes that Heaney attuned himself to foreign voices in the 1970s and 1980s 'in order to enrich his understanding of others' history' ('Fallout from the Thunder' 370), but such poems in *Station Island* show us how much foreign voices enriched his understanding of his own history, political and personal, and its dominant ethics. This enrichment happens when one takes a step away from identity politics: 'You could say that *Sweeney Astray* is a version of identity politics in Ulster. Now, one function of writing or of a writer, in fact, may be to disrupt all that. One of your functions is to say that your language and your consciousness are as wide as the world' (Heaney in Ni Anluain,

94). This is how we may understand 'Sweeney Redivivus' to be motivated by a different impulse from 'Sweeney Astray' – the poet has been
reborn as a fundamentally different voice, not a Catholic Nationalist
provocateur but a self-questioning exile from his own previous life, attuned to a foreign master and bitter towards his own backward people.
Although only certain poets of the wide world will produce work that
clarifies the speaker's situation, the flight from local ritual (such as the
Lough Derg pilgrimage at the centre of this volume) is seen in terms of
a generalized mastery of new vistas:

> I was mired in attachment
> ...
> so I mastered new rungs of air
> to survey out of reach
>   ... the people of art
> diverting their rhythmical chants
> to fend off the onslaught of winds
> I would welcome and climb
> at the top of my bent. ('The First Flight,' *Station Island* 102–3)

'Art' rhymes internally with 'divert,' forming a pair that encapsulates
the speaker's uneasy relationship to 'attachment' in this sequence,
which goes back in autobiographical time at the same time as it '[mas-
ters] new rungs of air' by fleeing parochialism. The compulsion of 'Station Island' *not* to divert itself from 'the fact' by employing 'tact' and art
instead of plain truth-telling is under question here. The art of attaining
a bird's-eye view, of leaving the communal 'chants' in order to embrace
that which they fear, the wind (of change; of the wide world's voices
sweeping across the local), is being mastered in 'Sweeney Redivivus.'
The sequence mediates between 'Station Island' and the aerated parables of *The Haw Lantern*.

The speaker has *not* fully 'mastered' these new rungs as yet, however
he may pride himself upon doing so; he is still a pupil, a searcher, one
who revisits without preordained conclusions, retaining some amus-
ing, almost juvenile resentment of the communities he has left behind.
The farming folk of his home community are 'pious and exacting and
demeaned,' while the intellectual 'Scribes' are 'petulant' even if 'excellent': 'In the margin of texts of praise / they scratched and clawed'
(111). Both Heaney's first and later communities are convicted of
narrow-mindedness, while the poet-speaker, much like Miłosz's, wishes

to devote himself to texts of praise rather than letters of resentment, even if they appear as books of withholding. The monastic scribe is different from the magus-like master, whose old rules provide relief and who is driven by 'purpose and venture' rather than 'myopic angers.' The speaker, meanwhile, is seeking guidance, and 'Sweeney Redivivus' echoes Geoffrey Hill's *Mercian Hymns* in its use of a doubled persona. The speaker is both a child, lonely among his brethren, and an adult retelling his coming of age, though the kingly nature of this Sweeney is certainly not emphasized. He is no ring-giver. He is no ruler. Indeed, the adult persona here is far more nebulous in character than Hill's King Offa. There is nothing historically verifiable about the adult Sweeney/Heaney. For this we must look at another poem in *Station Island*, in which Miłosz's words elicit bewilderment rather than satisfaction.

'Away from it All' and Metaphysical Bewilderment

Seamus Heaney speaks of the years composing *Station Island* as a politically brutal time of hunger strikes and sectarian killings when he himself 'was "away from it all" during those months: at a physical remove, living in Dublin, going on holiday in France' (O'Driscoll, *Stepping Stones* 259). In this context, living 'at a remove' itself seems tantamount to being on holiday. The remark shows how much these were years of self-accusation for Heaney; not an original point about *Station Island*, of course, but a necessary one for understanding Miłosz's role in its composition. 'My own mantra in those days was the remark by Miłosz that I quote in "Away from it All": I was stretched between contemplation of a motionless point and the command to participate actively in history' (ibid. 260). Read in the context of his reminiscences in interview, the remark gains an immediate historical context: the Catholic Heaney feels pressed to respond to the hunger-strikers' deaths, such as that of Francis Hughes, the son of his family's Catholic neighbours, and yet Hughes had essentially become 'a hit man' (260) and would have been seen as such by his other, Protestant, neighbours. We must briefly imagine this situation in order to contextualize Heaney's appropriation of Miłosz's remarks: Heaney learns of Hughes's death while dining at All Souls' College, Oxford, with Charles Monteith, erstwhile chairman of Faber and Faber, colleague of T.S. Eliot, and original commissioner of Heaney's poems. In other words, Heaney was enjoying himself in the company of English luminaries – partaking in a ceremonious dinner, to round out the irony at hand – while his neighbour punished and destroyed his own flesh by starvation to protest the British government. Although Hughes does make it into Heaney's verse, and Heaney admits to having some sympathy with the hunger strikers, he is afraid to build a myth of martyrdom out of it – especially wary, perhaps, because his earlier poetry had been reliant upon myth in order to understand the poet's home ground. *Station Island* wishes to stay clear of all processions (63) and from communal myths. Yet Heaney did participate in the 'usual ritual' of attending the wake for the eighth hunger striker to die (Thomas McElwee, Hughes's cousin and a near-neighbour), in order to pay his respects and to give himself 'some relief' (O'Driscoll, *Stepping Stones* 260). Relief from his feeling that he must participate actively in history? It was not a 'command' (to apply Heaney's own quotation to himself), as far as we know, to attend the wake; Heaney had been asked (possibly by Danny Morrison, a Belfast writer and ardent Nationalist) to address the hunger strikers' situation, an experience he wrote about many years later in *The Spirit Level* (1996), but 'command' must here be taken as an ethical compulsion before a physical or political exigency. Heaney's attendance at the wake may be called participation in history if we take 'history' as a term blanketing many different types of human activity. He recounts his confidence that McElwee's family would have known that his presence at Thomas's wake in August 1981 was 'above or beyond the politics that were distressing everybody' (O'Driscoll, *Stepping Stones* 260), since he was never an IRA supporter. McElwee, by contrast, had been a member of the much-feared Provisional IRA, and Heaney seems quite certain that his family would have put by politics for the occasion. His confidence seems rather utopian. It reveals the extent to which Heaney wishes that politics could be a matter of complex sympathy and not simple alignment, so that one could participate in history without 'active' duty in the service of dubious causes, whether they be formulated by paramilitary organizations or by idealistic patriots such as those heading the Warsaw Uprising and the Polish Home Army, which, we may recall, Miłosz did not join. He is far from sounding confident as he mulls over Miłosz's *Native Realm* in 'Away from it All,' which begins anecdotally with a lobster, the shade of 'sunk munitions,' being skewered by 'cold steel' in a restaurant. As the anecdote continues, the meditative speaker begins to balance the claims of lives inside and outside his own enclosure. The Polish poet's words come 'like ... alibis' for an undescribed wrongdoing. His immediate impulse,

however, is to question Miłosz's notion of active historical participation
and then metaphorize, and aestheticize, his sense of being caught between two conditions:

> '*Actively?* What do you mean?'
> The light at the rim of the sea
> is rendered down to a fine
> graduation, somewhere between
> balance and inanition.
>
> And I still cannot clear my head
> ...
> ... [of] the hampered one, out of water,
> fortified and bewildered. (*Station Island* 16–17)

It is safe to say that 'Away from it All' relies on a more awkward situation than Heaney's other poems, yet it occasions commentary *because of*
its internal disunity: we enter a descriptive and lyrical mode in which
one of Heaney's signature devices – the use of a word's secondary
meaning to broaden a poem's verbal reach – is juxtaposed with the banality of the represented action. 'Fortification,' however, is denied to
the vulnerable body caught on the edge of history. The obvious question to pose is the one Heaney's critics are baffled to answer: is the poet,
in all seriousness, being likened to a lobster by means of his exilic position (not 'in his element'), his confrontation with political exigencies
("*Actively?*"), and 'bewildered' position vis-à-vis the world of violence,
in which his own 'sunk munitions' are matched by 'cold steel' plung-
ing at him from outside? Is the parallel meant to hold? An intention-
alist question, to be sure, but one striking at the heart of this poem,
which negotiates the boundary between the political and the personal.
If so, must we understand the source of threat with direct reference to
Heaney's own life? The cold fork prodding and removing the lobster
from his 'element' may represent the Nationalist political demand to
'write something for us' ('The Flight Path') or, more broadly, reiterated
demands that Heaney show his political cards instead of maintaining a
tactfulness that could be seen as evasive.

This time, however, we must be wary of such a literal interpretation,
even if it centres the poem in a reassuring way, narrowing the scope
of our possible questions. Instead, the poem must be viewed in terms
of the volume, in which the speaker seeks to exorcise the demon of
local obligation in 'Station Island' and to 'master new rungs of air' that

allow for 'scope and neuter allegiance' in 'Sweeney Redivivus.'[10] It connects in a broad manner with Miłosz's work, which always balances itself between topical and – at the risk of using an unfashionable term – metaphysical relevance. Although both authors offer commentary that helps us to situate their poems biographically, it would be restrictive to take this as the only probable interpretation. The thematic, ethical centre of the poem is 'balance and inanition.' One word is positive – balancing competing demands – and one negative, from the Latin *inanire*, to void or empty; 'balance' holds elements in play, whereas 'inanition' empties the subject or its actions. The light may not be illuminating substance but emptiness. There is a 'fine graduation' between the two meanings.

The poem's lines also hover between rhyme (lyricism) and bathos (poet as lobster, let us remember). Their slant rhymes keep the poet out of his 'element.' They highlight the most complete, ringing rhyme in the poem, which occurs as the speaker grasps the quotation as a useful self-defence against charges which the poem does not utter. We may understand that they have to do with history – '"*Actively?* What do you mean?"' Heaney, of course, knows exactly what Miłosz means – he quotes the phrase often enough in his prose that we cannot, once again, impute unease to the man behind this mask. We must, instead, see this as the donning of a mask, one of feigned bewilderment, in which confusion serves as an alibi for not participating in history; and Miłosz is a master who (again like Yeats) is himself fond of donning masks. The poem's last turn, between its penultimate and ultimate stanzas, represents a swerve from incipient self-castigation (which would certainly cast the poem into autobiography in the manner of 'Station Island') to alibi making, here embodied by the bizarre metaphor of the lobster. This alibi works by casting the poet out of potentially fruitful contemplation (forwarded by the move from question to objective correlative) and into self-defensive metaphorization: inanition (emptying) is transformed into the colloquial 'clear my head,' and the speaker's *inability* to clear his head is seen as a sort of moral triumph. He vindicates himself by turning back to the doomed lobsters, back to his convivial meal – interrupted so unfortunately by philosophical speculation – despite the fact that he is responsible for the untimely death of the creature he has so enjoyed devouring.

The poem's obvious precursor is 'Oysters,' the poem beginning *Field Work* (1979). Here, another friendly meal and gustatory delicacy is seen 'Alive and violated,' representing the 'Glut of privilege' and provoking the speaker not to contemplation but to deliberate action:

... [I] was angry that my trust could not repose
In the clear light, like poetry or freedom
Leaning in from sea. I ate the day
Deliberately, that its tang
Might quicken me all into verb, pure verb. (*Field Work* 11)

Of course, 'verb' is here a noun; and how does one become a verb? Is it connected to active participation in history, which functions as a specification of the *type* of verb the speaker feels called upon to become? Yet 'Oysters' couches the demand for action in the speaker's psychology, not the outside world. He is angry at his own lack of trust, which, as Christopher Ricks has eloquently argued, is the central word of this poem. Ricks believes that *Field Work* is 'alive with trust,' dependent on it (Ricks 97); *Station Island* is a volume definitively taking that trust to task, prying it open and making a meal of the ensuing bewilderment. As we have seen, however, the objects under scrutiny in *Station Island* do not correspond to 'nouns of privilege (property and possessions)' (Ricks 96), but to bearers of judgment. 'Repose' is not made possible. The question is what the object of the verb should be, and how 'active participation' should be understood and directed.

When Life and History Rhyme: *Native Realm*

Considering Heaney's brief quotation from *Native Realm* has had such an international career, it is surprising that scholars have not troubled the fact that it is a translation. Its cultural translation into Heaney's work has, indeed, been considered, but not its literal linguistic translation, which struggles with a recalcitrant element of the original Polish. In Miłosz's *Rodzinna Europa* (literally 'Familial Europe') it reads thus: 'Byłem więc między dwoma biegunami: kontemplacja nieruchomego punktu i nakazem czynnego udziału w historii' (*Rodzinna Europa* 131). Literally, 'I was therefore between two poles,' and the image is one of *opposition*, of two poles exerting countervailing magnetic pulls. 'Czynny,' like 'active,' has the notion of results at its root – 'active participation' would bear fruit, have results. Thus we may answer the bewildered speaker's question in 'Away from it All.' Heaney has famously said that no lyric will stop a tank. 'Active participation' might. His ('rehearsed'?) puzzlement is a poor excuse; the actual poet has spent his life considering poetry's capacity for historical intervention and ruminating on

Auden's often-misquoted line ('Poetry makes nothing happen: it survives ...'). The real question is whether Miłosz's words can be taken as an 'alibi' for making things happen.

There were positive examples available for both men. Miłosz's youth was spent in Lithuanian schools where pupils of various nationalities mixed, and university life was a nonconformist freemasonry miraculously devoid of the anti-Semitism that plagued Europe (*Native Realm* 102). Heaney also attended a 'mixed' school as a child, yet 'race and resentment' were never far away. Both men could, then, 'actively participate' in history to uphold ideals of coexistence that they had, to some measure, directly experienced; yet Miłosz confesses, 'Quite early I learned to treat my literary triumphs as a compensation both deserved and somewhat discomfiting, because to me it was proof of my inferiority in other areas. Completely incapable of action, unfit for organizing or leadership or even blind obedience, I compared myself to my colleagues; they were drawing conclusions from their reading of Lenin' (118). The applicability of this sentiment to Heaney, erstwhile 'Incertus,' friend to eloquent Nationalists who called for alliance with their cause (we may recall his 1977 interview with Seamus Deane), is indubitable; yet both men refuse to 'jump in head first, to surrender completely to some cause,' realizing that the individual is powerless when he is involved in 'a mechanism that works independently of his will' (119–20).

This profitably complicates 'active participation.' How to participate while remaining independent of large-scale parties is an issue that both poets rethink throughout their lives. The adult Miłosz comes to embrace a rather Yeatsian sentiment: 'that the collective imagination is given shape through the discipline of form itself, and that poetry is political in a totally different sense from the conventional use of the term' (121–2). This leads to his frustration in the United States, when young poets would ask him how politically committed a poet should be, 'since I have the aura of a poet who wrote anti-Nazi poems' – and in the era of Vietnam War protests, his aura of dissidence would have been a powerful draw – but, Miłosz continues, 'I don't really know how to deal with their questions. Their concept of political commitment is naïve' (Czarnecka and Fiut 321). Collective imagination, the discipline of form, nonconformist commitment – it is no wonder that Heaney subconsciously brings together Miłosz with Yeats in 'The Master.' The idea that the giving of poetic form, imposing shape onto formless thoughts and feelings, can in itself be understood as a form of historical participation, is a rich concept that allows the poet to dwell between contemplation and action, even if we must forcibly banish naive notions of action and commitment from our minds to understand it.

Taken as a whole, the volume questions the poet's ability to write politically. Miłosz's *Native Realm* stands as a type of achievement that Heaney skirts but does not actually undertake: it is a cultural autobiography of 'an Eastern European' who realizes that his life and times are foreign to those in the West, and who realizes that the images of his life do not supersede each other easily and regularly, but 'collide' to form a tangled mass (*Native Realm* 3). To explicate this mass, one must start at the beginning. He does: the book provides a capsule history of Lithuania as well as a story of the poet's coming of age. The second strand is paramount, since, as Miłosz writes, 'much is said these days about history. But unless we can relate it to ourselves personally, history will always be more or less of an abstraction' (20). Heaney would agree. He does not, however, suffer from the same sense of exile and incomprehension as his Polish master: during his months in Ireland, he was perhaps too much surrounded by fellow-countrymen, though we must stress that the pressures to 'write something for us' and simultaneously to clarify 'that subject people stuff' to those abroad were correspondingly great, and this may well account for Heaney's interest in *Native Realm*.

The history that Miłosz relates is, however, extremely different from Heaney's socio-political background, and this bears mention. His father's work building roads and bridges for the Russian empire resulted in a 'nomadic life' for his family, who lived in covered wagons or army cars, a situation diametrically opposed to Heaney's rooted Mossbawn life. Miłosz draws the consequences: 'Such a lack of stability, the unconscious feeling that everything is temporary, ... can be the reason for taking governments and political systems lightly. History becomes fluid because it becomes equated with ceaseless wandering' (41). He is overstating the point, as even a cursory reading of his poems will attest, yet this early nomadism creates its imprint, and the sight of Eastern European borderlands being drawn and redrawn, lands bartered, languages vying for dominance and occasionally being illogically imposed, is foreign to Heaney. The life Miłosz started after 1918 becomes more similar to Heaney's: 'The contrast between the life I had known until then and the life I was to lead in the home of my birth was as great as, say, the contrast between the various circles of European hell and a farm in the American Middle West ... The days unfolded, just as they had for centuries, to the rhythm of work in the fields, Catholic feasts, solemn processions, and the rites of Christian-pagan magic' (47). This is the sort of life that Heaney experienced as a child and lost when he entered boarding school and then university; this is the life that furnishes a constant touchstone for both poets, one whose images are ceaselessly rejuvenating, and coalesce to form a sort of moral landscape for each one.

Yet the sentence that Heaney comes back to does not engage this reality but relates to Miłosz's coming of age politically and metaphysically, which forms the core of the book. The extent to which his metaphysics partake of 'Christian-pagan magic' is often underplayed, including by Heaney himself, who focuses on the shared Catholic childhood of both poets. Crucial as it is, we must remember that the 'motionless point' upon which Miłosz gazes has supra-religious significance.[11] Miłosz's Catholic education kindles a far-reaching interest in spirituality (in the broadest significance of the word); despite his continued exposure to the political (i.e., non-transcendent) dimension of his childhood religion, so does Heaney's: 'For a young lyric poet it is good to see the whole cosmos ashimmer with God and to know you, a pinpoint of plasma, are part of It, He, whatever. There is a sense ... [t]hat you are accountable. That every action and secret thought is known out there on the rim of eternity. It's a wonderful thing' (Heaney in Farndale n.p.). Poetry is seen as a 'visitation' by Heaney, just as it is for Miłosz, though the latter stresses its demonic quality and calls himself a Manichean. Although Miłosz writes poems in which a thousand hands of the dead seize his pen ('In Warsaw'), his core belief in a 'collective imagination' is less substantial and specific than such lines have it be. Poetry and art help to shape the collective imagination, while conversely, the poet writes out of a complex belonging to a metaphysical whole: Miłosz and Heaney's words cross, overlap, and mesh in a brilliantly irrational way. The poet's coming of age involves immersion in a reality set 'ashimmer' by a God that elicits awe at something that cannot be named ('It, He, whatever'). We can see why the young Heaney sought to emulate Hopkins. Heaney's description emphasizes the beauty of the transcendent realm; Miłosz often emphasizes its darkness and lack of concern for human welfare. Both are partially lapsed Catholics, and this background ineluctably colours their imaginings of transcendence, spirit, 'whatever' we may call it. This will come to the fore in Heaney's next volume inspired by the Eastern Europeans and especially by Miłosz, *The Haw Lantern* of 1987.

5 Unfortunate Nobility

The Alvarez-Miłosz Quarrel: Defining the Witness

Station Island meditates on what poetry is called upon to do and what it should do, realizing that they are not the same thing. *The Government of the Tongue* looks at other poets as examples of how to negotiate this difference. *The Haw Lantern* allegorizes the choice more abstractly than the extended metaphor of 'Sweeney Redivivus' had allowed, truly mastering new rungs of air by looking at the air itself rather than the ground beneath. This volume, called Heaney's first book of the virtual by Helen Vendler (in a refreshingly untechnological use of the term), is the repository of Heaney's allegorical 'parable poems.' Vendler identifies the two impetuses for this shift as the death of his mother and the reading of Eastern European poetry; hardly a natural pairing at first sight, these two events work together to attune Heaney to the invisible realm, that of 'clearances' and insubstantiality ('Seamus Heaney's Invisibles'). This is where Heaney's comment about words we are embarrassed to utter – abstract words, value-laden terms such as 'truth' – is put to the test, as he tries his hand at a newly abstract poetic register. Elegy and allegory do not appear to grow from the same root, though, and Vendler's scrupulous attention to form does not fully clarify the psychological or cultural wellsprings nourishing this unusual volume. In order to do so, we must attend to the continuation of Heaney's relationship with Miłosz, how the Polish master protested his Anglo-American reception in the early 1980s, why it matters for Heaney's view of him, and how this view dramatically changes in *District and Circle* (2006). Whereas we may never discover exactly what the experience of deep grief lends to the pursuit of 'invisibles,' we may begin by accepting their connectedness: 'In my fifties, I attended my first death beds – my mother's and my father's – and I found it an utterly simple and utterly mysterious thing to watch. Life goes, spirit goes, whatever, and abstract words that had previously had an ephemeral flimsiness to them were no longer abstractions' (Heaney in Farndale). The concrete and abstract are starting to change place. Miłosz is his tutelary presence here, and we may see in this statement what Heaney desired to see and emulate in Miłosz's work by experimenting with a radically new type of poetic language, and how uncomfortably this meshed with his cultural environment, though not with his personal circumstances.

A brief biographical digression is necessary to recall *where* Heaney was in the 1980s. While working in Dublin at the Carysfort teachers' training college, a job that ended up becoming onerous as the college expanded its programs and Heaney took on several administrative responsibilities, he was invited to come to Harvard University temporarily. In 1979, Heaney came to Cambridge, Massachusetts, with his family for one semester. He was lucky to have several friends in the area, and it was a positive experience. Two years later, Harvard made him another offer, this one a prestigious named professorship (Boylston Professor of Rhetoric and Oratory) that entailed teaching creative writing and lecturing on poetry for only half of the year (later, Heaney became Ralph Waldo Emerson Poet in Residence at Harvard), which he accepted. Heaney whittled his teaching stint down to four months a year, during which time he lived alone in Cambridge while his wife stayed with their three children in Dublin. This repeated separation, no doubt difficult, had the positive effect of allowing Heaney full immersion in each milieu on its own. We have to imagine a situation in which Heaney would plunge himself headfirst into the intellectually electrifying world of Harvard, teaching the craft of poetry and giving public and private readings of his own, writing and being written of in *The Harvard Review*, giving guest lectures and interviews, playing the part of public poet well before his 1995 Nobel Prize, and then spending the rest of the year with his family, gaining a bilocational perspective while tirelessly crossing the Atlantic.

Meanwhile, Eastern European poetry is at the zenith of its popularity. Heaney comes into close contact with Stanisław Barańczak, exceedingly prolific translator from English to Polish and vice versa, eminent poet (in Polish), and professor of Polish literature at Harvard. The two men collaborate on a translation of Jan Kochanowski's *Laments*, a series of threnodies grieving the death of the poet's daughter Urszula when she was two years old. Kochanowski's Renaissance poetic was translated into a modern idiom, and again, the subject of family grief, the 'clearances' left by death, became central for Heaney, albeit many years later. Barańczak, meanwhile, was a careful reader of Miłosz, and published a review essay on Miłosz's *The Collected Poems 1931–1987* in which he spent a good amount of space playing peacemaker in a quarrel that took place between Miłosz and Al Alvarez in the *New York Review of Books* that same year (1988). The issue, obviously, was unresolved, and the writers' feelings raw. Heaney had a front-row seat to this show of anger and cultural miscommunication.

What happened was that Alvarez published a laudatory review of Miłosz's *Collected Poems* in the *New York Review of Books*, entitled 'Witness': from the beginning, then, this was an international occurrence, since Alvarez made his name as a scholar and anthologist enjoining English writers in particular to look abroad for foreign models, pressing them to rejuvenate what he saw as their flagging poetic craft. The fact that Alvarez would enjoy and champion Miłosz's poetry was no surprise. In *Under Pressure – The Writer in Society: Eastern Europe and the U.S.A.*, he lauded the 'outward' impulse of Eastern European poetry and the role that 'pressure' played in galvanizing poetry into near-mandatory socio-political relevance. Even Daniel Weissbort states that it was 'a very tendentious anthology,' as is, of course, Weissbort's own (Weissbort 22). The fact is, the word 'witness,' and the concept of 'poetry of witness,' was extremely popular at the time. Such terms, and the histrionic language often attending their use, hearken back to the (then long-standing) vogue for Eastern European verse that we discussed in the first chapter. 'Witness' celebrates Miłosz's principled reactions to the sorrows befalling his country and, again, points to the value that such a writer could have for others. Alvarez presents the Pole as a quintessential Central European and a poet-in-exile; he points to the 'need for the beauty and order of poetry as an alternative to the disorder of homelessness' as a common theme in Miłosz's work ('Witness' 22). These remarks hardly seem surprising: does not Miłosz write, in 'My Faithful Mother Tongue,' that 'what is needed in misfortune is a little order and beauty,' has he not referred to himself as an exile and written extensively about this condition, and has he not *expressly* written, in the beginning of *Native Realm*, that the book aims to study himself as an exemplar of Eastern European consciousness for the benefit of Westerners who find his 'type' foreign (*Native Realm* 3)? Has not he written that the major theme of our times should be the interplay of poetry and history, yet that Americans in particular, and Westerners more generally, are losing the historical sense? In addition, why would he entitle his Charles Eliot Norton lectures – six public lectures delivered at Harvard in 1981–2, published in 1983 – *The Witness of Poetry*? The issue, for Miłosz, has less to do with inaccuracy than categorization: he deplores the implication that his poetic output could be *summarized* by the term 'witness.' He believes, with some accuracy, that Alvarez's fascination with poets of witness has to do with his distance from them, and that it effects a damaging exoticization. Miłosz, who has been writing for a half-century, protests being cast in one role: 'a poet repeatedly says farewell to his old selves and makes himself ready for renewals' ('A Poet's Reply'). Miłosz is not a chameleon poet, however, and does not see himself as such, but is still an exiled Eastern European who wishes to exist in the American present and not be frozen in a past that he evokes by using chameleonic personae. He realizes, as Heaney tacitly does, that the non-native audience *is* indeed crucial to his poetic success, however much both poets insist upon the primary importance of readers at home. There are considerable psychological complexities at work here. His piqued tone, however, justifies Alvarez's counter-reply ('A. Alvarez Replies'): 'In the world of letters there is no pleasing anybody,' he sighs, reflecting that he thought he had written a positive review. This reply, unfortunately, misrepresents the issue so that our sympathies tilt even more strongly in favour of Miłosz, who has pre-emptively acknowledged that Alvarez's *terms* of praise, not the relative praise or blame, are the problem.

Alvarez was not, however, the only one to thus describe Miłosz, and Heaney no doubt noticed the trajectory of Miłosz's career in the States. Bogdana Carpenter's exhaustively researched essay 'The Gift Returned' traces this career. She points to *The Witness of Poetry* as an event provoking revaluation of poetry's relationship with history (48), although Miłosz's reputation as a primarily political writer persevered, perhaps even longer than Carpenter opines. She cites a panoply of contemporary reviews, whether narrow and blinkered or extremely nuanced, such as translator Lillian Vallee's insightful assertion that Miłosz is 'ahistorical by predilection' but 'made historical by circumstance.' Leonard Nathan and Arthur Quinn's *The Poet's Work: An Introduction to Czeslaw Milosz* (1991), the first monograph of its kind, aimed to present Miłosz as a philosophical poet to the English-language reader. This may be seen as a turning point in his American career. A different sort of turn is represented by the criticism of Helen Vendler and, yes, Heaney, who turn their attention to Miłosz's lyricism, and particularly the formal features that prove unusual for the English-language reader schooled in Anglo-American modernism (57–8); we must add English Romanticism as an equally powerful background influence. In another article, Carpenter observes that Miłosz's work is *less* historically based from 1970 on, as he turns from history to ontology and metaphysics, from the 'native realm' to the 'unattainable earth' (Carpenter, 'Czesław Miłosz i Zbigniew Herbert' 180–1).

Critics such as Alvarez, therefore, who promoted Miłosz as a historical witness, were behind the curve of evaluative development. How epistemologically dire is this situation? One extreme conclusion is drawn by Mark Rudman in 1998:

> Be reconciled: Miłosz must remain somewhat unassimilable for the Anglo-American reader. The English-speaking world still has a long way to go in understanding Milosz. A lot of the criticism of Milosz, especially that which appears in journals with circulation beyond the merely literary, approaches him as a political writer or as a witness. This may have moral value, but it is the least interesting thing about him as a writer ... By 1980 I couldn't have been the only one who was becoming inured to a generic quality in the flood of eastern Europe poets [*sic*] appearing in translation. If another Milosz convert passed through New York said 'I have to read you Milosz's "Ars Poetica?"' I would have to devise a Rube Goldbergian contraption through which I could escape ... If there was anything I didn't care for in poetry at the time, it was advice. ('The Milosz File' 129–33)

Is Rudman going against his own words, though, by associating Miłosz's work with 'advice'? There is a trend wherein Miłosz's readers rework their own views, sometimes doubly contradicting their own assessments. Perhaps unsurprisingly, fellow poets often prove especially prone to self-reassessment. Charles Simic, for example, suggests, 'One could risk saying then that Miłosz plays an unwilling therapeutic function in the treatment of the modern ailment of dehistoricisation' (Simic in Jarniewicz, 'Eastern Recollections' 116). Barańczak's review of Miłosz's *Collected Poems* considers the terms of the Alvarez-Miłosz quarrel by conceding that the 'witness' label fits until the 1980s (*pace* Carpenter), but that by the 1988 *Collected Poems* we must reckon with him as a metaphysical poet, and must also recognize his persistent use of 'dramatic polyphony' (Barańczak, 'Between Repulsion and Rapture').

More recently and more surprisingly, Shirley Lim describes her reaction to the quarrel in *Reading the Literatures of Asian America*, narrating her gradual realization that what was at stake was not simply a writer's ego but a whole referential field and, even more broadly, a means of naturalizing foreign writers by subordinating them to local desires: as Alvarez describes Miłosz's natal Lithuania as 'a country that has vanished utterly into the Soviet maw,' so he stirs not just residual anticommunist fervour but a desire for exoticism that is predicated upon false mythologies of exotic descent, a form of hypostatized alterity. Lim connects this project to the struggles of immigrants discussed in Werner Sollors's seminal *Beyond Ethnicity: Consent and Descent in American Culture* (1986), thus allowing us to see how the publically divisive Alvarez-Miłosz quarrel may have broad, even global implications. Several points of this discussion are directly applicable to Seamus Heaney's career beyond Ireland, where he, too, is called upon to perform an exotic sort of identity (country boy, farm-dweller, son of a cattle dealer) in various metropolitan centres (his publisher's London office; the Bay Area; the Boston area). Miłosz's protest, then, would have been of particular interest to Heaney. Lim expands the significance of the quarrel yet further: 'Can it be possible that we hear in Miłosz's complaint the same protest against the stereotyping of exoticism, the same anger against a deeply engrained Anglocentrism as has been expressed by black Americans, Chicanos, Asian Americans, Latinos, and other ethnic minorities in the last three decades?' (Lim and Ling 17). With this question, Miłosz's protest definitively enters world – not simply European or Western – literature. There is more at stake than may have first been apparent.

Unfortunate Nobility

'History. Society. If a literary critic is fascinated with them, that's his choice; if, however, he is insensitive to another dimension, he risks to curtail his right to reflect on literature ... [T]he voice of a poet should be purer and more distinct than the noise (or confused music) of History' (Miłosz, 'A Poet Replies'). Nobody could accuse Seamus Heaney of insensitivity to poetry's many dimensions. Now that we have quickly surveyed Miłosz's changing reception in the 1980s, we can see how the 1987 *Haw Lantern* came out at an unstable point at which his reputation was a highly contentious issue. The project and the effect of *The Haw Lantern*, though, are somewhat at cross-purposes. Whereas we *hear* a 'pure' and 'distinct' voice emanating from the newly abstract parable poems, their origin is rather bathetic: 'There was an exercise I used to set the students in my poetry workshop at Harvard – to make up a poem that pretended to be translated from an original in a foreign language. The parable poems were that kind of exercise ... I'd just finished *Station Island* and was trying to dodge documentary' (Heaney in Brown 85). The language of the poems is 'a kind of translatorese.' Such comments are unfairly deflationary. Let us recall their occasion: spoken well after *The Haw Lantern* had garnered several negative reviews and *Seeing Things* (1991) extremely positive ones, Heaney begins to position *The Haw Lantern* as a transitional volume of modest scope. Yet we do not have to believe him. The volume represents a serious attempt to reckon with the legacy of Eastern Europe, not merely to good-humouredly undertake a student exercise. The implication that *Station Island* could be referred to as 'documentary' is rather reductive in light of the complex realignments and re-imaginings of its sequences, and our focus will now be on the manner in which *The Haw Lantern* takes on a 'foreign' style and how to situate it against the background of the Alvarez-Miłosz quarrel over poetry of witness. The use of a typical style ('translatorese') is exactly what Miłosz wishes to avoid by protesting the act of typification itself.

'From the Land of the Unspoken' reaches into Miłosz's thematic territory:

> Our unspoken assumptions have the force
> of revelation. How else could we know
> that whoever is the first of us to seek
> assent and votes in a rich democracy
> will be the last of us and have killed our language? (*The Haw Lantern* 19)

The 'exercise' aspect of the poem is visible on the surface: as in 'North,' it begins with an act of evocation rather than *in medias res*, so that the hypothetical ('I have heard of ...') melts into the plural indicative ('We are a dispersed people ...'). Like most of Heaney's parable poems, this one employs a paratactic style for a vaguely didactic aim: the poet is presenting matters of interest. But for whose interest? The ominous tone of Heaney's allegories is unusual, and here does little except add a tinge of apocalyptic melodrama ('will be the last of us'). Miłosz informs the poem's story: he has written about the price of selling one's soul to a rich democracy and to a ruling party (Marxism). He has written about exile, about changing cultural landscapes, and the sometimes-absolute division between individual and communal values (the 'Land of the Unspoken' depends upon necessarily communal values – we must all recognize the unspoken for it to be revelatory). He has written against the debasement of language, as has Herbert, and any reader of Eastern European writing will recognize the indictment of political language as a common theme. Yet Miłosz rarely utters blanket condemnations, precisely because his subtle mind is always leaping underneath the visible to the hidden or unspoken (this is especially visible when he writes about politics, in *The Captive Mind* or the chapters on the Marxist 'Tiger' in *Native Realm*). Thematically, Heaney's poem about solidity, silence, and exile runs counter to Miłosz's desire to be considered part – albeit an exotic part, telling of the faraway – of the American poetic landscape.[1] In his protest against Alvarez's review, Miłosz insists that we allow the poet's voice to change, and the poet to enter new environments, so that the 'metal core' admired by Heaney's speaker does not seem an apposite symbol for the mind or heart of Miłosz or, for that matter, Herbert (whose speaker tries to imbue his dignified bit of stone with false warmth).

When we look closer at the language of the parable poems, though, we can see a complex *un*working of the parable taking place as it is drawn out, which impels us to ask whether Heaney is winking at his own effort (a manoéuvre that would be typical of an ironist such as Miroslav Holub, or even of his two favourite Poles):

you can't be sure that parable is not
at work already retrospectively,
...
... those old revisionists derive
the word *island* from roots in *eye* and *land*.

'Parable Island' is a place where allegory has no fixed signifying foundation, where the ground of meaning has washed away from underneath symbols that float upon the surface of a barely present reality. The meaning-filled word, for which Heaney and Miłosz repeatedly affirm their respect, is skipped over by scholars whose revisionary etymologies reveal only what they wished to see in the first place. How much is this a critique of revisionist, tendentious historiography – a possible yet narrow interpretation – and how much does the poem's critique cross over to the (dare we say it?) universal, as a humorous dismissal of *all* top-down ideologies?

Now archaeologists begin to gloss the glosses.
...
One school thinks a post-hole in an ancient floor
stands first of all for a pupil in an iris.
The other thinks a post-hole is a post-hole. (11)

Heaney himself has written poems in which he takes on the voice of anthropologist for his tribe; Miłosz does the same in sequences such as 'Lauda.' What is being mocked is the manipulation of material history for obscure purposes, which could easily become narrow-minded and ideological, and not the act or trope of excavation itself. But how do we know when a post-hole is merely a post-hole? The answer may be furnished by Miłosz's poetry and, more specifically, its *difference* from poems like this. 'Translatorese'? Heaney misrepresents his own effect when he uses this neologism. The poem mocks the very project it undertakes, both in its statements, its humorous tone, and its prosaicism – poetically, it is not among his most accomplished lyrics; thematically, it enacts a critique of interpretation that shows how inspired emulation can skirt bathos, thus showing what it tells. Just as Herbert states that he hesitates and appeals to conscience through the conditional, whereas Heaney writes enthusiastically of poems that stand their ground in the indicative, so Miłosz asserts the urgency of recognizing a poet's development instead of petrifying him in one posture – such as the one-track symbolism of Parable Island's revisionists – and of allowing his work to become part of his host culture instead of cultivating an exoticizing 'translatorese.' Does Heaney actually mis-read and mis-construe, though, and is it so easy for Miłosz – or any others from beyond the Iron Curtain – to resist a quality that we may translate as 'unfortunate nobility'?

It is all well and good for Miłosz to aver that the poet's voice should purify the language of the tribe rather than embroil itself in the din of history, but the fact is that with the advent of martial law on 13 December 1981, Polish literature was under more pressure than ever. Although martial law only lasted for a year and a half, the 1980s were altogether a dark decade, and Polish literature reflects this circumstance. As in Northern Ireland after the Special Powers Act, internment was practised arbitrarily. The people were paying the price for their oppositional (anti-communist) activities: spiritual and intellectual independence was being punished. In such a climate, the question of literature's responsibility and its obligation to witness was paramount ('The act of writing a poem is an act of faith; yet if the screams of the tortured are audible in the poet's room, is not his activity an offense to human suffering?' Miłosz, *History of Polish Literature* 458). At this point, however, the Poles – indeed, all of the Eastern Europeans – had done a good deal of witnessing already. This new crisis was, in a way, nothing new at all, merely another step on the road for the so-called Christ of Nations. Miłosz had enough: 'Yet again, *La Pologne martyre*, a jealous goddess, drew the total attention of writers' (*Eseje* 123–4, my translation). Literature was an instrument serving the nation, and bore the mark of an 'unfortunate nobility.' This concept allows us to perceive why Eastern European poetry would stay separate from the work it inspired in the West: in times of national misfortune (on a scale unknown to most Westerners), nobility of feeling becomes conflated with artistic quality. The more 'noble' the art, the higher its national service; its hallmark is a politicization of the imagination. It is useful to note the difference of this nobility from the concept formulated by Wallace Stevens in the early years of the Second World War, in the United States: for Stevens, art provides a pressure from within countering a pressure from without; it represents the imagination pressing back against reality. Stevens' famous 'nobility' defends the integrity of the imagination; Miłosz's Polish nobility subsumes individuality into collective need. Polish nobility is 'unfortunate' (Miłosz's Polish essay is entitled 'Szlachetność, niestety'), a moral positive born of a historical negative; yet it is also a cage from which a poet such as Miłosz longs to escape. Taking on the role of noble witness may call forth politicized and moralistic readings of one's work; meanwhile, the nation's desire is precisely to escape the conditions that necessitate 'nobility.'

A paradoxical situation becomes evident: although he repeatedly disclaims this role, Miłosz is persistently associated with nobility. Aleksander Fiut reminds the American immigrant, 'In Poland you have become a symbol of integrity, a moral authority.' Miłosz replies: 'It's very good that you've raised that point. Me a moralist – I find that a little humorous. Do you understand? I've never seen any especially moral principles in my work.' Later: 'Morality was not in fact a great concern of mine' (Czarnecka and Fiut, 323–4). But of course it was, and it always has been. Why else would a stanza of 'You Who Wronged' have been inscribed on a monument to shipyard workers killed by riot police? The inscription contains the following lines: 'Do not feel safe. The poet remembers ... The words are written down, the deed, the date.' These certainly sound like the words of a moralist, and a representative one, at that. The image of the poet here is clearly that of a witness, even though this poem (first published in *Światło dzienne*, 1953) was written once its author had left Poland and had published essays admiring the use of irony in Anglo-American poetry, speaking out against the legacy of Polish Romanticism. This latter point proves crucial to understanding how Miłosz wished to be seen and the conflict that this occasions with Heaney's parable poems.

'That you should visit us no more': Miłosz's Anti-Romanticism

Miłosz responds to Alvarez by relating that 'my struggle as a writer-in-exile has consisted in liberating my neck from those dead albatrosses; in fact for a long time my name was connected with my books in prose available in translation, while the poetry that I have been publishing since 1931 only slowly made its way to the reading public' ('A Poet's Reply' 42). The quality of unfortunate nobility is a by-product of a long cultural trajectory, one which produced 'dead albatrosses' whose compulsions must be symbolically vanquished. Miłosz is speaking of Polish Romanticism, and his metaphor, though borrowed from an English Romantic poem, blurs the difference between the two traditions, and their differing attractions in the late twentieth century. Heaney can safely look back to Wordsworth because it does not involve him in the 'gloomy national ecstasy' that Miłosz discerns in the Polish Romantic legacy of martyrdom, Messianic teleology, and bardic lyricism. Heaney's Romanticism is ideologically safer than Miłosz's, and, indeed, less ideologically fraught altogether. In addition, there had been a more powerful backlash against British Romanticism than Polish, so for an English-language poet the example of Wordsworth is always usefully counterpointed by that of Eliot and Auden, whose names appear often in Heaney's writing, or even Yeats, who progressed beyond his own self-styled Romanticism in his later work. Miłosz, by contrast, is everywhere confronted by Romantic shadows, by Romantic political movements (as he saw the Warsaw Uprising), and by Romantic style: whenever one wishes to touch on 'the great themes,' he complains in an early essay, one 'falls into the Romantic manner' ('wpada w romantyczną manierę,' *Kontynenty* 236–80). This may explain why the *tone* of a poem such as 'Dedication' may seem rather Romantic – and we should note that the poet participated heavily in his own translation – while its subject is the laying to rest of a Romanticized spectre:

You whom I could not save
Listen to me.
Try to understand this simple speech as I would be ashamed of another.
...
What is poetry which does not save
Nations or people?
A connivance with official lies ...
...
They used to pour millet on graves or poppy seeds
To feed the dead who would come disguised as birds.
I put this book here for you, who once lived
So that you should visit us no more. (*New and Collected Poems* 77)

'Dedication' bears the inscription 'Warsaw, 1945,' and may be read as an *ars poetica* that is, itself, a ritual farewell marking the beginning of a new epoch – culturally, stylistically, but also personally, as the title of the volume *Rescue* (Polish *Ocalenie*, 1945) must be understood. In order to situate this much-quoted, much-misquoted poem in the context of our current argument, we must place it against the historico-psychological contours within which *Native Realm* allows us to understand Miłosz's wartime work. On the directly referential surface, the poem is 'about' a young poet killed during the Uprising – one who gave into the lethal force of the 'gloomy national ecstasy' grounded in the Romantic epoch, premised upon the conjuncture of lyricism and martyrdom, blindly opposing – at the price of one's life – what would only crush such tragic idealism. On another surface, metaphorical yet also superficial, the poem embodies the moral call to arms (grounded in dire historical realia) that fascinates Western readers, and it is easy to read it as a call for poetry to witness, to 'save' by means of hortatory zeal, to take Auden's (also much-misquoted) dictum, 'Poetry makes nothing happen,' in blindly direct opposition. On a deeper level, the poem chimes with Auden's lines ('Poetry makes nothing happen; *it survives* / In the valley of its making, ... A way of happening'; emphasis mine). It survives the events that felled the young idealist; it offers a way of happening that is *not* the 'happening' of historical necessity *or* of Romantic teleology. Because its way is different, it survives. It is not cut down. It survives – to Auden, to Miłosz, and also to Stevens – *because* it changes, because it does not freeze, paralysed by the sight of atrocity or by assumptions of its own inefficacy. It survives because it is modified by those still living, because it enters the living stream instead of petrifying in a posture that ultimately proves mortal.

The poem mediates between the individual and the collective and, in parallel mode, between Romantic invocation and post-Romantic dedication to a persistent revenant and, in Janus-faced style, to the era coming after him. This era will only be free once he is ceremonially put to rest;[2] unfinished ethical questions form a temporal block against the new. The time is out of joint because it has stalled. The poem is an act of release. Despite its thematics – destruction, atrocity, ruin, rubble – Miłosz's wartime poetry is, the author holds, triumphal, signalling his recovery of poetic health. The gulf between aestheticism and socially 'committed' poetry vanishes so that in his own work, he proudly asserts, 'now even the most personal poem translated a human situation and contained a streak of irony that made it objective' (*Native Realm* 247). 'Objective' may be understood as 'anti-Romantic' and, more broadly, anti-subjective, anti-sentimental. Miłosz greets the arrival of this new style with an enthusiasm that he makes little effort to conceal: 'Had I been given the chance, perhaps I would have blown the country to bits, so that mothers would no longer cry over their seventeen-year-old sons and daughters who died on the barricades ... Because there is a kind of pity that is unbearable' (257). Such a reaction against pity, which is so central an unstated term in the appreciation of Eastern European poetry, may be surprising but is comprehensible and salubrious.

'Parable Island' had, on a smaller scale, turned against the very mode it instantiated; so 'Dedication' fulfils the role it casts off. 'Playing the traditional role of a Polish poet, Miłosz simultaneously rebels against it,' asserts Bronisław Maj, noting the strange and pathetic irony of being a poet of a nation that possesses only the words of the poet – and, we may add, living *in* a different nation that may only come to know the first by means of the poet's evocations. Maj notes Miłosz's lifelong attention to history's multi-dimensionality, which we may oppose both to the relatively narrow way in which Eastern European history was summoned by participants in so-called 'Slavic chic,' and to the teleology of Polish Romanticism.[3] We can understand his rebellion against the 'witness' label even more clearly and broadly when we view his 1980s remarks, and Heaney's 1980s poetic interventions, in light of the earlier essays written in the 1940s and 1950s, published in *Kontynenty* and *Prywatne obowiązki*, in which Miłosz speaks out sharply against the Romantic myth. These dates compel mention because they signal decades when poetic testimony would seem necessary. Miłosz was not insensitive to this need, and did not wholly refuse to write testimonially and collect 'invincible' poems by others (see *The Invincible Song*, originally published in 1942). Yet of his wartime poems there is little reportage, and 'The World: A Naïve Poem' stands as their centrepiece. This is, we will recall, the work that provokes his ire when it is translated in virtuoso style. It surprises by its omissions:

> Faith is in you whenever you look
> At a dewdrop or a floating leaf
> And know that they are because they have to be.
> Even if you close your eyes and dream up things
> The world will remain as it has always been
> And the leaf will be carried by the waters of the river. (*New and Collected Poems* 48)

Its inscription reads 'Warsaw, 1943.' But, the historical materialist may ask, where is the poem's 'context'? The ethicist may ask, how can one legitimately say that faith is perpetual, and that what is may be justified in its being by some transcendent exigency? Sceptical readers of all stripes may ask, how can one believe for a minute that 'the world will remain' when it shows – in Warsaw of 1943 – every sign of perishing before our eyes? 'A Naïve Poem,' indeed.

Of course, omissions are not accidents. The poem captures Heaney's attention: its sing-song, he maintains, is the poet's answer to destruction, and its naivety is a mask assumed with full knowledge of the demands placed upon art in a time of war; he opposes it to poems that self-indulgently refuse self-scrutiny (Heaney in Thomas 46–7). Because of its omissions, we are able to interpret the poem in widely divergent ways – as a poem of shellshock, as psychosocial balm, or, perhaps, as a dark version of 'The Hollow Men.' There is also a cultural backdrop with which to contend, such as Miłosz's hyperbolic desire to blow up the world crying out for pity, obtruding its Romantic martyrology upon what could be modernity; 'what appeared to be the end was not the end of either tradition or literature or art' (*Native Realm* 247). This is *not* the way the world ends, and the virtue we feel upon uttering commonplaces about the end of culture, civilization, or art is falsely self-satisfying. Adorno has protested the misuse of his dictum about lyric after Auschwitz: after mass tragedy we must, of course, continue to think, produce, create. The statement that we cannot do so out of adherence to some ostensibly virtuous vow of silence is not helpful or healthy. Miłosz responds to the presence of what appears to be real, actual catastrophe by writing a series of versets that he likens to a metaphysical tract in simplified shapes and colours (more specifically, to Thomist philosophy [248]). The truth of simplicity and naivety is equal to the truth of complexity and corruption.

Miłosz is not, however, associated with simplicity, with naivety, or with easeful diction. In 'The Master,' he cuts a vatic figure for Heaney, he is called an 'Old Master' in Poland, and is seen as a philosopher-poet writing in slightly archaic, patently serious language.[4] Words such as 'stern' and 'didactic' inevitably colour even the most positive assessments of his work. As we have seen, Heaney's own work tends towards this opinion in the 1980s, although it is crucial that *Heaney himself* is usually the one to point out the breadth of Miłosz's influence. His readers sometimes prefer to narrow this influence so that Miłosz emerges as a safely one-dimensional figure, a historical moralist. Heaney, however, constantly stresses his multi-dimensionality, even while not all of these dimensions make it into his poems on the Master – at least not at once, not in the same volume. The baffling 'World' is, Heaney tells us, the influence behind his 'Alphabets,' composed in 1984 but published in *The Haw Lantern*. 'Alphabets' has garnered sufficient scholarly exegesis that it need not be replicated here, but virtually none of its exegetes have discussed this Miłoszian influence.[5] This fact alone shows us that Heaney – *despite* his image of Miłosz as a magus unclasping a book of withholding – is willing to encounter, and take influence from, multiple Miłoszes. His Master would be happy, since he spends a good portion of his life battling the Romantic legacy that has, paradoxically and yet understandably, helped to form his image. He insists that he is no bard and no moralist, and yet his work of the 1940s and 1950s often sounds bardic. Ian Balfour makes a useful distinction between prophetic modes which helps to understand Miłosz's authorial persona: 'The major difference between the prophet and bard lies in the way history functions for each of them,' Balfour writes, so that the bard 'is much like the epic poet, an individual repository of a people's histories, legends, and myths, whereas the Biblical prophet ... tends to be concerned above all with the people's impending crises, the demands of what Martin Buber called "the historical hour"' (30). Miłosz combines aspects of both by believing staunchly that the poet, representing the people's histories (including their everyday, unheroic lives), may put himself 'on the side of life in times of impending catastrophe – which, in the twentieth century, are numerous.' He does not place himself above the people's morality, however, and this is the substance of his complaint to Aleksander Fiut ('Me, a moralist ...?'). Central to Miłosz's belief in the salvational power of poetry is his belief that the poet has a particular role to play in the world *but* that this role is not that of hero, martyr, or moralist. Because British Romanticism does not insist upon the poet's heroic mission, the point may not seem central to Anglo-American readers, but it is for Poles: Miłosz's anti-Romanticism focuses its rebellion upon the particular role that the Romantic poet is called upon to play in Poland (a role that is familiar to other Eastern Europeans). At the same time, he insists that the poet *has* a special role. Elżbieta Kiślak, in a book devoted entirely to this topic, hypothesizes that Miłosz's 'Romanticophobia' is rooted in his dislike of Messianism – in other words, one aspect of Polish Romanticism, which effects the 'ideologization' (Polish 'ideologizacja') of martyrdom. This useful semi-neologism links the poet's rebellion against the Romantic legacy to his rejection of various ideologies, speaking against right-wing and left-wing excesses alike. His insistence on making politics personal in *Native Realm* (and in *The Captive Mind*) links up to his lifelong dislike of 'ideologizing' events or emotions. His own emotions rise up when he speaks out against the 'ideologization' of religion, which is, for him, a deeply felt impulse rooted in the heart and ramifying outward, into metaphysics and ethics; when religious thought is politicized, it loses the organic meaningfulness that makes it powerful and appealing in the first place. Miłosz is aware that his religious sense is irrational. In his lifelong defence of it, he repeatedly separates religion – or, rather, religious feeling, the religious impulse – from domains that are (or should be) guided by reason, such as science or politics.

Yet 'the sacred exists and is stronger than all our rebellions' (*Visions from San Francisco Bay* 33). He insists upon an attitude that must be called old-fashioned, because it stubbornly rejects so many aspects of modernity, yet that concurrently rejects Romanticism, the pre-eminent precursor of the modern period. This is the root of so many readers' bewilderment with Miłosz: should we label him the most incorrigibly old-fashioned of Christian poets or the most modern, obsessed as he is with the contours of 'my century,' as he so often calls it – or, perhaps, so contemporary that he is post-postmodern, insisting upon a *return* of beliefs that were opposed by modern thinkers and upon a mode of expression that makes good on twentieth-century quests for a 'more spacious form' than that of the traditional lyric?

This lattermost point is at the heart of Heaney's fascination with Miłosz, and although he occasionally gestures towards the national value of poets such as Herbert, Mandelstam, or Miłosz, their stances towards the so-called national question do not absorb him. Miłosz, however, insists upon his distance from certain national(ist) currents, and at the risk of overstating the point, the link between Heaney's often 'invisible' backdrop of nationalist politics (to appropriate Vendler's term) and Miłosz's extremely visible political views is worth suggesting. The type of transcendent 'invisible' space sought by both poets must be separated from the tainted and dangerous 'beautiful ideas' allied with destructive (or self-abnegating) politics *and* from narrow, politicized, often nationalistic versions of Catholicism. In both Poland and Ireland, religion and politics go hand in hand, and the legacy of Polish Romanticism impels a provocateur like Witold Gombrowicz to assert that in Poland, ethics constitute a writer's sex appeal. Working off this statement, Miłosz laments that as soon as Poles make a writer into a bardic figure, they clothe him in 'the romantic, the heroic, and so forth' ('Separate Nations' 30). Yet he is concerned with ethical questions and with the maintenance (perhaps restitution, if we believe it gone) of a religious function to language – this is what sometimes bewilders Anglo-American commentators who insist on its completely secular character (such as Bruce Murphy), and why a reader such as Heaney differs from them, with his obstinately sacramental outlook. It is hard to see Miłosz's affirmations that a respect for mystery enriches one's life, that a Catholic upbringing teaches this respect, and that mystery compels humble submission to a higher authority (*Visions from San Francisco Bay* 85) as paradigmatically modern statements. Of course, it is also easy to forget how many modern poets underwent religious conversions or never abandoned the faith of their childhoods. Be that as it may, there is an archaic tinge to Miłosz's assertions, and they would smack of pride (despite their call for humility) were it not for his concomitant longing for a 'path that leads into the heart of the fortress.' There is genuine emotion behind them, in Polish and in English. Thought and feeling, the individual ego and the man who is part of a great community (the human family; dwellers in the twentieth century), are united. In his work – as, often, in Heaney's – we may discern a desire for the unity of subject and object, and a desire for a vitalizing force to imbue matter with meaning that comes from the presence of spirit. Such a desire may be called Romantic.

We have discussed Miłosz's perceived similarity to Adam Mickiewicz in the second chapter; the critical paradox here is not only that the 'Romanticophobic' Miłosz has some rather Romantic desires, but that he allies the greatest Polish Romantic poet with the Enlightenment in an early article pitched at an English-language audience ('Mickiewicz and Modern Poetry,' 1948). It is not unusual to see Mickiewicz as a superhuman literary figure who is a master of many voices, but Miłosz seeks to re-envision the Romantic master in a way that almost foresees the comparisons that would be made between them. He insists that we view him as a reader of Voltaire and a poet whose style is more classicist than people like to admit, and opposes the manner in which Mickiewicz is, in his view, conventionally taught – namely, as an arch-Romantic steeped in folk customs and mythologies, writing work whose main function is to elicit pathos (363). Even more surprisingly, Miłosz informs us that Mickiewicz was not as naive as his critics claim, but merely imitated a folksy credulity while maintaining religious solemnity and, simultaneously, evincing a detachment from his subject matter (365). These are remarkable statements. They make not an Enlightenment-era classicist out of Mickiewicz but something even stranger: a proto-modernist. In particular, they place him beside T.S. Eliot, whom Miłosz had been reading and translating during the Second World War.

Miłosz as Anti-Modernist? The Influence of T.S. Eliot

The story that Miłosz had been translating T.S. Eliot in wartime Warsaw is not new, and much has been made of its dramatic circumstances. We have discussed Eliot as an influence mediating between him and later generations of Polish poets, and the importance of Eliot's Dante for both Miłosz and Heaney. When viewed against the backdrop of Miłosz's reputation as a witness poet, and his anti-Romanticism, a different Eliot emerges. Instead of Eliot's tone, what comes to the fore from this perspective is his place in literary history and how it fits in – surprisingly – with Miłosz's very conscious literary-historical self-positioning. This positioning is perversely inflected by the pressures of history: in circumstances that would press a poet most forcibly into Romantic patriotism, Miłosz threw himself full force into eminently un-Romantic poetry. He had journeyed at great peril *to* Warsaw during the war – an almost suicidal undertaking – and had done his best not just to survive but to work on poetry and translations, particularly from English-language poets. Shakespeare drew him, as did Thomas Traherne, whose poems he likened to 'The World' – again this is a point of contact with Heaney, who is attracted to the childhood meditations of Traherne's *Centuries,* in particular his recollection of 'immortal' wheat seeming to stand 'from everlasting to everlasting' in the child's mind. Traherne, then, calls forth a reminiscent naivety that fits somewhat uncomfortably with the counter-apocalyptic tone of 'The World'; yet he has also written that 'order the beauty even of order is,' which, decontextualized, could serve as a classicist credo.

Heaney reassesses his own childhood reminiscences in 'Sweeney Redivivus,' and we will have to wait until *Seeing Things* until he can finally view the soul as an entity 'snagging on nothing' in its ascent to the empyrean. Miłosz impels Heaney to reconsider his own influences and motifs, and motivates this progression towards *Seeing Things.* Eliot appears an odd man out, not fitting obviously and organically into this developmental arc. We now need to triangulate Miłosz's often-eccentric assessments of his mentors – his de-Romanticization of Mickiewicz, his darkening of Traherne's meditations, and his transnationalization of Eliot – with Heaney's position in the 1970s and 1980s, and Heaney's view towards his English-speaking cultural surroundings. What comes clear is that Miłosz strenuously protests against the Romantic context within which he starts to be viewed by both English-language and Polish readers well before his fame has become incontrovertible, and he tries to nip this phenomenon in the bud by reaching for the most un-Romantic exemplars he can find in the thick of war and insisting that we view Poland's arch-Romantic as a distant, self-aware classicist. This protest, in turn, affects Heaney, who re-encounters Eliot *through* Miłosz.

It may have been a matter of chance that Miłosz would have carried Eliot's poems (Faber edition) around with him as he saw Warsaw's falling edifices and burning rubble, and it would be far too romantic to ascribe symbolic significance to the fact that he was felled by a nearby explosion – and, from that point, forced to seek safe lodging with his wife like two fugitives, unable to return to their city apartment – as he was going to discuss his English translation project with a friend. It is too easy to liken Eliot's Waste Land to smouldering Warsaw, and the comparison would effect a detrimental historical flattening. Miłosz had been feeling poetically unsettled before the war, and had been searching for a new type of form for his work – a so-called dry form. This dryness, which is connected to anti-Romanticism, 'simple speech,' and the notion that one could view the poem as a space for working out intellectual problems, allies him naturally with Eliot. Heaney reacts to the 'purity' of Eliot's influence in his not uncontroversial statement that 'the one thing you read in Eliot is what he wrote,' as manifested by the lack of ancillary baggage, unlike, for example, Thomas Hardy; Eliot is 'a pure precipitate of sensibility' (Heaney in Brandes 14). The opinion is mildly outrageous – how can we *not* bring the ancillary baggage of Eliot's emotional crisis to bear on our reading of *The Waste Land*? – but most important here is the fact that Heaney presents Eliot in a way that makes his influence upon Miłosz far more comprehensible than would a heavily contextualized portrait; after reading Heaney's words, it becomes clearer still why such a figure would have appealed to the Polish metaphysician. Although Eliot had not been a large influence upon Heaney, poetically speaking, his *view* of Eliot is noteworthy as we clarify the Eliot-Miłosz-Heaney nexus. His comments (made in the 1980s) reveal what Heaney is looking for during this time period: Hardy has been, and always will be, influential, but at the moment Heaney does not want to read of 'landscape, ... sentiment, ... nostalgia, ... thatch and pewter mugs and yokels' (13). Neither does Miłosz. Heaney describes Eliot as a late Symbolist (14); Miłosz does the same in 'Reflections on T. S. Eliot.' Eliot's place in literary history, the mode of writing he makes possible, is more important to Heaney and Miłosz than his reputation, his biography, his culture, or the literal 'messages' of his works; this differs crucially from Eliot's importance to commentators or even to later generations of poets.

   Miłosz links Eliot to American poets' fight against Romanticism, and this qualifies Eliot to serve as a guide to a poetic path not taken by the Poles, who, according to him, preferred 'emotional gibberish' during the war. Even more surprisingly, he suggests a link between Eliot and his much-admired cousin Oscar Miłosz and, indeed, with other poets of 'metaphysical orientation' (he does not mention Eliot's essay on the subject), who explore man's isolation in relation to the objects that surround him (a theme that links Miłosz with Herbert). This is seen, by Miłosz, as part of the fight against a scientific world view that is 'emptied of values' – by putting his own quotation marks around the phrase, he recognizes its controversiality and perhaps its overuse in discussions of modernity – and the concomitant effort to view art (if one could) as a value-creating act. This is a global struggle, and Eliot stands as an exemplar of the struggle itself, yet *not* as one who has triumphed. In an

Anglo-American context, Eliot's work also serves as a counterweight against the poetry of self-absorption that Miłosz sees ascendant after the war (in the United States especially); of course, the poetry of the first person, as we may call it, can be viewed as a backlash against Eliot's often-maligned theory of impersonality. Reading contemporaneously, we may view these types of poetry as poles of a literary-historical dialectic that begins to seem eerily deterministic in itself. Miłosz, however, searches for egress from the time-bound into the timeless, eternal realm, and Eliot's desire to escape subjectivism is attractive for Miłosz. So is what Miłosz sees as his struggle to rebuild the world from fragments, which links the *Four Quartets* together with *The Waste Land*.[6]

This remains Eliot's greatest legacy for Miłosz. Eliot's formal dislocations fascinate the poet in search of a spacious, cross-generic form, but the effort to discern direct formal influence in Miłosz's poems will not bear convincing results. Instead, Eliot stands as a formal *example*, not an influence; he tacitly opposes the aestheticism of the Polish avant-garde that Miłosz dislikes (*Kontynenty* 78), knows how to use meter without achieving songlike cadences (something Miłosz wants to be able to avoid), uses ordinary as well as 'poetic' language, is unafraid of employing abstraction and composing lines virtually devoid of imagery, and, crucially for a Polish reader, intellectualizes poetry by allowing it to reach beyond the personal and the sensual to a realm that can only be called metaphysical, in which one could examine emotion through the lens of intellection rather than giving in to expressionism, vagueness, or indeed Romanticism. Eliot offers a bridge between seventeenth-century metaphysical poetry and contemporaneity for Miłosz. Surely Edward Hirsch exaggerates when he states that Miłosz teaches us how to think in poetry; this is, however, one of the skills for which Miłosz turns to Eliot for guidance, and which fascinates his own readers, including Seamus Heaney. The way Miłosz thinks, though, is not easy to place (as we have seen in 'Dedication'), and his 'dry form' prevents us from readily trusting the poet. Trust is the key term that Christopher Ricks applied to Heaney, and it becomes extremely complicated when we interrogate its place in Heaney's use of a mentor who takes Eliot as his precursor. Expressivity naturally allies with trust; 'dryness,' abstraction, obliquity, and irony do not. Heaney induces *our* trust and wishes to trust others. This springs from his Romantic grounding, which Heaney has never disowned, though he is willing to submit it to self-examination. What happens when one attuned to Romantic expressivist criteria – which call for trust – reads a patently anti-expressivist, abstract, dry poem?

Irony versus Prophecy: Heaney's Reading of 'Incantation'

If one were to compile a list of Miłosz's favourite words, 'incantation' and its cognates would surely be on it. When asked about his health upon the occasion of a severe illness in old age, he apparently responded, 'I survive by incantation' (*Selected Poems* xiii), as if the word had real power over the failing flesh. His lifelong desire for a language that holds weight, that contains a measured and dignified rhythm, whose nobility is a matter of cadence rather than of topical concern, would seem to set him at odds with 'his century,' yet it does not preclude him from imbuing even the most cerebral, (seemingly) abstract poems with irony:

> Human reason is beautiful and invincible.
> ...
> It establishes the universal ideas in language,
> And guides our hand so we write Truth and Justice
> With capital letters, lie and oppression with small.
> ...
> Beautiful and very young are Philo-Sophia
> And poetry, her ally in the service of the good.
> As late as yesterday Nature celebrated their birth,
> The news was brought to the mountains by a unicorn and an echo.
>
> (*New and Collected Poems* 239)

Seamus Heaney thrills to this poem when he first encounters it in Berkeley, sensing that it 'did things forbidden within an old dispensation' (*Government* 37). The Anglo-American orthodoxy associating the lyric with particularity, especially of imagery (as a long-lasting legacy of Imagism), conditions the ear in such a way that it baulks at the 'torpor' of abstract language and 'unembarrassed didacticism' (37). What is even worse, the poem appears to contain a 'message,' that which we have been taught to eschew. We have discussed Anglo-American poetry's predilection – or even imperative – for concreteness in chapter 1; Heaney's view of it as a 'dispensation' captures the iconoclastic thrill his pleasure gives him, and he is unafraid to view 'Incantation' as a spell uttered in 'argent speech' to bring about a utopian state of affairs. Behind it lie the trials of the poet's life and the wisdom gained from them. Heaney is not relegating the poem to an exotic otherworld but querying why he could have not written it; Robert Pinsky, one of

Miłosz's translators, refuses to believe it could not be emulated by an English-language poet, using his own envy as a modest test case: 'I wish I had found that mode ..., I wish I had heard that imagined music of meaning ... Which again I take to mean that it was possible: it was there to be written' (Pinsky in Thomas 17). A 'music of meaning' is not strictly national, Pinsky implies. We should not let literary history close our minds to different dispensations, thereby excusing us from writing in new ways. Nor should literary critics' fascination with otherness and exotic witnessing exempt us from taking language on our own individual terms.

Is this, however, the sort of poem Heaney wishes it to be? His assessment is also a sort of 'incantation' meant to establish an exotically heretical space for poetry in which Miłosz serves as patriarch. This is a space in which truth and justice rule writing so that, eventually, the end of art might be peace. Heaney does not, however, actually *interpret* the poem extensively, astounded as he is by its form; neither do most of Heaney's scholars. Yet it remains his touchstone. In an editorial optimistically entitled 'Poetry's Power against Intolerance,' he quotes from 'Incantation' in order to assert that it reveals the 'fundamental beliefs upon which the fight against racism can be based.' He even opines that the poem puts forth the 'ideal possibilities' of life 'unambiguously and unrepentantly' by wiping the historical slate clean and returning us to 'the bliss of beginnings.' In Heaney's foreword to Miłosz's 2006 *Selected Poems*, he cites it as proof that the Pole considered poetry the ally of philosophy, and the whimsical unicorn and echo impart 'trust in the delicious joy-bringing potential of art and intellect' (xiv). In other words, he puts by any doubt in the poem's affirmative intent while maintaining that there is 'nothing disingenuous' about this experienced poet's beliefs.

What happens when we cease to view the poem as a totem and review its content with a sceptical eye? A different poet – one trained, perhaps, by Eliot's 'dry form' – emerges. Its opening line ('Human reason is beautiful ...') becomes a challenge rather than an affirmation. 'Universal ideas' will become one of Miłosz's favourite phrases to deconstruct, though here we encounter these ideas as linguistic manifestations of a quasi-divine force ('reason' is masculine in Polish; the godlike 'he,' rather than the neuter 'it,' governs the poem). Its circularity – that reason should establish idea, whereas it is pure idea itself – does not raise Heaney's eyebrows, though the proposal that we view reason as the progenitor of Truth should nettle a reader sensitive to the 'preoccupations' of language. A reader of *Native Realm* and *The Captive Mind* should look askance at the statement that reason puts 'what should be' above things 'as they are,' given these books' exposé of utopian ideology. A reader attentive to literary history should certainly look askance at the ludicrous 'unicorn' (a rare icon of the Incarnation) and echo (which makes a tautology out of a philosophical premise, and narcissistic solipsism out of poetry). Even at the most obvious level, if read with Miłosz's biography in mind – which his readers most often do – then the assertion that '*Human* reason is ... invincible' should turn heads.

Heaney ruefully admits that he has been told Miłosz's meter and tone in Polish are slightly comical, and that the poem is saved from sentimentality by its irony. In Polish only? Granted, the original has a catechetical tone that does not fully carry into English, but the translation is quite literal. 'A unicorn and an echo' remove any possible suspicion of poker-faced seriousness. Why does Heaney repeatedly proffer a naive reading? He recognizes the dark foundation of 'The World,' a poem with a more utopian bent than 'Incantation.' The answer lies in Heaney's desire to read Miłosz's work as essentially affirmative, to associate him with positive values, and to ally him with his Romantic mentors in the service of the good. He is not alone in his tendency to view Miłosz as more of an anti-modernist than an anti-Romantic, and the necessity of choosing between these postures has unfortunate heuristic results. Heaney does not wish to turn his back on his Romantic fathers, who set the foundations for his poetic thought, and he wishes to see Miłosz as more Romantic than he is or wishes to be. This is why he is seen as a tower-bound 'Master' reminiscent of Yeats, and why Eliot does not enter into his discussion of Miłosz. It is easier to see Miłosz as an anti-modernist whose essentially affirmative aim situates him comfortably prior to Eliot's dislocations. This is not altogether inapposite, but it tempts us into the tacit equation of anti-modernism with Romanticism – choosing the lamp over the mirror – whereas Miłosz does not actually support a dualistic understanding of literary history. Refusing Romanticism does not equal acceptance of Modernist aesthetics. Nor can we, of course, equate Polish with Anglo-American Modernism, despite certain features that appear international, and we cannot equate Polish with British Romanticism ... yet Miłosz is ready to paint in broad strokes when he enthusiastically writes, 'I am learning a lot in America: the battle against Romanticism in poetry is taken seriously here, and its foundation is, of course, English 17th and 18th-century poetry' (*Zaraz po wojnie* 278, my translation). He finds that the resultant verse is weakened, however, by tricky intellectual game playing that reveals the lack of a deeper message. In light of such pronouncements, Eliot's attraction for Miłosz becomes even more clear: his call to renew our acquaintance with the metaphysical poets, his eschewal of the intellectual game for the metaphysical-religious quest, and his willingness to allow the fragmented, desiccated forms of *The Waste Land* to be irrigated by human emotion in 'Ash-Wednesday' and the *Four Quartets* allow us to understand what sort of example he provided for the anti-Romantic Miłosz. Similarly to Eliot, we cannot equate Miłosz solely with affirmation or with irony; the cutting edge of 'Incantation' does not slaughter his ideals. They exist previous to the poetry and beyond it. Their basis and their reach are also questioned, often with ruthless directness, by autobiographical verse of a sort *not* written by Eliot but also differing from the Wordsworthian model favoured by Heaney.

Ethical Comings of Age: 'Bypassing Rue Descartes' and 'From the Republic of Conscience'

It should not surprise us that Heaney does not take much influence from Eliot: his project is different. Eliot, by Heaney's own admission, might be too 'pure' an influence (Heaney in Brandes 13), as opposed to Hardy, or Kavanagh, or Hughes ... the list could stretch on. Heaney does not look for 'pure' influences, even though he is attuned closely to form. There are always 'impure' considerations – an unfortunate term because of its suggested corruption – such as the material histories and biographies that fascinate Heaney even as he admires language that is 'a pure precipitate of sensibility' (13). As we have seen, an abstracted view of language tempts Heaney, but he cannot embrace it himself. It comes as no surprise that Miłosz's autobiographical tour de force, 'Bypassing Rue Descartes,' should attract Heaney through its *personalization* of historical and ethical coming of age. The topic has attracted Heaney throughout his life, but his exposure to Miłosz allows him to explore it in a different light, as it were, and a different focus – panoramic, allegorical, and indeed, more abstract – than he has in previous volumes. Miłosz's broad-range perspective confers an authority upon the lyric speaker that is justified because it opposes arbitrariness, generalization, and self-justification: let us recall, 'unless we can relate it to ourselves personally, history will always be more or less of an abstraction' (*Native Realm* 20), and this leads to the crimes against humanity against which both Miłosz's and Heaney's poems protest. 'From the Republic of Conscience' was originally commissioned by Amnesty International as a poem responding to human rights abuses, and although no crimes are enumerated in either Heaney's or Miłosz's poems, the backward journeys both undertake are motivated by the need to reckon with their moral roles. Miłosz's poem, however, *critiques* the abstraction and universalism that makes his work so compelling for Heaney, and that motivates Heaney's *Haw Lantern* experiments.

The poet begins in the past as a 'young barbarian' arriving in Paris, which is allied with 'the universal,' leaving him 'dazzled and desiring.' Differently from Heaney's poem, the speaker here is one of many from the provinces of empires, fought-over territories with complex identities that produce travellers who are killed for their desire 'to abolish the customs of their homes,' even while their coevals achieve power 'in order to kill in the name of the universal, beautiful ideas.' There is an immediate reality, too, that of the city, also an actor in the poem, 'baking long breads' and 'pouring wine into clay pitchers,' 'indifferent as it was to honor and shame and greatness and glory.' A massive destabilization is put in motion: the speaker's difficulty of reckoning with the variety of temporal and identitarian levels in the poem results in a near-epiphany, a spatio-temporal kaleidoscope:

> Again I lean on the rough granite of the embankment,
> As if I had returned from travels through the underworlds
> And suddenly saw in the light the reeling wheel of the seasons
> Where empires have fallen and those once living were dead.
>
> There is no capital of the world, neither here nor anywhere else,
> And the abolished customs are restored to their small fame
> And now I know that the time of human generations is not like the time of
>   the earth. (*Collected Poems* 393–4)

'Bypassing Rue Descartes' casts its referential nets broadly *as* it reveals the basis of individual morality in local custom. It is structured by an alternation of perspective between young and elderly speakers, singular ('I') and plural ('We,' 'many'), and between named place and grand time spans ('the time of human generations,' 'the time of the earth').[7] In the original Polish, Miłosz's own home city of Wilno takes its place in a list of provincial locations yet then drops out, as the 'I' recedes and then approaches. The poem grips down on its roots in the empirical at the same time as it breathes the rarefied air of wide-ranging pronouncement. Its movement between the specific and the general puts in motion its central difficulty, that of determining how much ironic distance is present in the present-day speaker's words. The traveller passes by a location dedicated to France's most influential rationalist philosopher, who premised existence upon thought, although he is, presumably, motivated not by the *cogito* but, perhaps, *sentio* or *percipio*, by his feelings and perceptions of the sensual capital of the world, which split from 'beautiful ideas' in their effects upon history. Without a synthetic understanding of universalizing ideologies, though, and without the context of Miłosz's lifelong battle with dualist philosophy, the poem would not be possible.

Interestingly, the attraction of the 'dazzling,' sensual city is left intact in 'Bypassing Rue Descartes.' For all his concreteness, Heaney does not actually replicate this appeal to the senses in 'From the Republic of Conscience,' though the poems share the same thematic focus, dichotomization of local and universal, and definitive moral conclusion. Heaney's poem does not directly engage history *or* summon the sensuality of the morally indifferent city from which the poet travels, starting with his arrival in the silent 'republic of conscience' and proceeding straight to immigration. He is greeted by an elderly man, in 'homespun coat,' who displays a picture of the immigrant's grandfather. This forms part of a ritual of recognition which grounds the speaker in his own local mores:

> The woman in customs asked me to declare
> the words of our traditional cures and charms
> to heal dumbness and avert the evil eye.
> ...
> He therefore desired me when I got home
> to consider myself a representative
> and to speak on their behalf in my own tongue.
>
> Their embassies, he said, were everywhere
> but operated independently
> and no ambassador would ever be relieved.   (*The Haw Lantern* 12–13)

Although Heaney tries to emulate Miłosz's mixture of empirical particularity and ideational scope, this, his best-known parable poem, does not 'sound' like a Miłosz poem even if some of its formal hallmarks – end-stopped lines, the interplay between 'I' and 'you,' allegorical figures – are similar, though not quite 'translatorese'; the task of direct comparison, though, would result in frustration. This poem must be seen as a *response* to Miłosz, an attempt to speak his poetic language, *not* a poem enabling neat image-for-image comparison.

The two poems' themes, though, are close, and show them negotiating similarly rocky cultural terrain: each poetic speaker is concerned with the values taught by locality. Lest this seem banally oversimplified, let us attend to their complications: both poems are premised upon an act of physical 'translation' from one locale to another (province to city and vice versa) that is also a translation of value, yet certain values cannot translate but require the individual to undertake a realignment and reinterpretation of himself and his culture. Miłosz's poem goes further: certain types of *time* cannot be translated. This untranslatability leads to a vision of incommensurability. The speaker is left confounded – Miłosz's more than Heaney's, having undergone a more total upset. Crucially, though, the journeys both speakers undertake between different sets of cultural values both lead away from relativism. The speakers learn they must not scant the local by forgetting or relativizing it. Instead, they learn, during the epistemological journey of each poem, to recognize, honour, internalize, and then represent values inhering in the local ('no ambassador would ever be relieved') rather than the putatively universal ('the universal, beautiful ideas'). Their parabolic technique achieves an almost-paradoxical universality even while the poems condemn the false grandeur of universals that require blood sacrifice. Values must be concrete, not theoretical. Morality must be based on specificity; one enters the republic of conscience by reckoning with embarrassingly local truths ('traditional cures and charms').

Despite its insistence upon locality, though, 'From the Republic of Conscience' does not summon it with a great deal of precision, whereas the sensual city is at the centre of 'Bypassing Rue Descartes.' Its physicality – remembered and current sights, smells, sounds – disorient the speaker, so that his epiphany, if we can call it that ('I ... suddenly saw in the light the reeling wheel of the seasons') *un*settles and *de*stabilizes perceptual, structural, and intellectual categories. Instead of providing a sudden epistemological key to link cosmopolitan and rural, collective and individual perspectives, universal ideas and singular bodily experience, it sets these terms whirling. Although Heaney associates Miłosz with assurance (even 'complete certitude about the shape of things,' 'command[ing] our emotional assent,' *Government* 115), these lines cry out with self-distrust. The epiphanic moment itself is hypothetical ('As if I had returned ... And suddenly saw'), and it seems that the greatest certainty the poem offers is that of sensual memory ('Again I lean ...').

This aspect of the poem is central for Heaney: 'He recollects the fresh bread smells on the streets of Paris when he was a student at the same moment as he summons up the faces of ... young revolutionaries,' he writes, obviously attracted to precisely the aspects he does *not* replicate in his own poem. Is this an accident? Must we conclude that Heaney does not know how to write 'translatorese'? In some respects, yes, but not necessarily to his detriment: his parable poems ('From the Republic of Conscience,' 'From the Canton of Expectation,' 'From the Frontier of Writing,' 'Parable Island,' et al.) are extremely self-conscious. They are an experiment, not an ongoing mode. Heaney has stated his fascination with abstraction, with the abstract noun and words that Western writers are embarrassed to utter, and these poems do their best to utter them, yet Heaney, under the tutelage of Miłosz, is led back to the local concreteness he has been trying to escape. 'From the Republic of Conscience' may originally have been requested as a straightforward morality tale, but it was only after Heaney initially refused the commission that he created a poem beginning with an actual experience (landing in a small plane in Orkney, which magically becomes a republic of conscience). The point is not that Heaney does not write an exact replica of a Miłosz poem, that Richard Wilbur's 'Shame' (comparing the emotion to a small, cramped country) helped his writing to get off the ground, or that the poem has inorganic roots in a Human Rights Day commission. The more interesting point is that Heaney draws himself away from the sensual details that actually attract him in Miłosz's poem; this subliminal attraction works in spite of his intent to embrace the abstract noun, which he fulfils. By banishing sensuality (the roughness of the granite embankment propping up the bewildered elderly traveller; the warm smell of baking bread; the temptation to join in laughter, eating, and drinking of delicacies in a city that is ready to overlook and level the unfortunate nobility of one focused on honour and glory, but drawn by secular bread and wine), Heaney does not replicate the sensual dimension of Miłosz's poem in his own. It is less *physically* compelling. Yet Heaney can write poems so sensually vivid that they are referenced on Irish tourist brochures (abstract nouns will never draw visitors; concrete evocations will). He is here trying to write in a way that inaccurately represents the texture of the poems he loves. Vendler accurately speculates that Heaney does not feel at home in allegory, but the poems that inspire him are not simple allegories. Heaney recognizes, and also attends to, other (non-allegorical, non-testimonial, non-moralistic) aspects of Miłosz's work in his later writing.

He is unashamed to interpret 'Bypassing Rue Descartes' as a poem about the poet himself, and to see it as the product of two types of admirable extremity: '[Miłosz's] merciless analytic power coexisted with helpless sensuous relish.' This poem – as opposed to 'Incantation' (and 'Child of Europe,' 'Dedication,' and 'Ars Poetica,' all mentioned in the same spirit) – awakens his sympathy as well as his awe ('*help-less* ... relish'). Heaney offers this encapsulated discussion in a 2004 obituary tribute ('In Gratitude for All the Gifts'). 'Bypassing Rue Descartes' functions as a turning point in his assessment of the Master: instead of viewing him as a tower-bound magus slowly exposing his book of withholding, he now sees him as a man at his own mercy, prodigious of intellect yet unable to fully harness either his 'merciless' mind or his pleasure-loving body. This accords with the self-castigations, confessions, and often merciless self-analyses that Miłosz had published for decades, most visible when brought together in the *New and Collected Poems*: 'So what kind of prophet am I? ... Who would have trusted me? For they saw / How I empty glasses, throw myself on food, / And glance greedily at the waitress's neck' ('A Confession,' published in English in 1985, 461).

'Bypassing Rue Descartes,' then, functions in two different ways for Heaney, at two different points in time: it helps to inspire his moral allegories of the 1980s and also inspires a re-evaluation of Miłosz nearly two decades later. During the period in between, Heaney definitively steps away from Anglo-American critical opinions focused upon Miłosz's witness function, and begins to attend to a different cluster of themes and a different poetic movement.[8] In doing so, he focuses attention on a new dimension of Miłosz's work.

The Sensual and the Transcendent: Reviewing Miłosz's Character

After *The Haw Lantern*, Miłosz's poetic influence wanes. It does not disappear. How could it? The fact that the vogue for Eastern Europe disappears after the Cold War ends, there is no more evil empire to vilify, and no totalitarian oppression to decry, is culturally central, but we cannot ascribe the waning of influence to cultural and material factors alone. Heaney does not always go along with the crowd. He revels in his own distaste for the ascendance of theory in the academy at the expense of humanistically based scholarship, for example, and makes clear that he is of a different ilk than the post-structuralist crowd. In the late 1980s and 1990s, Herbert and Miłosz are still writing and publishing poetry, even if the Anglo-American public is not as interested in their native lands as it once was. Their influence does not disappear altogether, because it motivates the great abstract and ethical turn in Heaney's poetry. Heaney continues to refer to their example in the 1990s, yet they are not directly summoned by his poems until he elegizes their deaths.

His summative obituaries cover enormous amounts of ground in large strides, as in the recent 'A Quality of Wisdom' (2011), which presents Miłosz as a compendium of qualities ('abundance and spontaneity,' 'at-homeness in so many different genres and landscapes,' 'desire for belief and ... equally acute scepticism'). The difficulty of pinning down Miłosz's legacy to one precise quality or 'gift' increases with time. Miłosz is a rooted man, an Antaean drawing strength from his home ground; he is, however, spoken to by a 'daimonion,' a concept Heaney has not much considered before, and he places the word in quotation marks to mark his questioning of it. Many years removed from his *Haw Lantern* experiments, he expresses a slight dubiety regarding Miłosz's 'unabashed ... readiness to pull out all the stops' rhetorically, seeming to view his dramatic, maximalist lines as somewhat excessive, even while the boldness of Miłosz's approach is admired. Heaney recognizes, however, that Miłosz's 'unabashed' faith in poetry drew strength from his 'impulse towards the transcendent' and certitude that 'an elsewhere' exists ('A Quality of Wisdom' 20). This is, finally, Miłosz's greatest gift, a broadly affirmative one, in which his role as secretary of invisible presences is recognized, by Heaney, as the model for an attunement to the visionary sensitive enough to recognize the transcendent in the mundane.

Meanwhile, a different shift is occurring within Heaney after the responsibility-laden 1980s, not so much a dramatic turn as the intensification of a primary need for the luciferous and miraculous. Because Heaney has focused his gaze on Miłosz's abstraction, Herbert's bare tests of fortitude, the moral exemplarity and the verbal 'toughness' of both, their influence seems to be at odds with his need for 'the heart to lighten.' A good decade after *The Haw Lantern*, we are surprised to see the hyperborean Herbert conjoined with Apollo the sun-god. Miłosz's image is also transmogrified, yet this is a longer, more complex, and ultimately more dramatic process, culminating in the celebratory 'Out of This World' in 2006.

This poem is one of Heaney's many recent elegies. Tripartite in structure, it surprisingly focuses on the two poets' Catholic grounding, not on the political themes that had started to tire both poets in their older age. Its first section, a single long quotation, links these two sceptical Catholics to all who worship: '"Like everybody else, I bowed my head / during the consecration of the bread and wine, / ... / believed (whatever it means) that a change occurred"' (*District and Circle* 45). To readers of *The Haw Lantern*, this summons the seventh 'Clearances' sonnet: 'High cries were felled and a pure change happened' (31). Matter into spirit, the movement goes, and yet after the death of the poet's mother, he feels that the space previously inhabited by her 'had been emptied / Into us to keep,' and that the atoms of space charged with her presence were suddenly encountering emptiness, 'clearances,' in the material world. In the later poem, the charged space of faith – with its spirits, demons, and possibility for transubstantiation – meets the emptiness of unbelief. The supposed miracle of holy communion is a matter of ritual ('like everybody else,' one goes through the motions) and demands an unquestioning belief ('whatever that means'). But this speaker knows 'what it means'; both Heaney and Miłosz have written moving poems upon belief and loss (occasioning change). That is not the question; rather, faith and knowledge threaten to part ways. This should not surprise us: we have seen how passionately Miłosz insists that we set apart art and science, belief in metaphysical reality from science-inspired determinism. More surprising is the conclusion:

> ... There was never a scene
> when I had it out with myself or with another.
> The loss occurred off stage. And yet I cannot
> disavow words like 'thanksgiving' or 'host'
> or 'communion bread.' They have an undying
> tremor and draw, like well water far down.

The first tonal upheaval occurs in the parenthetical 'whatever that means' of the first stanza, and here it threatens to tear apart the ground itself. Its jump into the demotic – 'had it out' – and, correspondingly, the cinematic – 'a scene' – is accompanied by a cynical sort of pride that the great fuss occurred offstage, and that the celebrant-turned-actor played his part well. Its swing back up into the hieratic ('disavow,' 'undying') is forcibly pushed through, though effectively so: the poem ends on a note of rejuvenating mystery, and finds a distant imagistic echo of the wellspring present in 'The Master.' Our Miłoszian touchstones are all in place. But what has happened to the Catholicism linking these poets? Is this poem admitting a loss of faith, and offering a (merely) linguistic faith in its stead? The question is not rhetorical, and the five-page poem is meant as a complicated answer. The poet's changing diction plays an integral role in his process of thinking. We hear and feel the hieratic register as an auditory pleasure, as the 'draw' of the trembling water holds us gazing into the image. What we see are also Heaney's previous images: the wells that drew the child and refreshed the adult, the underground springs intuited by the diviner's rod, and the wellspring of inspiration. We end by legitimating our enjoyment: surely no puritanical soul would deny us the sensual pleasure of language, which here has to do with the residue of religious awe present in words such as 'thanksgiving,' 'host,' and 'communion.' An unsteady faith trembles but also draws.

The re-explorations of the later parts of the triptych continue this serious play with belief and doubt, the visible and invisible. 'Brancardier,' the least thrilling of the parts, finishes up a pilgrimage to Lourdes (a 'brancardier' is a stretcher-bearer; the speaker helps the ill to be cured) with a plastic canteen of miracle water, a snow globe featuring Bernadette and the Virgin, and a certificate for his 'stretcher-bearing work.' This is hardly uplift and reaffirmation. Instead of encountering Eleusinian mysteries in Christian form, the speaker faces into his disenchantment. His unusual enjambment of 'Mystical Body' across two stanzas breaks what should be whole (the mystical body of Christ is the church), while his quotation from the Latin Credo – *unam, sanctam, catholicam* – leaves out the last adjective of the sequence, *apostolicam*. Instead of affirming his belief in a united church of which he would be an apostolic representative, he leaves off this obligation-inducing adjective (*apostolicam*). His foray into the past brings not epiphany but fuel for doubt, his slant rhymes offering a smirk rather than a harmonic chord. This poem shows Heaney in an unusual guise: aching to celebrate and justify mystery, he gives voice to partial disenchantment. Miłosz's confessions of doubt and incapacity are legion, but this is a new stage of Heaney's relation to them: he has not, until now, taken proper cognizance of the Master's self-proclaimed weaknesses. He has been a tower of fortitude and a well of wisdom. Heaney's poet has been tested, bewildered, and made a representative (of the Republic of Conscience); he has approached the Master's poems head-on, using them as ethical guides; yet we have seen how the Master, time and again, abdicates from this role, declaring himself unfit. He is 'on the side of man, for lack of anything better,' doubting the faith that he feels necessary for his existence, and declares that 'the history of my stupidity would fill many volumes' ('Account,' *New and Collected Poems* 395). Heaney is finally responding to this strain of Miłosz's writing by offering a de facto verse dialogue on the subject of their wavering Catholic faith. The sub-poems of 'Out of This World' are acts extending their fellowship.

'Saw Music,' the last of the triptych, will turn seemingly lacklustre art into the re-enchantment for which the poet aches, though it will do so suddenly, with a turn towards the Master, who, at last, withholds nothing either spiritually or emotionally. Beginning with a Christian pledge of renunciation as its epigraph (*'Q. Do you renounce the world? / A. I do renounce it'*), the poem veers from catechism to banal fact – 'Barrie Cooke has begun to paint "godbeams"' – which will arouse a sceptical smirk in those of us who doubt the medical efficacy of Lourdes water (as in 'Brancardier'), the bewitchment of religious kitsch, or the artistic quality of 'godbeams.' So much the worse for us. Instead of re-enacting the let-down of 'Brancardier,' 'Saw Music' earnestly transfigures Cooke's 'godbeams' into a spiritual allegory that leads into the precise, lyrical memory which dominates Heaney's most recent work: the Belfast beggar squeezing music out of a saw, surrounded by the gaudy trappings of Christmas (tinsel, neon), is recalled as Miłosz lies 'coffined in Kraków,'

> as out of this world now
> As the untranscendent music of the saw
> He might have heard in Vilnius or Warsaw
>
> And would not have renounced, however paltry. (*District and Circle* 49)

The Pole has become a heretical guide to the seemingly 'untranscendent' world that serves as a portal to the otherworld. The banal colloquialism is both literalized and ironized: the pleasures afforded by a lowly reality cast us out of the truly banal into the freshened, lightened space beyond, where the world need not be renounced because it serves as our imaginative stimulus, the source of our iconography and the literal representation of what must remain figurative. Renunciation becomes tantamount to dour narrow-mindedness, rejecting the music that could deepen, not jeopardize, spiritual experience. The poem's final outrider allows the speaker to fully break the pattern of slant-rhymed quatrains that have served as his thought-units, and to speak *for*, not in response to, his elder predecessor. The emotional mood of the poem deepens. The stress is on Miłosz's affirmation: Heaney has come to view Miłosz as a force of inclusion, refusing to renounce the sensual world which holds him helplessly in thrall, yet ennobling that refusal as a positive choice rather than a weakness.

This is a new Miłosz, and 'Out of This World' is the most detailed, complicated, and stirring testimonial to Heaney's changed view of his Polish master. His experiments with the parable form did not last, but were necessary for testing the ability of his poetry to invigorate the abstract register that fascinated him in 'Child of Europe' and 'Incantation.' Heaney's refusal to discern irony in the latter is opposed by his subtle use of irony – together with Miłoszian high seriousness – in his memorial poem. The truism that a poet's prose does not always satisfactorily account for the work of his poetry may be recalled, but the issue is not that Heaney's prose is ineffective – quite the opposite – but that certain of his prose genres (the review essay, the commissioned article, the public address) restrict his tonal range in a way that the lyric does not. Therefore, when he writes an article tendentiously entitled 'Poetry's Power against Intolerance' and uses Miłosz as his example of said power, it is understandable that 'Incantation' and 'Dedication' are put to work in a certain manner that may be decried as naive. His statement that poetry addresses itself to the individual conscience, though, is not naive, and what we see in this later work is an individualization, as it were, of Miłosz's legacy. In 'From the Republic of Conscience,' the poet does not allow himself to individualize the journey he undertakes, even though the poem we may hold as its Polish counterpart does. Heaney seems to assume, in *The Haw Lantern*, that the individual and the instructive must part ways at some point, and that philosophical heft must rely upon a purging of personality. 'Out of This World' shows that Heaney is able to dive into memory, to write of and from the self, to ironize the self's position and admit to disillusionment in himself and the world outside him, at the same time as the whole work of the poem is to brilliantly conjoin the luminous and the humble.

Miłosz's influence lingers and changes: Vendler believes that Heaney's Oxford lectures, *The Redress of Poetry*, demonstrate a broadened application of Heaney's renewed conviction that poetry *can* serve as 'redress,' which conviction is strengthened by close readings of Eastern European poets in *The Government of the Tongue*. Miłosz, Herbert, and Mandelstam stand as invisible presences behind the lecture series's guiding assumption, a triad of Slavic father figures watching their Northern Irish colleague apply what he learned to a different complex of texts and situations. Even in the lectures, though, we can see that something is changing: Heaney's quarrel with Miłosz over Larkin's 'Aubade' turns on Heaney's insistence that we read implicit hope, joy, positive value, into the poetics of a poem whose darkness Miłosz deplores. Poetics, not thematics: by disentangling the two elements, Heaney is able to argue – politely, with due deference – that Larkin's poem does not dwell entirely in darkness. In the same lecture series, he takes up the distinction established by Miłosz's beloved philosopher, Simone Weil, between gravity and grace. By interpreting Weil so that her idea of balancing these two forces is made comparable to Heaney's notion of redress, 'tilting the scales of reality towards some transcendent equilibrium' (3), he also tilts his own poetic philosophy towards the standards established by Miłosz. Even when he does not invoke him directly, the elder Pole stands behind him, and these words indicate a profound realignment of alliances after *The Haw Lantern*. Whereas the earlier volume recurrently re-imagined frontiers, the *Redress* lectures focus on a meta-frontier, as it were, that between two forms of knowledge, the practical and the poetic, of which each addresses the other, with an easily traversable border between them. Heaney had, we may recall, aligned Eastern European poetry as a whole with the *utile* dimension of poetry, with clear use-value, and here he even more usefully effaces the strict distinction.

Heaney is speaking *after* the influence of Eastern Europeans has waned, but this new stage of thinking is a direct result of his long reading of their work. The *Haw Lantern* parables were marred by the unhelpful distinction between useful and pleasurable poetry; whereas it is valuable for heuristic purposes, for poetic purposes it proved restrictive. His longing to find the 'transcendent equilibrium' between gravity and grace, groundedness and transcendence, shows him travelling down an intellectual path that the Master helped him recognize, even if its benefit seems self-evident. This does not mean that Heaney would not have found it himself. A prolonged reading of Miłosz helped him to recognize, however, that the abstract register of language can correspond to a transcendent register. The truth of words such as Justice, Philosophy (Miłosz's miraculously birthed Philo-Sophia), and Truth is not only a hard-nosed political truth, an abstract intellectual truth (arrived at by not-so-invincible human reason), or a local truth for which we need an interpretive key; it is not just 'previous to poetry,' as Heaney states, but a truth of the spirit, and it can also be reached subsequent to our reading, as a state of truthfulness we reach *through* the lyrical act. Miłosz allies himself with Eliot in the search for a 'time lifted above time by time,' for the eternal reached through movement, and holds that hope lies in assimilating the historical – learning the movement of time – and then leaving it for the metaphysical, 'to seek the ontological dimension after passing through the purgatory of historical thought' ('Treatise on Poetry,' *New and Collected Poems* 143; Miłosz in Czarnecka and Fiut, 181–3). Heaney comes to recognize that Miłosz is an unwilling witness to history, and that his greatness inheres in his role as witness to a certain 'plane of consciousness' (*Redress* 4) that is established in poetry. Just as ontology – the *esse* that is Miłosz's ultimate desire – must be reached by passing *through* history, as a desired eternal moment, so poetry may pass into a luminescent realm that appears to be 'out of this world' through a celebration *of* the things of this world, whose music only appears to be 'untranscendent.' Let us not fear abstraction, Miłosz teaches his readers, but let us also not locate the source of this language in a high tower *or* in the unfortunate nobility of suffering. Instead of locating ideals in grandiose statements which conceal an ironic cutting edge – one that slices through their own grandeur, which proves to be apparent, not intrinsic – let us learn that the concrete can lead us *to* the metaphysical. We need not disavow either the one or the other, but can face into the bright light allowing a pure change to happen. It may allow us to enter the realm of the marvellous.

Conclusion: Considering the Gift

The Oracular and the Virtual

Seeing Things is universally acknowledged as Heaney's book of the marvellous, yet it would not be possible either without the hard-edged explorations conducted under the tutelage of Zbigniew Herbert or the mastery of new rungs of air conducted under the gaze of Czesław Miłosz. It is tempting to take Heaney at his word when he writes that he had to wait until he was nearly fifty to credit marvels ('Fosterling'), but poems do not always make reliable autobiographies. He has actually been attuned to the marvellous ever since his first poems; the degree to which he 'credited' it is up for speculation. In this context, we may credit Miłosz with making a sustained defence of the marvellous available. He does so poetically and intellectually, yet despite his careful thinking through the problem of political witness, of religious faith, and of poetic responsibility, Heaney must ultimately *feel* his thoughts in order to make them poetically powerful, and this process has its twists and turns. When he reaches *District and Circle*, he has come to feel the influence of Miłosz in a new way, and it translates into a complex act of thinking in verse.

Feeling and thinking, though, need not be opposed. They represent separate acts of knowledge; they do not necessarily work at cross-purposes. They can, however, root themselves in different sets of symbols or texts. When Heaney writes that Miłosz's work 'liberate[s]' one into 'the authentic solitude of one's own being,' he connects the Polish poet to his long-beloved Wordsworth, whose 'authentic solitude' is attuned to the world around him – and often enough to the world within him – in *The Prelude*, a text through which Heaney feels his way into self-expression. This is his preferred image of Wordsworth, and 'authentic solitude' summons this continuing Romantic guide even as the phrase is used in praise of another poet. Heaney's feeling centre remains Romantic. This is why he has such trouble recognizing the anti-Romanticism of Herbert and Miłosz. He senses the difference between their poetics and those of the English Romantics, but is loath to create an either/or choice. His dramatically changing response to Miłosz eventually results in a glimpsed alliance between his Romantic and Eastern European mentors, so that his youthful conviction that poetry offers a revelation of the self to the self finds continuation in his later response to his Polish master. Paradoxically, this poet who feels himself connected to every living thing reinforces Heaney's sense of individuality, no doubt because of his 'head-clearing' examinations of conscience and constant re-examinations of selfhood.

The other major Romantic predecessor whose letters, in particular, helped to form Heaney's poetic views, is aligned with Miłosz on thematic grounds: 'Miłosz would have deeply understood and utterly agreed with Keats's contention that the use of a world of pain and troubles was to school the intelligence and make it a soul' (Foreword to *Selected Poems* iv). As an analytical comment, it risks over-simplification (is Keats's conception of soul making truly parallel to Miłosz's thoughts about history and ethics?), yet as an act of literary alignment, it effects a conjunction that Heaney needs to *feel* works. It allows Heaney to integrate Miłosz's influence, to allow these putatively separate figures to fraternize. The awkwardness that so many critics discern in *The Haw Lantern* and occasionally *Station Island* may stem, at least in part, from the difficulty of integrating Eastern European with British and Irish poetry. As we have seen, its otherness generated its glamour. Yet in order to send roots down into Heaney's imagination, it cannot function as a self-enclosed anomaly, but must find a way to link into the root systems already in place. Heaney's momentary parallels of Miłosz with Wordsworth and Keats begin to accomplish this linkage.

It is not easy to encapsulate the total influence of Eastern Europe because, in the final stages of its spell, it connects to other strands of Heaney's poetics, it leads out from itself, and it reaches deeply into Heaney's mind and work. Defining one phase of a writer's career is risky. Must it imply that the phase ended? It is easier to determine the beginning of Heaney's Eastern European 'phase,' if this word is indeed applicable, than its ending (for instance, Herbert's 1968 *Selected Poems* are a germinal influence, as is Heaney's exposure to Miłosz in 1970–1). Calling it a phase risks diminishment or at least excessive modesty: we grow out of behavioural phases and look back with bemusement at their excesses. As we have seen in his elegies for Herbert and Miłosz, Heaney grows *into* a new awareness. We can safely say that the phase during which he felt tempted to compare life in 1971 Belfast to life under martial law ended fairly quickly, since this sentiment does not recur; a poem such as 'From the Frontier of Writing' depends upon a far broader understanding of subjection than the straightforwardly political. The final effect of the parable poems (all published between 1985 and 1987) is to move from the political to the virtual, from seeing things happen to 'seeing things' in the abstract. Due to their 'foreign' form, the seam between the two areas is made visible. 'From the Frontier of Writing,' 'From the Republic of Conscience,' and 'Parable Island' deploy this form self-consciously, which may be why it is easy to group them together; other poems hover between self-consciousness and self-immersion.

'The Riddle' (*Haw Lantern* 51) asks whether we should credit its own narrative – the man who carries water in a riddle is, on the one hand, squandering water by letting it drain through a sieve; on the other hand, he is sifting 'the sense of things' from 'what's imagined.' The author self-consciously uses the riddling story to 'hold water,' in this case its own allegorical potential to mean something that is questioned in its very telling: 'was it culpable ignorance,' he asks, or a '*via negativa*' materialized? Is the man a figure of foolishness or wisdom? Do we learn through immateriality, through 'what's imagined,' as truly as from the real? Material conditions hold themselves more firmly in place, and yield answers more readily, than imagined ones, and the poem's placement at the very end of *The Haw Lantern* questions the movement of the volume as a whole from 'bonded pith and stone' in its eponymous poem to the water almost escaping the poet's allegorical grasp. Plato relates that the impious and unjust must fetch water in a sieve in Hades (*Republic* 2.363d), and Socrates relates a fable in which the insatiable souls in Hades must carry water in sieves, which resemble their thoughtless, unbelieving souls (*Gorgias* 493a–c); as the great allegorist himself concedes the story rather absurd, Heaney follows suit, so that just as 'Parable Island' and 'From the Land of the Unspoken' are subtly tongue-in-cheek, so the story of 'The Riddle' may simply illustrate 'culpable ignorance.' The ultimate ignorance here may turn back on its own interpretive terms: instead of creating dichotomies, we must query whether 'what's imagined' may *contain* the actual 'sense of things.'

This is, after all, the guiding hypothesis of Heaney's work in the 1980s and 1990s. *Station Island* begins a trajectory that culminates in *Seeing Things* in 1991. It starts with the scathing self-assessments of the former, in which Zbigniew Herbert's tough minimalism serves as a formal and ethical guiding strategy, and the dichotomy of inscrutable, judgmental object and 'complaisant pith' of the human functions as a Herbertian conceptual leitmotif. The abstraction of Herbert's knocker, which merely raps out 'yes' and 'no,' represents the extreme of self-denial to Heaney at this time, yet also helps to establish and justify a level of abstraction, minimal and uncreative as it may be, and it is a short step from 'yes' and 'no' to 'truth,' 'justice,' and the other words Heaney wishes to restore to his poetic vocabulary. Herbert's *type* of abstraction is different from Miłosz's, and Heaney tacitly creates a division between the two when he appropriates them in radically different ways. The infernal stone of 'Sandstone Keepsake' and the sharp-edged 'Granite Chip' are imagistic and psychological miles away from the advice-giving scholar of 'The Master' or the disembodied voice breaking through a postprandial silence in 'Away from it All.' *The Haw Lantern*'s poems answer the desire of the speaker, who wants greater closeness to his master, by allowing him the scope he seeks in 'Station Island.' This scope brings him closer to the master than before. *This* is the volume displaying his mastery of 'new rungs of air.'

After *The Haw Lantern*, Heaney is no longer the poet of roots and graftings. He has finally become a celebrant of 'the diamond absolutes' in all their clarity and brilliance. 'Absolutes' are no longer necessarily incarnated in acts and persons but are often thought through in sublimated, supra-physical terms. Whereas there is an oracular quality to some of this poetry, its voice is not authoritarian (despite some of the charges levelled against him at this stage, addressed below), but claims its authority based on access to vision. When we reach *Seeing Things*, the lyric voice is unafraid to interrogate itself and others, to question how it may gain access to all the nooks and crannies of the spirit and how to express them in art. It should serve as no surprise that a poem on mnemonics ('Squarings' xix, 'Memory as a building or a city ... ,' *Seeing Things* 75) is connected to Miłosz himself, as a second-order metaphor for metaphor: 'His head was like one of those renaissance theatres of memory,' Heaney writes in his obituary piece 'In Gratitude for All the Gifts.' The poem suggests the development of a 'code' to learn the mind's own contents, enclosing its metaphors within a tight formal structure.[1] As an extension, we have the obituary essay: 'Part of the secret and much of the power [of Miłosz's poetry] came from his immense learning,' Heaney writes. The poem's surprisingly dry figuration – 'Memory as a building or a city, / Well lighted, well laid out' – is thus complemented by the obituary, which connects the academic discipline of mnemonics with the power of creative art. The secret discipline of shaping one's mind, learning it, and then rousing it creatively, undergirds finished poems. This is not a model of divine inspiration – Heaney never mentions Miłosz's *daimonion*, whose promptings Miłosz claims help inspire poems – but of discipline that allows for transcendence. The virtual, however, is not empirically verifiable, even if it springs from empirical as well as abstract knowledge; it is in many ways antithetical to the concrete. This antithesis makes some critics uncomfortable. It seems unaccountably hard to find a place for *The Haw Lantern* and *Seeing Things*, and the adjectives used to describe them – airy, abstract, virtual, visionary – run the gamut from deprecatory to laudatory. They can be seen as volume-long *artes poeticae*, self-regarding yet not self-enclosed, and the *ars poetica* is a notoriously risky genre that will inevitably call forth a poet's detractors. The easiest part is finding terms for the volume's Eastern European influences; Miłosz points the way by identifying himself with a group, and affirming that it should indeed have a place in scholarly discussion of contemporary writing.

Despite his stated opinion that Polish literature did not live up to the 'chance' of taking on truly 'universal' themes, Miłosz does concede that its high visibility has engendered an identity for Polish poetry in particular: 'I myself used this expression the "Polish school of poetry" because ... something like this exists and it has its international place in world literature thanks mostly to translations into English ... The literary milieu, the poetry milieu, in the United States or in England would understand what I mean by the "Polish school of poetry"' (Miłosz in Kosińska). Speaking in 1997, Miłosz refers his interviewer back to what the 'literary milieu' had read in the past three decades. What Polish poetry offers the English-speaking world, then, is a new literary paradigm, not just individual names of suffering poets. The moniker helps us to recognize the literary phenomenon to which Heaney reacted, though its boundaries extend well beyond Poland, making it a sort of 'Slavic School,' as it were. We may define it by its willingness to directly

engage the dangerous topic of values and to face into this danger, discussing the limits of human value systems, the seduction of ideologies
promoting one set of values, the wrongfulness or hypocrisy of one's
own values or actions, and the ambivalent role of religion in promoting value. These authors do not shirk self-condemnation or its more
benign variant, self-questioning, and, as Herbert would say, the use of
the conditional mood.

Schools and Reassessments

The task of assessing this group's complex cross-cultural influence has,
hopefully, been at least partially undertaken by this book, at least in
direct reference to two of its most famous representatives, Herbert and
Miłosz. As we turn to a summatory assessment of its legacy, we find that
one particular aspect of the Polish School's poetics – shared as well by
several other Eastern European writers – draws fire from Anglo-American critics when deployed by one of their own, by an Irish poet. The
quality in question is abstraction. I have used this word to denote the
type of language that strikes us in poetry from Eastern Europe. Heaney
calls it 'aerated.' Yet there is nothing objectionable about an aerated object; he comes closer to the emotional mark when he speaks of words
we are 'almost too embarrassed to utter.' This formulation allows us
to perceive a possible chink in the armour of Eastern European poetry,
which we may call its *potentially* embarrassing use of abstract words,
most often connected to values (spirit, truth, justice) or entities in which
we are not sure we believe (God, angel, spirit), or those that seem simply old fashioned (in short, anything capitalized: History, Truth). We
can understand why Heaney's critics are so divided by *The Haw Lantern*
and certain poems anticipating it ('Chekhov on Sakhalin,' for example).
Embarrassment may get the better of them, or conformity to an unspoken code of literary conduct. As we have seen, however, Heaney does
not commit all of these supposed sins, though when he does it tends to
be all at once, employing abstract words, celebrating spirits and nothings and metaphysical frontiers, and using old-fashioned allegories
('the republic of conscience').

Is this why several critics react so strongly to the volumes we have
just considered in this study? Dennis O'Driscoll calls him a 'pasticheur'
of Eastern European styles, noting with apparent relief that this role
did not last long and simultaneously noting that Heaney was formally
ill suited to mimic or paste together the sort of writing he admired

(O'Driscoll in O'Donoghue 59–60). Douglas Dunn is glad that the confident *Seeing Things* issued 'from the transitional disgruntlements of *The Haw Lantern*' (Dunn in Curtis 208). Michael Allen asks, 'What Has Happened to Heaney?' and then answers his own question in two different ways, one surmising that Heaney has gone too far out on a limb in *Station Island*, the other postulating the opposite about *The Haw Lantern*, that the limb has dried up, so to speak, and Heaney's youthful creativity might have subsided ('Writing a Bare Wire: *Station Island*,' 'Holding Course'). Unusually, he holds that Heaney shirks the great Joycean responsibility of forming the uncreated conscience of his race in *The Haw Lantern*, satisfying himself with 'moderate, international' statements of conscience (in opposition to Longley's equally negative opinion, quoted below). Allen construes the poems' abstractions and sublimations as avoidances or refusals to shoulder 'a burden of guilt,' which results in 'paranoia' ('Holding Course' 110) and a severance of moral issues from psychological truths. These are serious charges. There are lighter ones, too: Terence Brown thinks Heaney's poetic sins are venial, proceeding from his fortunate fate not to have experienced the realities prompting the 'urgent and risky' parables of Eastern European writers. Since Heaney's parables are not 'urgent,' they read as forced exercises, collapsing into banality at their worst, obviously lacking the 'stark imprint of necessity' that marks successful Eastern European work ('The Witnessing Eye' 62). The most innocuous negative opinions relegate *The Haw Lantern* to the status of 'transitional' volume. Unfortunately, the ever-self-critical and genial Heaney sometimes encourages this view, and he has pleaded for the merits of the volume's fanciful, self-gratifying dedicatory couplet rather than for the more substantial and controversial poems within (Heaney in J. Campbell, n.p.).

Under such negative pressure, it is no surprise that Heaney should slight the volume himself, and point towards *Seeing Things* as the final fruition of *The Haw Lantern*'s efforts. In interview, he cites the last line of 'The Disappearing Island' – 'All I believe that happened there was vision' – and continues, 'After that, I did a book called *Seeing Things*' (Heaney in Morgan, n.p.). This comment hints at a rather delusory causality: *The Haw Lantern* has as many 'visionary' poems as *Seeing Things*. Its connection to ethical and aesthetic questions need not be seen as proof positive of a destructive 'gravity' at work, in Simone Weil's use of the term, but may be seen as an extension of the beneficent grace towards which Heaney wishes to tilt the scales. His poetry hangs in the balance but certainly does drop in quality in *The Haw Lantern*, as his harshest critics believe. Nor is it truly 'transitional': we have seen how the influence of Herbert comes visible in *Station Island* and shades over and into the influence of Miłosz, who appears in both volumes, and, as an inspiration eventually allied by Heaney with the ascension of grace over gravity, stands as a virtual progenitor of the metaphysical poems in *Seeing Things* as well as *The Haw Lantern*. It would be exaggeration to state that Miłosz is solely responsible for Heaney's visionary turn, but the depth, breadth, and height of his influence cannot be disclaimed. We are critical of transitions because we prefer auspicious beginnings, brilliant apexes, or grand conclusions, but Heaney's 1980s work must be read together with *Seeing Things* as one sustained, brilliant period of cross-cultural visionary exploration.

His essays receive their share of criticism as well: 'Seamus Heaney in *The Government of the Tongue* ... would have all Western poetry go to Poland, go spiritually and aesthetically to Herbert and Miłosz.' Perhaps it makes sense that Edna Longley, distinguished celebrant of the Protestant imagination in Northern Irish poetry, proponent of local roots, and frequent critic of Heaney's aesthetic choices, would employ such hyperbole. She reacts to the declarative meta-descriptive language of *The Haw Lantern* as well, noting with relief that Heaney does not quite disappear into the ether but stays grounded in 'more corporate *loci*,' though she is obviously averse to what she calls 'a United Nations poetry-keeping force, [which] ... smacks of ultramontane hegemony and an Irish Literary Counter-Reformation' (Longley, 'Putting on the International Style' 75–9, 80). Her linguistic choices, however, betray her own partiality, perhaps purposefully so. Longley clearly prefers British over foreign influences, local and concrete over abstract poetry (she believes MacNeice *disparages* Muir's parables by comparing them to abstract paintings), and a reformed Protestant sensibility over a 'Literary Counter-Reformation.' This acute, nuanced critic, alive to the subtlest of verbal effects, is roused to antipathetic ire by *The Government of the Tongue*. She does not note the fact that the Eastern European poets extolled in the volume are obsessively anti-dogmatic in their ethics as well as their aesthetics, a distinction they actually efface. This fact is, however, crucial to understanding how Heaney's assessments set him apart from other readers. The criteria Longley establishes, at times implicitly, pass ambivalent judgment on *The Haw Lantern* as a whole and negative judgment upon its Slavic-styled poems. She rightly notes that we may discern Anglo-American influences as well as Continental ones on

Heaney's work, and holds that the former inevitably take precedence over the latter, intimating that there is an inevitable schism between the two. By summoning safely English-speaking influences who, Longley holds, inevitably obtrude themselves into the English-language poet's work, and asserting a dichotomy between sounding like Zbigniew and sounding like George (Herbert, that is), she not only disclaims any possible crossover between them – echoes of Frost, Wilbur, or Auden are not anathema to Heaney, even in the 1980s, and happily harmonize with the echoes of Continental European poets – but skips over the important conjunction essayed by Heaney, among many others, between Auden and the Eastern Europeans. As we assess Heaney's work at this juncture in his career, we cannot scant the possible – perhaps not fully realized – conjunctions towards which he gestures as well as the oppositions that are rather more easily established.

Flint and Fire, Cognac and Chains: Auden and Chekhov

Of course, not *all* of Heaney's readers share such negative opinions: there are those who admire everything he has produced, those who may be afraid to say differently, and even those, like the author of this book, who are captivated by *The Haw Lantern* and believe it represents one pinnacle of Heaney's achievement. It is, though, undoubtedly heterogeneous in style. Dawe believes that it veers between the picturesque and the 'flinty Audenesque,' by which he denotes the parable poems (Dawe 1987, 24–5). The adjective is worth interrogating beyond the confines of his criticism, if criticism it be: for Heaney, Auden stands as the great mediator between Western and Eastern European style, a harbinger who sketched out the possibilities that the 'historically tested' Eastern Europeans would bring into being. For van Nieukerken, Auden links contemporary Polish with Anglo-American poetry. For Carpenter, Auden is one representative of 'the poetry of rigor' for Miłosz, notable for writing 'objective, impersonal' poems that read like philosophical essays. Miłosz notes that 'New Year Letter' lacks intellectual sophistication but is admirable formally, and brings this sub-genre (poem as philosophical essay) to fruition in his own work. Heaney, who puts Auden's verse side by side with Miłosz's, seems surprised to discover a cleverness in Auden that suffers by comparison with Miłosz, but pushes his essay ('Sounding Auden') through these straits.

Far more troublesome is the issue that these scholars and poets do not engage: it is often hard to say exactly what Auden means. Mean he does, all the critics agree, but it can be devilishly hard to elucidate how some of his most telegraphic, quickly-shifting poems do it, and Christopher Isherwood is no help when he relates that Auden would sometimes tack together lines that pleased him without overmuch trouble about coherence. Heaney modestly describes his early struggles to clarify a daunting poem and describes an epiphany that occurs upon realizing, with the help of Geoffrey Grigson, that Auden could be discussed in terms of his music and imagery rather than, or in addition to, political and intellectual meanderings. Critical assessments that focus upon poetics are worth more in the long run, Heaney hazards, because they are sensitive to language as art, and verify 'the reality of poetry in the world' (*Government* 119–20). Worth more than what, we may ask, and Heaney does not wish to speak ill of others, so he proffers Stan Smith's deconstructionist Marxism as an example *as* he praises it (a miniature tour de force of diplomacy). A focus upon poetics reveals different pleasure-giving dimensions of a poem than a focus upon politics would. He assures us that he is now content with Auden's opacity; his continued sense of perplexity does not diminish his enjoyment of Auden's work.

This turn should not surprise us, since Heaney always wishes that we credit the form of poetry as well as its content, even when this means swimming against the grain of fashionably anti-formalist theories. His admission of feeling that Auden's work excludes him, though, is striking, since it could be immediately applicable to the other poets discussed in *The Government of the Tongue*, those parabolic and abstract Eastern Europeans. He does not, however, feel excluded by their work. Auden's exclusivity originally bothers him because the English tradition is – should be – familiar and comprehensible (as opposed to the Polish or Russian traditions he dips into later), but also because Heaney, despite his statements about musicality, is convinced that poetry must also communicate. He is willing to fight for music but music is not a sufficient end in itself. The task of putting Auden together with the Eastern Europeans, then, is not just a matter of pedantically delineating the precise area of overlap between Western and Eastern poetic forms, but a harder task: to strike sparks between a poetry he approaches by means of form (Auden's) and by means of meaning (Herbert and Miłosz's).

This is too stark a dichotomy for Heaney to ultimately uphold, and again, his *poems* always usefully complicate the structures established by his essays. Music and meaning come together, but do not easily mesh, in a poem such as 'Chekhov on Sakhalin':

> So, he would pay his 'debt to medicine'.
> But first he drank cognac by the ocean
> With his back to all he travelled north to face. (*Station Island* 18)

This poem is in the storytelling mode prevalent in *Station Island*, and goes on to describe the young doctor's symbolic smashing of his cognac glass, its noise echoing that of the convicts' chains on the prison island of Sakhalin. It 'rang on like the burden of his freedom' while he turned his face back to the grim world he had come to assess. We are back in the penitential mode of *Station Island*, yet looking back from the clearances and luminosities of *Seeing Things* and *The Haw Lantern*, we can see the first stirrings of Heaney's later modes: with its conjunctive 'So' beginning the poem, it sighs, as it were, and continues an already-begun dialogue. The truth previous to this poem is that Chekhov – and, by extension, the poet – *must* 'pay his debt.' It has been perversely incurred *by* the fact of his freedom. We know the story: Heaney, too, feels his debt to the socio-political world, and secretly longs for release just like the young doctor, who downs his bottle of cognac to allow himself one last luxury before the hard work.

This thematic point, however, would not guarantee the poem's interest. What does is the poem's failure to be as darkly sonorous as it could be if its pentametric lines sounded like blank verse – which they do not – and the poet's gaze dwelt long on the darkness of this penance – which it does not. It turns its back on 'all he travelled north to face' at its outset, and its quatrains skip from image to image, creating a collage of fire and ice that corresponds to the brilliance and abjection of Chekhov's situation, juxtaposing the multi-tonal smashing of glass with the smooth ringing of crystal. Its music, in other words, brings together the wildly contrastive in a strangely brilliant collocation (do chains 'ring'? does freedom 'ring' if it is a burden, or rather, if the burden has been lifted?). A similar collocation is present in 'Holly': sprigs of sharp-edged holly, fresh from the rainy cold, gleam 'like smashed bottle-glass' or like Moses's burning bush (*Station Island* 115). Their sharp reality lends a hard edge to their illuminating power; we are not entering the warm glow of a familial hearth but the illumination of Yeats's cold heaven. It is a new aesthetic for Heaney. As he negotiates the stark circumstance of being 'riddled with light,' so he works through the consequences of only having a 'small light' on offer for his 'small people,' of failing Diogenes's test, of not living up to the 'yes' and 'no' of Herbert's knocker, and is finally able to recognize the *music* of such difficulties and to face into it, recognizing the call of a supra-reality in its untranscendent tones.

Against Renunciation: The Legacy of Eastern Europe

We can read Heaney's changing opinions on 'content' and 'form,' in the brief space of 'Sounding Auden,' as emblematic of a larger negotiation. Heaney feels released into appreciation, into aesthetic pleasure, when he puts by his diligent pupil's insistence on figuring out 'what it means.' We should not exaggerate the point: Heaney *always* cares what it means. But the self-conscious move from meaning to rhythm and music is telling. The imagistic phantasmagoria of 'Chekhov on Sakhalin' runs between the extremes of affront and luxury, material (chains) and ideality (freedom), dark northern penance and diamond absolutes. Obligation can also be an ideal. But it is easier to credit obligation – to believe in its existence and exigency – than to credit illumination (which may blind by excess). At least, it is easier for Heaney.

He has always been known as a scrupulous poet, which is why his penitential self-questioning is so serious and so long, why his reading of poets such as Zbigniew Herbert is so deep (to whom the pebble represents a literal 'scrupus'). It has taught him to reinvigorate his use of metaphorical emblems and more generally to rethink the relation between word and thing. It has led him to re-interrogate the relation of art to conscience, of the 'petrified nightingale' at Apollo's feet to the single-note howl of the suffering Marsyas. It is a worthy legacy. But if this were *all* that Heaney learned from his Eastern European masters, then we could justify a certain amount of carping that Heaney may have lost his imaginative spark. He knows, though, that poetry must put expressive considerations first in order to survive. 'Chekhov on Sakhalin' contains in miniature, in intermittent sparks, the material that will glow, catch fire, and spread out in later volumes. There are two ways to read the trajectory of *Station Island*: one as a penitential exercise examining the poet's mistakes and inabilities in order to correct and reappraise his writing, and another way, as the beginning of a gradual efflorescence into Weilian 'grace,' in which the poet readies himself to find, accept, and eventually credit the 'diamond absolutes.' Herbert shows him the process he must undertake to position himself vis-à-vis these absolutes, and Miłosz shows him how to intellectually justify and take pleasure from them.

This is contrary to the popular views of Eastern Europe with which we began this book: instead of continuing to see Miłosz as part of an Eastern European group that collectively seeks to rub our noses in the dire realities of life, Heaney comes to see him as a guide who teaches us to credit the musicality of poetry's form, which is its highest aim – to give form to the formless, to make that form strong and meaningful, so that it can bear the weight of the experience it supports and encloses. A thousand voices cry out to us, a thousand hands seize our hand and command it to write, Miłosz sighs, and yet disobedience to one's gift is also a shirking of responsibility. Narrow-minded, moralistic refusal to hear 'untranscendent music' is not just a sin against aesthetics but a sin against being, an ontological sin.

Heaney has been concerned with paying his debt, fulfilling his obligation, and yet what reading Eastern European poets teaches him is that poetry's soteriological function comes about through its discovery of grace even where we were convinced the force of gravity held us in thrall. His Simone Weil is different from Miłosz's: the latter sees her as an ascetic and a heretic, whereas Heaney approaches her as an aesthetic philosopher, perhaps in order to allow her distinction to open Miłosz's verse yet farther to the luminous and numinous. Heaney's idea of formal redress was already present, yet not fully developed, long before *The Redress of Poetry*. With the help of the Eastern Europeans, Heaney had come to see that conscience comes in many forms, not just the 'bare wire' kind associated with these poets; they are the first ones to express this truth. The legacy of Eastern Europe is present in Heaney's process of rethinking how poetry may be informed by and saturated with particular kinds of conscience. *The Haw Lantern* had come to see attunement to the intangible as one of its forms, and the effort to reach it as a moral *and* aesthetic endeavour. Miłosz impelled him to credit his own effort, and not to renounce the unfashionable concept of the metaphysical. As this dimension is embraced and one learns not to be blinded by its illuminatory power, one of Heaney's original desires – to escape the first-person singular by means of this poetry from the 'other' Europe – comes close to being fulfilled. The 'second space' that transcends person and tension comes into view:

> Have we really lost faith in that other space?
> Have they vanished forever, Heaven and Hell? (Miłosz, *Second Space* 3)

Miłosz concludes by begging us to desire: 'Let us implore that it be re-turned to us,' he writes more in entreaty than command. His appeal is on behalf of the creative imagination. Perhaps even the word 'witness' can be re-imagined – to use Heaney's word, aerated – so that accepting and celebrating Miłosz's 'second space' itself becomes an act of witness. It would be a shame and an oversight *not* to witness this radiant space where invisible guests come and go at will, where the self spreads out into spirit, and obedience to grace redresses the force of gravity.

Notes

Acknowledgments

A portion of chapter 3 will be published, in revised form, as 'Seamus Heaney, Zbigniew Herbert and the Moral Imperative,' in *Comparative Literature Studies;* reprinted by permission of the Pennsylvania State University Press. Several pages of chapters 4 and 5 formed the basis of an article entitled 'Dialogues across the Continent: The Influence of Czesław Miłosz on Seamus Heaney,' published in *Comparative Literature* 63.3 (Spring 2011); reprinted by permission of the University of Oregon and Duke University Press.

Introduction

1 For an interesting slant on this issue, see Emily Apter's discussion of Alain Badiou's ostensible belief in untranslatability, and his own pragmatic contradiction of this belief (Apter in Saussy 54–61).
2 Meanwhile, let us not forget that the best theorists are often excellent close readers themselves, alive to the subtlest reverberations of the written word. Scholars such as Gayatri Spivak, one of the driving forces behind the expansion of Derridean theory and 'post-colonial backlash,' insists on the importance of such concrete, untheoretical skills as foreign language comprehension (how can one engage in comparative literary studies with no language training?) and interpretive ability (how can one engage in literary studies without the ability to interpret literature?). Her *Death of a Discipline* (2003) immediately became a seminal, much-debated text. It continues to stand as a major attempt to diagnose the ills of literary studies; Spivak is mostly concerned with comparative literature and area studies, but the slew

of recent publications, both academic and popular, seeking to come to terms with the perceived crisis of the humanities, shows no signs of abating. The periodic 'state of the discipline' reports written on behalf of the American Comparative Literature Association (the Bernheimer report; the Saussy report) fuel the flames of debate, and make for fascinating reading partly because of the responses they stimulate. Heaney's occasional outbursts of irate impatience with an academy that privileges 'politically approved themes' and critical fashions over probing examinations of works and themes that continue to matter, whether 'approved' or not, should be added to the extant literature upon our disciplinary crisis, which is basically a crisis of faith.

3 I have considered it myself in other publications, though the key source text for understanding the early days of the Northern Irish Renaissance must surely be Heather Clark's *The Ulster Renaissance: Poetry in Belfast, 1962–1972*.

4 I cannot resist a recent example: Heaney's 'Audenesque,' an elegy for Brodsky published in *Electric Light* (2001), explicitly invites this question by referring to its own predecessor, Auden's 'In Memory of W. B. Yeats': 'Joseph, yes, you know the beat. / Wystan Auden's metric feet' (77). This is begging for trouble, as Edna Longley notes, since such explicit revision of a great poem will immediately summon critics; the poem's success will have to depend on the success of its adaptation of the predecessor poem. In this case, 'Audenesque' loses in comparison with Auden's elegy – its tone is not quite as varied, its self-consciousness excessive, its form not as complex (adapting only the first section of Auden's tripartite structure) – yet, for all that, it is, *would* be, a fine poem in its own right. As a jocular elegy that is also a light glance at the conventions of poetic rhythm, ending with Brodsky among the shades – one of Heaney's recurrent classical tropes – it is stronger and more confident when it stands alone than when it is read comparatively.

1. Looking Eastwards

1 Heaney's own early verse participates in the culture of what is called the well-made poem. He starts to experiment in earnest in the 1970s, particularly in *Wintering Out* (1972). Bernard O'Donoghue examines Heaney's use of Irish poetic techniques, his fusion of English and Irish prosody and the cultural implications of this fusion, in *Seamus Heaney and the Language of Poetry*. Jason David Hall surveys Heaney's prosodic (particularly rhythmic) choices in *Seamus Heaney's Rhythmic Contract*, which includes a useful chapter on Heaney's earliest poems and their play with English convention (24–56). For the current analysis, it is worthwhile to bear in mind that Heaney does at times participate in the very cultural patterns that he

decries. His remarks on detrimental tendencies in contemporary verse should be read as self-criticisms as well – hence his frequent use of first-person plural forms ('my,' 'our'), which I find to be usefully inclusive, and use in my own work to mark our participation in the cultural events and analyses of the present study.

2 Parkinson's conference paper was originally delivered at the Modern Language Association convention in 1979 as part of a panel entitled 'Current Unstated Assumptions about Poetry.' It was published by *Critical Inquiry* in 1981 and worked into Parkinson's *Poems, Poets, Movements* thereafter (published in 1987). Heaney participated in this panel as well; his paper will be considered shortly.

3 In a phrase that echoes Heaney's own statement cited earlier, Justin Quinn posits that British and American poets, to Heaney, had stopped 'confronting fundamental truths' (Quinn in O'Donoghue 94); to Quinn, this is largely to do with the influence of New Criticism, which lauded poetic restraint and irony. The point is apt but not strong enough: Heaney has always been salubriously suspicious of critical orthodoxies, and *literary* history is the most persuasive. We must cast a glance at the poetic landscape of Heaney's day – which also contained a high number of ironists, and whose irony differed radically from that of the Eastern Europeans – to see how Heaney, and others, would have responded to Eastern European writing.

4 Heaney reputedly told Derek Mahon and Michael Longley (all precociously talented young men at the time), 'I'd like to write like you boys, but I have to do my own thing.' See Parker, *Seamus Heaney* 53 (Michael Longley relates this anecdote in an interview with Michael Parker).

5 Daniel Weissbort, in his own anthology *The Poetry of Survival: Post-War Poets of Central and Eastern Europe*, the title of which echoes this mystique, critiques Alvarez's principle of translatability but ends by accepting it (Weissbort 22–6); this is a salient example of how the terms in which such poetry was discussed came under critique but not erasure, which allowed them to survive. This is a delicate point: a translator motivated by admiration and enthusiasm would need to weigh the *terms* in which the translation was presented to his audience.

6 Joseph Brodsky points out that Herbert's resistance to 'oversaturated aestheticism' and to the corrosive communist system was stylistic: his opaque, understated and ironic style *is* the language of survival. It is also the language by which he may resist the simplification of reality: Herbert's real enemy, Brodsky claims, is 'the vulgarity of the human heart,' which glories in expounding symptoms instead of diagnosing the cause of suffering, which requires a certain cold precision. Writing near the end of his own life,

Brodsky sums up a brief introduction to Herbert by stating 'to me, though, his irony is no more than the safety valve of his compassion, since human tragedy is repetitive.' In order to guard against vulgar and repetitive exhibitionism, and to guard himself against emotional evisceration, Herbert – and, by extension, ironists like him, who are writing in similarly difficult circumstances – chooses a plain, unostentatious voice. See Brodsky in Paine 253–5.

7 Helen Vendler makes a similar point about Miłosz, though earlier than Heaney (1984), affirming that 'there are no direct lessons that American poets can learn from Miłosz' (Vendler, 'From Fragments' 146). Miłosz's position in the American literary landscape will be discussed in greater detail in chapter 4; for now, it is noteworthy that Vendler believes that Americans are hampered by their incomprehension of the historical experiences of which Miłosz writes (as Miłosz himself proclaims).

8 Piotr Sommer believes that this constitutes a pattern: although Poles will read English-language poets in translation, their lack of interest in taking influence from poets who write parabolically (i.e., through allegorical parables), such as Heaney or Charles Simic, is striking (155). He speculates that Poles may not be inspired by poetry with a clear intent (Heaney, for example, seems as if he knows exactly why, for what, and for whom, he writes). This may help to explain why Frank O'Hara – a poet far, far away from the abstract and allegorical, from tight formalism and moral seriousness – was the most important English-language influence upon late-twentieth-century Polish poetry. His verse was antithetical to the dominant mode of post-war Polish writing until around 1990 (he was introduced into Poland in 1986, also in Sommer's journal; for a useful introduction to this event, see Niżyńska, 'The Impossibility of Shrugging One's Shoulders'). Sommer also lets us know, with refreshing candour, that the very few Polish attempts to emulate Heaney's work have not been successful (159–60). Arent van Nieukerken opines that major Anglo-American *modernists*, such as Eliot and Auden, actually proved to be most influential on contemporary Eastern European poetry taken as a whole (van Nieukerken 117).

9 Timothy O'Leary discusses this point with reference to Plato's notorious notion that poetry can be too effective, so that it creates a corrupting force in the *polis*. Whereas Heaney rejects Plato, his reflection on the political obligation of poetry (or lack thereof) should be viewed as an engagement with Plato, who underlies every defence of poetry from Sidney to Stevens (O'Leary 662–70).

10 Significantly, in *Minotaur: Poetry and the Nation State*, published in 1992, Paulin writes differently: 'The lyric speaks for unchanging human nature, that timeless essence beyond fashion and economics' (233). Although his previous statements are topical and his later ones general, the difference in tone between the two is noteworthy.

11 Henry Hart makes one of the earliest attempts to view Heaney in deconstructive terms in *Seamus Heaney: Poet of Contrary Progressions* (1992), while Eugene O'Brien applies the terminology of post-structuralist theory to Heaney's work in his triad of books about the poet. Both scholars undertake their attempts in a positive spirit, though Heaney's frequently voiced resistance to theory is famous (some would say notorious). Ultimately, the effort to view Heaney as a writer amenable to theorization will run aground, the poet's insistence on self-transformation, 'second thoughts,' and linguistic suppleness evading any and all paradigmatic readings. An indictment of Heaney upon ideological grounds will prove as fruitless as a celebration of him on theoretical grounds unless such readings take cognizance of the linguistic complexity of his work – and some do; few scholars, including Hart and O'Brien, would actually endorse rigidly paradigmatic reading practices.

12 A middle ground between the two positions (separation versus complicity) is represented by Jonathan Hufstader, who reflects that while mired in 'the marshes of complicity with violence and implicit guilt, the liberal poet's ship of self would, no doubt, prefer to weigh anchor and depart, but another force, the anchor-line of the traditional self, restrains it' (20). The conclusion he draws from this elegant meditation is, however, problematic, albeit subtly so: he insists that Heaney locates 'wrongness' outside, not within, the self, which absolves him from the guilt of participation in violence, even while he does not disclaim participation. Yet Heaney's 'traditional self,' rooted in his community, *necessarily* participates in the community's guilt, and the numerous poems of testing and self-judgment in *Station Island* and *The Haw Lantern* testify to this. They do not pose merely aesthetic critiques, but moral ones.

13 At the same time, however, his own 'sense of exclusion' is not the only factor underpinning his promotion of poets on the peripheries, as Tim Kendall implies it may be, stating that Heaney's current position at the centre of the literary establishment helps him champion poets who, Kendall remarks, often bear some resemblance to Heaney himself (Kendall in Curtis 233). The Eastern Europeans cannot be put into this category: they do not need championing, as Heaney's own comments on the 'chicness' of their

writing admit, and the difference – not similitude – of their lives inspires his expository meditations on their exemplary status.

14 This is a young Mahon. The older Mahon – post-*Hudson Letter* (1995) – does not apologize for his engagement with topical issues, such as ecological devastation and foreign wars. Clearly he reconciles himself to the fact that the Irish will care what he thinks.

15 John Healy controversially reads 'Requiem for the Croppies' as a commemoration made from the vantage point of a 'symbolic priest-poet' affirming the legitimacy and potency of blood sacrifice, thus transforming the slaughtered Irish rebels into resurrected martyrs. Healy adduces this poem as exemplary of Heaney's myth-making tendency (Healy in Lynch et al. 53–65). Edward Picot uses the same poem to link Heaney with the Yeats of 'Easter 1916.' His emphasis is upon the Marian Catholicism that suffuses Heaney's work (Picot 214–20).

2. Heroic Names

1 Maria Janion is the pre-eminent scholar of Polish Romanticism. For general background and discussion of the Romantic legacy, see her *Gorączka romantyczna* (2000) and *Romantyzm i historia* (2001); a translated article entitled 'Romanticism and the Beginning of the Modern World' is useful for English-language readers. In *Czy będziesz wiedział, co przeżyłeś* (1996) she discusses the significance of the fall of communism, and how it must inevitably change the regnant Romantic paradigm.

2 There is much to be said about how Anglo-American critics tend to view the politics of Romanticism. In general, the trend has been to reintroduce politics into a realm traditionally characterized as visionary and private. Jerome McGann famously argued that poetry cannot simply liberate us from history, and referred to the grand illusion of liberation as quintessentially Romantic. Yet contemporary critics such as Nicholas Roe argue that Romantic poems are basically escapist, enacting 'dramas of idealization' that variously displace, repress, obscure, or even deny the claims of history by means of the force of the imagination; Alan Liu stresses the eternal truths that Romantic poetry seeks to communicate over and above the contingent. A poet such as Miłosz severely complicates such a dichotomy, not because of his critique of Romanticism but because in his work the eternal is a grand edifice – a real edifice – to be built *upon*, not in place of, the contingent. David Duff and Catherine Jones, however, boldly proclaim that Romanticism in the twenty-first century is seen as archipelagic rather than monolithic, and that politics and culture (i.e., contingent, not 'eternal concerns') imbue Romantic discussions of the literary more than ever

before: 'Romantic literature as self-expression takes second place to Romantic literature as expression of national identity' (Duff and Jones, Introduction, 27). Yeats's Romanticism, meanwhile, needs careful compartmentalizing; his love of order and courtliness seem classicist rather than Romantic, and Ellmann's time-tested view regarding his not-quite-Romantic character is apt: 'His nature is not Wordsworthian, his heroes are not Byronic, his emotional expression is not Shelleyan' (*The Identity of Yeats* 4).

3 Brodsky's own work is exceptional for its extremely strong, cadenced rhythm – in other words, its musical quality. His poetry readings are truly performances. Brodsky's insistence upon the primacy of formal music, particularly rhythm, must be kept in mind while we consider his remarks on other poets. His bold statements about the importance of form, of eccentricity in the face of pressure, and of poetry's inherent ethics are useful for contextualizing his own assertions, and for allowing us to see how a complex and subtle network of voices is created for Heaney in which Mandelstam and Brodsky (and, in the background, Akhmatova) speak to and through each other about the interrelation of poetry and ethics.

4 David-Antoine Williams offers an informed view of this idea in 'Tête-à-tête, Face-à-face: Brodsky, Levinas, and the Ethics of Poetry,' *Poetics Today* 30.2 (2009): 207–35.

5 David Wheatley believes that this pattern effectively 'short-circuits any Bloomian anxiety of influence' (Wheatley in O'Donoghue 124), although this view scants the momentous stature of Yeats and the implied need for *all* Irish poets to position themselves in respect to him (this need not entail vanquishing him *or* assimilating him). Wheatley aptly notes that when it comes to Eastern European poets, Heaney often abjures straightforward description (a qualifier is needed: Wheatley obviously has Heaney's essay on Mandelstam in mind, and not, say, 'Atlas of Civilization' on Herbert [130]). Hence Heaney's statements that Mandelstam sounds like late Yeats or Hopkins (two different tones, to be sure), even though it is unclear how much of Mandelstam's *poetry* Heaney has read; its tone is at least slightly obscured by translation.

6 Ryszard Nycz argues against viewing Miłosz as a Modernist, claiming that any similarity of style is largely due to the effect of English translation (which may, presumably, summon forth Eliotic rhythms). His poems appear more 'clean' and stylistically unified in translation, he holds, while they appear multivocal in their original Polish (*Literatura jako trop rzeczywistości* 159–60). Nycz's point is sound and is an almost-inevitable effect of the translation process, though we must note that Miłosz himself, who was perfectly fluent in English, had a large say in translations of his own work. We must additionally discern stylistic qualities that are difficult to

translate – such as voice – and those that can be readily translated (thematic and temporal jumps, shifts between prose and poetry, the collage form in general) and echo Modernist techniques. Thematics, of course, are a whole different matter, and the interest that *The Waste Land* and *The Four Quartets* would hold for Miłosz is both obvious and profound.

3. Zbigniew Herbert and the Moral Imperative

1 For an etymological discussion of authority and its Roman roots, see Docherty, *On Modern Authority.*
2 Annas cites Kurt Baier and Geoffrey Warnock's separate content-based definitions of morality (as an adoption of principles with the particular aim of furthering the common good and counteracting the limitations of human sympathies) and opposes them to 'purely formal' (and therefore, presumably, less useful) definitions (citing R.W. Hare). For a larger study of morality and its relation to ancient virtue, see Annas's *The Morality of Happiness.*
3 Herbert initially came, in 1968, at the invitation of the Poetry Center in New York. A grant from the State Department allowed him to travel around the country, giving several readings. He came again in 1970, this time to be a visiting professor at California State University in Los Angeles, teaching poetry and drama. He did not meet Heaney, who was several hundred miles north at the time, in Berkeley; he did, however, keep in contact with Miłosz. Miłosz introduced him to several other poets living in California, whom Herbert analysed with an anthropologist's glee ('I have met many Californian poets and am trying to get a look at them, how they think and live' – letter dated 13 December 1970 to Jerzy Turowicz, Herbert and Turowicz 182, my translation).
4 See, for instance, his extremely long letter to Barańczak dated 6 August 1990, in which he takes it upon himself to expose the previous corruption of life under communism to an émigré who knew it all too well. This is part of Herbert's unfortunate late correspondence, when the ailing poet was seized by a sort of moralistic mania, and perhaps it is unfair to refer to it at all. Yet it remains available to the public – in fact, it was published in the popular newspaper *Gazeta Wyborcza* that same year (vol. 203). In this letter he turns on his Anglo-American hosts, whom he had praised for their beneficence in 1970, by claiming that Westerners' fascination with Eastern Europe was not based on the quality of its literature, which they did not know, but on a repellent desire to condemn their own democratic systems in favour of communism. I will not linger on this unfortunate phase of Herbert's life, during

which his mind clearly suffered, since it does not provide an accurate image of the 'real' healthy Herbert, who eagerly threw himself into his travels with an open mind. See Herbert and Barańczak 34–43.

5 As if Catholics were never nationalists!

6 Although Heaney generalizes the 'hard-bitten aesthetic' of Eastern European poets, the first two decades after the Second World War were not uniform in their difficulty: the early years of post-war Stalinism were followed by a 'thaw' in the 1950s (in Polish, 'odwilż'). This period was, in turn, very different from the dark years of martial law in the 1980s. In brief, while Heaney is reacting to work written during different manifestations of communist oppression, he is publishing *Station Island*, *The Haw Lantern*, and *The Government of the Tongue* at a time when this oppression was at a peak (in the mid-1980s).

7 The early 'Antaeus,' composed in 1966, celebrating the strength of one nourished by 'the earth's long contour, her river-veins,' is bitterly matched by 'Hercules and Antaeus,' wherein the earth-born titan offers the 'pap for the dispossessed' instead of strength-giving nourishment. Although both poems are printed in *North* (1975), they represent two distinct stages in which Heaney thinks through the Antaean myth.

8 Heaney's early exemplars – Wordsworth, Lowell, Hughes, and Kavanagh – may be unified around this quality. Even the 'messianic' Kavanagh, to use the poet's own term, grounds his poems in an expressive self, a *personalized* self. This vision of the lyric is a post-Romantic inheritance.

9 Heaney enumerates 'Mr Cogito – The Return,' 'The Abandoned,' 'Mr Cogito's Soul,' and 'Report from the Besieged City' as poems of this type. One receives the impression, however, that Heaney is wishing this intimacy into existence. Consider the following lines from 'Report from the Besieged City:' 'and if the City falls but a single man escapes / he will carry the City within himself on the roads of exile / he will be the City' (Herbert, *Selected Poems* 151). There are hardly any more stirring proclamations of deep-rooted collective allegiance than this; the poem is spoken by an individual (a chronicler too old to bear arms) but its emotion is entirely invested in the creation of this human synecdoche by which an individual becomes, by necessity, a part containing the whole. Its voice moves between intimacy and hortatory zeal. It is an emotional poem but not a personal poem.

10 In his seminal *Inventing Eastern Europe*, Larry Wolff opines that Rousseau was the first major figure who challenged the Poles to 'preserve Poland in their own hearts' (Wolff 281), before Polish Romanticism took up this synecdochal relation of the individual to the imagined ideal of the nation

as its central tenet. Adam Mickiewicz elaborates this concept in *Books of the Polish Nation and of the Polish Pilgrimage* (*Księgi narodu polskiego i pielgrzymstwa polskiego*, 1832).

11 Heaney explicitly connects metrics to vocal pitch: 'Those thin small quatrain poems [of *North*], they're kind of drills or augers for turning in and they are narrow and long and deep ... after those poems I wanted to turn out ... [and make] a return to an opener voice and to a more – I don't want to say public – but a more social voice. And the rhythmic contract of meter and iambic pentameter and long line implies audience' (Curtis 104–5). The pentametric line, then, becomes a bearer of sociopolitical intent, even while the work of the poem may or may not function in tandem with this intentional pitch. The uncertainty of the formal 'contract' here, though – as seen in its metrical ruptures, tonal stumbles, irregularities of shape – are as important as the traditional nature of this 'contract' (Jason David Hall examines this term in *Seamus Heaney's Rhythmic Contract*). The poem, after all, vivifies a test, not a declaration.

12 'The Pebble' first appeared in a volume entitled *Study of the Object* (Polish *Studium przedmiotu*), 1961.

13 Thomas Docherty asks a seminal question about contemporary poetry – 'whether, in an age of globalization, poetry can serve the functions that it used to when it was firmly and clearly located, tied to a local habitation and a name; when poetry was, as it were, a matter of imagination, and not an imagination of matter' (Docherty in Pilny and Wallace 18). Docherty's chiasmus captures one of the major differences between Herbert and Heaney. Heaney's sandstone keepsake and his stone verdicts balance upon this line, but their function is pre-established as 'a matter of imagination' by means of the speaker's situation in his 'free state of image or allusion.' Herbert's 'concrete' art of matter consciously pushes away the Romantic imagination in order to attempt to align itself with the 'calm and very clear eye' of the object world. It can never be fully objective or exist in a zero temporality, but Herbert's poems reach for these states as vanishing points on an absolute moral horizon.

14 Barbara Hardy concludes that '[t]he full implications of veneration utterly destroy the innocence of the stone.' The reference has the effect of politicizing contemplation and veneration, and of complicating the speaker's conclusion by showing that the seemingly 'free' image is actually bound to a bloody history (Hardy in Curtis 162).

15 Stanisław Barańczak usefully troubles this view in *A Fugitive from Utopia* by claiming that Herbert should be viewed both as a classicist and a self-proclaimed barbarian in the garden of Western civilization. His barbarity

inheres in his attachment to Polish historical experience. This duality creates a contradiction: on the one hand, Herbert is attached to the values of the Western cultural heritage; on the other hand, he is aware of Eastern Europe's irreversible state of disinheritance (Barańczak 2).

16 Neil Corcoran holds that the implicit association of Joyce with the Martello tower is enough to justify reading 'Granite Chip' as a dialogue with Joyce's 'arrogance and absolutism,' which is the source of the chip's maxims: Joyce's example, in turn, makes the speaker aware of his own 'complaisance.' These maxims also frustrate the search for communion: ' "*You can take me or leave me*" may be read as the convinced self-assurance which will always embarrass the solidarity of community' (Corcoran, *Poets of Modern Ireland* 112). Yet we do not need Joyce to come to this conclusion; Herbert's reistic poems serve as richer and, indeed, closer intertexts for 'Granite Chip.' Rather, Heaney uses Herbert's form, and imbues it with references from his own cultural sphere.

17 Herbert's original poem allows 'completely' to stand on its own apart from the final full stanza of the poem. The translation Heaney uses does not follow this original formatting.

In order to further complicate the possible readings of this poem, we may take into account the variety of Herbert's treatments of Apollo. Ryszard Przybylski usefully enumerates these treatments, which include a view of Apollo as a redeemer (in Polish, 'Apollin Zbawiciel') as well as the god of cruelty ('Apollin Okrutnik'), in addition to the more conventional Nietzschean Apollo, god of harmony and measure. See Przybylski in Franaszek 87–99.

18 Herbert is angered by readers who associate irony with humour, especially, in his view, the Americans; he proffers an anecdote as an example of his cultural difference: 'When I was being translated by an American, he wrote me enthusiastic letters but was amused by my quoting the Bible. He was anxious to find irony in work which was meant to be quite serious. He was trying to uncover the allegedly comic undertones so that his students might laugh like mad ... I sometimes get furious when others laugh at moments that make my throat go dry. They ... "tick differently." The Americans are pragmatic, but they lack our sense of history' (Oramus 327–8).

19 A similar situation is stunningly ironized in 'A Box Called the Imagination' (contained in *Elegy for the Departure* 50–1). In this antiseptically structured poem, the speaker describes, stanza by stanza, the acts he can perform in order to elicit fanciful pictures from the mind (seen as a jack-in-the-box of images). Unlike 'The Knocker,' the poem never allows the speaker to hazard an opinion, to accept or reject the magical box.

20 When considering these inconsistencies, we may bear in mind that the
    initial poem was written extremely quickly: it was sent for publication on
    1 August 1998, four days after Herbert's death on 28 July, but there was
    plenty of time for revision before the 2001 publication of *Electric Light*.
    Bogdana Carpenter notes that the poem was first published not in the
    New Yorker but in the Polish journal *Tygodnik Powszechny*, on 9 August.
    It had already been translated into Polish by Barańczak. The *New Yorker*
    version was printed several months later, on 18 January 1999. See 'Hiper-
    borejczyk,' trans. Stanisław Barańczak, *Tygodnik Powszechny* 32 (9 August
    1998) 9.

4. Approaching the Master

1   Dennis O'Driscoll states that 'direct poem-by-poem comparison would
    be difficult to sustain' (O'Driscoll in O'Donoghue, *Seamus Heaney* 59–60),
    yet he goes out on a critical limb to hazard that the verbal compactness of
    certain poems in *Seeing Things* show the prior influence of Eastern Europe-
    ans. O'Driscoll's remarks, however offhanded – certain poems bear resem-
    blance to certain poems, he writes – evince a frustrated desire to take on
    the very subject matter whose importance he attempts to downplay. This
    is a telling moment. By concluding that Heaney's language *could* never
    become like that of Popa or Pilinszky, he tacitly justifies his refusal to con-
    sider whether it could become like that of Herbert or Miłosz. Even a reader
    as sensitive to verbal texture as O'Driscoll automatically groups together
    radically divergent Eastern European poets, implying that we could iden-
    tify a composite Eastern European voice. Asking whether Heaney's voice
    resembled this composite would be begging the question.
2   Heaney does, however, state very similar opinions on the dangers of being
    a successful writer in the United States: he has to learn to 'survive his
    career' and fulfil the expectations that being 'a success,' in Miłosz's term,
    brings. 'If I came here to live, I would be just an "ethnic curiosity,"' states
    Heaney in an uncanny echo of Miłosz's earlier statements (Beisch 164).
3   Miłosz chose different translations for his *Collected Poems* than had been
    previously published in certain cases, leading to some obvious confusion
    over which translation should prove definitive. The most salient example
    of this for our analysis is 'The World,' a poem that surprised and im-
    pressed Heaney, and that was ingeniously translated by Robert Pinsky and
    Robert Hass. This version appeared in *The Separate Notebooks* (1984). Miłosz
    chose a far flatter, more prosaic translation for inclusion in the *Collected
    Poems* (Pinsky claims it was based on a literal translation by Lillian Vallee;
    see Pinsky in Thomas 17). Miłosz ultimately decided that 'The World,'

subtitlted 'A Naïve Poem,' should not sound *more* sophisticated in English than it did in Polish, and the later translation does away with all rhyme. This is one of the most contentious examples of his participation in the translation process, given that the final 'World' is less euphonious than the first.

4 Miłosz reiterates (and re-defends) his choice to conserve his past as a source of inspiration in the later *Beginning with My Streets: Essays and Recollections*: 'An immigrant in America, I was confronted with a choice: either to leave behind what existed only in my memory and to find in what surrounded me material for my reflection or, without renouncing the present, to try to bring back the streets, landscapes, and people from my past ... I chose the second solution, that of living simultaneously here and there, both in California and in the city of Wilno, now Vilnius ... And since I am primarily a poet, I have always believed I was a better writer in my mother tongue ..., so I kept writing all my poems and the majority of my essays in Polish' (ix–x).

5 One of the greatest poets of the American West, Robinson Jeffers, embraces 'inhumanism,' which Miłosz seriously studies but cannot accept. Herbert, Miłosz, and Heaney all defend the embattled and unfashionable concept of humanism. To them, the word conveys a salubrious respect for the Western tradition, yet not a necessary connivance with its evils; we need only read one or two of Herbert's poems to realize that his deep attunement to the cultures of the Mediterranean includes a struggle with its ethical (or unethical, as the case may be) underpinnings; Herbert is, I believe, already a few steps ahead of our late-twentieth-century reaction against humanism in his early poems.

6 The reader will no doubt deduce that I am at variance with several critics on this point. For examples of opposing viewpoints, see Parker, 'Changing Skies'; Allison, 'Beyond Gentility'; and Allen, 'The Parish and the Dream.' Allen argues that the greatest turn towards American audiences happens after Heaney starts teaching at Harvard. He tends to eschew close reading, however, which makes his central claim questionable: we could choose poems countering his argument from several stages of Heaney's career, which never truly abandons what Allen calls his 'parish'; the abstract poems of *The Haw Lantern* (allied with 'a self-reflexive aesthetic' by Allen) are certainly *not* influenced by American poets.

7 Arent van Nieukerken provides a meaningful gloss on Błoński's statement: 'It would be more accurate to say that its "anecdotalness" [("anegdotyczność")] and stylization occur simultaneously, and precisely this tendency ... to clothe the "I" in various costumes (Renaissance, Baroque, Enlightenment, Romantic), which demand that the subject play

different roles, decides the precise extent to which it is autobiographical. The confessional "I" is [only] one of these roles' (44–5). Caveat lector, van Nieukerken warns: the poems that appear anecdotal, almost as a form of life-writing, are, in fact, stylized. Let us not draw hasty biographical conclusions. His stress on Miłosz's use of historical personae is necessary, and his theatrical metaphor helpfully explains the way in which Miłosz *can* be seen to write autobiographically *through the guise* of his personae.

8 See, for example, Peter McDonald's remarks about Yeats's placement into a group of male proponents of seriousness and difficulty, which exerts a somewhat negative effect upon his reputation and his influence ('Difficulty, Democracy, and Modern Poetry' and *Serious Poetry*).

9 The translation appeared in the weekly newspaper *Tygodnik Powszechny*, which, in Poland, fulfils the function of a cultural journal more than a traditional newspaper. Barańczak's translation appeared in the 9 April 1996 issue of the paper.

10 This latter phrase comes from 'The Cleric' (*Station Island* 107–8), and shows how these qualities are, for Heaney, associated with the 'kingdom' of religion as well as literature. This will become an important point in the next chapter, where Heaney's growing interest in transcendence and 'clearance' will be seen to reach its apex in *The Haw Lantern*, in which Eastern European poetry is constantly a shadow presence.

11 We must note that Miłosz variously paraphrases this point; in his Nobel lecture, for instance, he draws his dichotomy 'between being and action' and then 'between art and solidarity with one's fellow men.' Each dichotomy could be unravelled on its own, yet here, the operative one is between contemplation of transcendence and historical action. Given that Heaney's *Haw Lantern* focuses upon the transcendent realm in a manner that betokens a debt to Miłosz's writing, this particular dichotomy will allow us to deeply comprehend the transition from *Station Island* to *The Haw Lantern*.

5. Unfortunate Nobility

1 'I am grateful to America and proud of being now one of its poets, reaching young audiences who treat me primarily as a poet' [as opposed to a political essayist] ('A Poet's Reply' 42).

2 Interestingly, Clare Cavanagh holds that the poet links himself to Adam Mickiewicz through the ceremonial offering of millet and poppy seeds – a Lithuanian folk custom mentioned in Mickiewicz's *Forefathers' Eve* – and deliberately summons an old multi-ethnic Lithuania, placing it in tacit contradistinction to the current state of the land. See *Lyric Poetry and Modern Politics* 254.

3 Maj speaks to a predominantly American audience in these remarks, which no doubt affects his choice of emphasis. His talk is available in a compendium of scholarly presentations, 'Miłosz's World Today: ABC's to Road-side Dog,' *Partisan Review* 66.1 (Winter 1999): 100–14.

4 Ryszard Nycz insists that English translations of Miłosz's poetry substitute unity of tone for Miłosz's famed multivocality, and that they unjustly 'modernize' and homogenize his stylistic complexity (Nycz 159–60). It is an apposite point, but *even* in English, a good deal of his variety and complexity comes through, even if it is not frequently associated with the influence of Eliot. Eliot is not the sole English-language influence on Miłosz's poetry, but he is a key figure influencing Miłosz's search for a 'dry form' and – were his influence stressed even more than it is in Anglo-American scholarship – further complicating our ability to associate Miłosz with the 'witness' label, political parables, or moralism.

5 Since I will choose to focus on 'Bypassing Rue Descartes' as an even more complicated and fascinating influence, most notably upon Heaney's 'From the Republic of Conscience,' I will not undertake the analysis of 'The World' and 'Alphabets' that Heaney tacitly calls for us to consider here, for reasons of space and focus: I prefer to continue pursuing the important point of Miłosz's anti-Romanticism, and its importance for his Irish and Anglo-American legacy. Were I to undertake it, I would insist that we place Miłosz's 'Sentences' as a more logical partner to 'Alphabets,' and consider why Heaney pinpoints 'The World' instead. Because of the dates involved, Heaney must have the early, overly virtuoso 'World' in mind, rather than the re-translated, flattened-out version published in *Collected Poems* (1988).

6 Miłosz's placement of Eliot in a *re*constructive tradition is crucial to his attraction to Eliot, and Jesse Airaudi scants this fact in his comparison of Eliot and Miłosz as 'protest poets' fighting against bourgeois materialism in the name of spiritual values. He importantly links the authors' belief in memory as a corrective force against cultural decay and discerns a related belief in hierarchy that underlies their cultural protest. This lattermost term, though, is overvalued, and it obscures the questions of form and literary history that must underlie any discussion of Eliot and Miłosz. See Airaudi 453–7.

7 The poem situates itself by bearing the inscription 'Berkeley, 1980' at the bottom of the poem, though its first version read 'Paris, July 1980,' and was published in the Polish literary journal *Twórczość* in June 1981 during a triumphal post-Nobel trip to Poland by the poet (his first, in fact, after his defection thirty years previously). Its publication occurs six months before the imposition of martial law and the renewed domination of 'unfortunate nobility' in Polish writing. These facts would have been noted by Polish

readers. Additionally important for English-language readers would be the date that Miłosz's Nobel Prize was announced: October 1980. The poem consciously dates itself *before* the Nobel, then, attempting to ensure that we do *not* equate the bewildered, self-conscious speaker of the poem with an internationally recognized 'success' (to use the sarcastic terminology of 'My Faithful Mother Tongue'), though it was only printed after the Nobel (English readers had to wait until 1984). We may surmise that Miłosz wished to highlight the developmental narrative of the poem.

8 As an example, let us take the following opinion by a major critic: 'Bypassing Rue Descartes' implicitly bases the speaker's 'claim to having witnessed momentous events' with 'the sense that only one who has seen what was unimaginable in fact occur can understand the transience of governments and institutions,' writes Robert von Hallberg in an otherwise illuminating discussion of Miłosz's *Visions from San Francisco Bay* (von Hallberg in Bercovitch and Patell 181). In other words, the poem can be interpreted in light of Geoffrey Hill's 'Language, Suffering, and Silence.' The witness understands more than we; von Hallberg's emphases ('*momentous*,' '*only* one') accent his resentment. Heaney's opinion is noticeably different.

Conclusion

1 For additional information on Renaissance mnemonic theory, see Draaisma's helpful *Metaphors of Memory* 38–44.

Bibliography

Note: All entries are print sources, unless indicated otherwise.

Adams, Hazard. *The Offense of Poetry*. Seattle: University of Washington Press, 2007.

Airaudi, Jesse. 'Eliot, Miłosz, and the Enduring Modernist Protest.' *Twentieth Century Literature* 34.4 (Winter 1988): 453–67.

Alcobia-Murphy, Shane. *Sympathetic Ink: Intertextual Relations in Northern Irish Poetry*. Liverpool: Liverpool University Press, 2006.

Allen, Michael. 'The Parish and the Dream: Heaney and America, 1969–1987.' *Southern Review* 31.3 (Summer 1995): 726–38.

Allen, Michael, ed. *Seamus Heaney*. New York: St Martin's Press, 1997.

Allison, Jonathan. 'Beyond Gentility: A Note on Seamus Heaney and American Poetry.' *Critical Survey* 8.2 (1996): 178–85.

Alvarez, A. 'A. Alvarez Replies.' *New York Review of Books*, 21 July 1988: 42.

– 'Introduction to the Poetry of Zbigniew Herbert.' In Zbigniew Herbert, *Selected Poems*, 9–15. Harmondsworth, Middlesex: Penguin Books, 1968.

– *Under Pressure – The Writer in Society: Eastern Europe and the U.S.A.* Baltimore: Penguin Books, 1965.

– *Where Did It All Go Right?* New York: William Morrow, 1999.

– 'Witness.' *New York Review of Books*, 2 June 1988: 21–2.

Anders, Jarosław. *Between Fire and Sleep: Essays on Modern Polish Poetry and Prose*. New Haven: Yale University Press, 2009.

Annas, Julia. *The Morality of Happiness*. New York: Oxford University Press, 1995.

Apter, Emily. 'Global *Translatio*: The "Invention" of Comparative Literature, Istanbul, 1933.' *Critical Inquiry* 2 (Winter 2003): 253–81.

Arac, Jonathan. 'Anglo-Globalism?' *New Left Review* 16 (July/August 2002): 35–45.

Articulations: Poetry, Philosophy and the Shaping of Culture: Seamus Heaney, Royal Irish Cunningham Medal, 28th January 2008. Dublin: Royal Irish Academy, 2008.

Audi, Robert, ed. *The Cambridge Dictionary of Philosophy.* Cambridge: Cambridge University Press, 1995.

Balfour, Ian. *The Rhetoric of Romantic Prophecy.* Stanford: Stanford University Press, 2002.

Bandrowska-Wróblewska, Jadwiga. Conclusion ['Nota Biograficzna']. In *Poezje wybrane*, Zbigniew Herbert, 135–51. Warsaw: Ludowa Spółdzielnia Wydawnicza, 1973.

Barańczak, Stanisław. 'Between Repulsion and Rapture.' *The Threepenny Review* 38 (Summer 1989): 23–4.

– *A Fugitive from Utopia: The Poetry of Zbigniew Herbert.* Cambridge: Harvard University Press, 1987.

Barańczak, Stanisław, and Clare Cavanagh, ed. and trans. *Polish Poetry of the Last Two Decades of Communist Rule: Spoiling Cannibals' Fun.* Evanston: Northwestern University Press, 1991.

Becker, Lawrence, and Charlotte Becker, eds. *Encyclopedia of Ethics.* 2nd ed. Vol. 1. New York: Routledge, 2001.

Beisch, June. 'An Interview with Seamus Heaney.' *Literary Review* 29.2 (Winter 1986): 161–9.

Bell, Marvin. 'Homage to the Runner.' *American Poetry Review* 7.1 (January–February 1978): 37–42.

Bercovitch, Sacvan, and Cyrus Patell, eds. *The Cambridge History of American Literature.* Vol. 8: Poetry and Criticism, 1940–1995. Cambridge, New York: Cambridge University Press, 1996.

Bernheimer, Charles, ed. *Comparative Literature in the Age of Multiculturalism.* Baltimore: Johns Hopkins University Press, 1995.

Bibliografia anglistyki polskiej 1945–1975. Warsaw: Państwowe Wydawnictwo Naukowe, 1977.

Bielik-Robson, Agata. *Romantyzm, niedokończony projekt.* Cracow: Universitas, 2008.

Blackburn, Simon. *The Oxford Dictionary of Philosophy.* 2nd ed. Oxford: Oxford University Press, 2005.

Błoński, Jan. *Miłosz jak świat.* Cracow: Wydawnictwo Znak, 1998.

Boss, Michael. 'Roots in the Bog: Notions of Identity in the Poetry and Essays of Seamus Heaney.' In *Ireland: Towards New Identities?* ed. Karl-Heinz

Westarp, Michael Boss, and Tim Caudery, 134–45. Aarhus, Denmark: Aarhus University Press, 1998.

Brandes, Rand. Interview with Seamus Heaney. *Salmagundi* 80 (Fall 1988): 4–21.

Brearton, Fran. 'Poetry of the 1960s: the "Northern Ireland Renaissance." ' In *The Cambridge Companion to Contemporary Irish Poetry*, ed. Matthew Campbell, 94–112. Cambridge: Cambridge University Press, 2003.

Brearton, Fran, and Justin Quinn. 'Reports from Central Europe.' *Metre* 12 (Autumn 2002): 85–7.

Brodsky, Joseph. *Less than One: Selected Essays*. New York: Farrar, Straus & Giroux, 1986.

Brown, John. *In the Chair: Interviews with Poets from the North of Ireland*. Cliffs of Moher, County Clare, Ireland: Salmon Publishing, 2002.

Campbell, James. 'The Mythmaker' [interview with Seamus Heaney]. *The Guardian*, 27 May 2006.

Campbell, Matthew, ed. *The Cambridge Companion to Contemporary Irish Poetry*. Cambridge: Cambridge University Press, 2003.

Carey, John. Review of Seamus Heaney, *The Haw Lantern*. *Sunday Times*, 21 June 1987.

Carpenter, Bogdana. 'Czesław Miłosz i Zbigniew Herbert: Poeta wygnania i poeta powrotu.' In *Literatura Polska na Obczyźnie*. Vol. 5, ed. Józef Bujnowski, 176–92. London: Polskie Towarzystwo Naukowe na Obczyźnie, 1988.

– 'The Gift Returned.' In *Living in Translation: Polish Writers in America*, ed. Halina Stephan, 45–75. Amsterdam, New York: Rodopi, 2003.

Carpenter, Bogdana, and Carpenter, John. 'Zbigniew Herbert: The Poet as Conscience.' *Slavic and East European Journal* 24.1 (1980): 37–51.

Cavanagh, Clare. *Lyric Poetry and Modern Politics: Russia, Poland, and the West*. New Haven: Yale University Press, 2009.

– 'Poetry and History: Poland's Acknowledged Legislators.' *Common Knowledge* 11.2 (Spring 2005): 185–97.

Clark, Heather. *The Ulster Renaissance: Poetry in Belfast, 1962–1972*. Oxford, New York: Oxford University Press, 2006.

Coetzee, J.M. *Giving Offense: Essays on Censorship*. Chicago: University of Chicago Press, 1996.

Corcoran, Neil. *The Poetry of Seamus Heaney*. London: Faber & Faber, 1998.

– *Poets of Modern Ireland: Text, Context, Intertext*. Cardiff: University of Wales Press, 1999.

– 'Seamus Heaney and the Art of the Exemplary.' *Yearbook of English Studies* 17 (1987): 117–27.

Cornis-Pope, Marcel, and John Neubauer, eds. *History of the Literary Cultures of East-Central Europe: Junctures and Disjunctures in the 19th and 20th Centuries.* Amsterdam, Philadelphia: John Benjamins Publishing Co., 2004.

Crowder, Ashby Bland, and Jason David Hall, eds. *Seamus Heaney: Poet, Critic, Translator.* Basingstoke, New York: Palgrave Macmillan, 2007.

Cuda, Anthony. 'Heaney, Eliot, and the Epigraph to *North.*' *Journal of Modern Literature* 28.4 (Summer 2005): 152–75.

Curtis, Tony, ed. *The Art of Seamus Heaney.* 4th ed. Bridgend, Mid Glamorgan: Seren, 2001.

Czapliński, Przemysław, and Piotr Śliwiński. *Literatura polska 1976–1998. Przewodnik po prozie i poezji.* Cracow: Wydawnictwo Literackie, 1999.

Czarnecka, Ewa, and Aleksander Fiut. *Conversations with Czesław Miłosz.* Trans. Richard Lourie. San Diego: Harcourt Brace Jovanovich, 1987.

Czerniawski, Adam. 'Are Poets Necessary?' *Poetry Review* 77.3 (Autumn 1987): 7–10.

– 'Polish Poetry and the Polish Predicament.' *Bête Noire* 5 (1988): 66–76.

Davie, Donald. *Czesław Miłosz and the Insufficiency of Lyric.* Knoxville: University of Tennesee Press, 1986.

– 'Responsibilities of *Station Island.*' *Salmagundi* 80 (Fall 1988): 58–65.

Dawe, Gerald. *The Proper Word: Collected Criticism – Ireland, Poetry and Politics.* Ed. Nicholas Allen. Omaha: Creighton University Press, 2007.

– Review of Ciaran Carson, *The Irish for No,* Seamus Heaney, *The Haw Lantern,* and Paul Muldoon, *Meeting the British. The Linenhall Review* 4.3 (Autumn 1987): 24–5.

Deane, Seamus. 'Unhappy and at Home' [Interview with Seamus Heaney]. *The Crane Bag* 1.1 (Spring 1977): 66–72.

Desmond, John. *Gravity and Grace: Seamus Heaney and the Force of Light.* Waco, TX: Baylor University Press, 2009.

Dettlaff, Karol. '*A gdyby nas lepiej i piękniej kuszono?* O ocaleniu i zagładzie Miasta wartości. *Raport z oblężonego miasta* Zbigniewa Herberta.' In *Literatura i/a tożsamość w XX wieku,* ed. Adrian Gleń, Irena Jokiel, and Marek Szladowski, 15–26. Opole: Wydawnictwo Uniwersytetu Opolskiego, 2007.

Dimock, Wai Chee. 'Literature for the Planet.' *PMLA* 1 (January 2001): 173–88.

Docherty, Thomas. *On Modern Authority: The Theory and Condition of Writing, 1500 to the Present Day.* Brighton: Harvester Press, 1987.

– 'The Place's Fault.' In *Global Ireland: Irish Literatures for the New Millennium,* ed. Ondrej Pilny and Clare Wallace, 13–32. Prague: Litteraria Pragensia, 2005.

Draaisma, D. *Metaphors of Memory: A History of Ideas about the Mind*. Trans. Paul Vincent. Cambridge, New York: Cambridge University Press, 2000.

Duff, David, and Catherine Jones. *Scotland, Ireland and the Romantic Aesthetic*. Lewisburg, PA: Bucknell University Press, 2007.

Eliot, T.S. *Poezje wybrane*. Trans. Władysław Dulęba et al. Warsaw: Instytut Wydawniczy Pax, 1960.

Ellmann, Richard. *The Identity of Yeats*. London: Faber and Faber, 1964.

– *Yeats: The Man and the Masks*. New York: The Macmillan Company, 1948.

Farndale, Nigel. Interview with Seamus Heaney. *Telegraph*, 5 April 2001. www. telegraph.co.uk.

Filipowicz, Halina. Review of Charles Kraszewski, *Essays on the Dramatic Works of Polish Poet Zbigniew Herbert*. *Slavic and East European Journal* 48(3) (Autumn 2004): 521–2.

Foster, John Wilson. *Colonial Consequences: Essays in Irish Literature and Culture*. Dublin: Lilliput Press, 1991.

Franaszek, Andrzej, ed. *Poznawanie Herberta*. Cracow: Wydawnictwo Literackie, 1998–2000.

Frängsmyr, Tore, and Sture Allén, eds. *Nobel Lectures, Literature 1981–1990*. Singapore: World Scientific Publishing Co., 1993.

Goodby, John. *Irish Poetry since 1950*. Manchester: Manchester University Press, 2000.

Gorczyńska, Renata. Interview with Zbigniew Herbert. Republished posthumously in *Zeszyty Literackie* 17.68 (Fall 1999): 156–65.

Grudzińska Gross, Irena. 'Poles Apart.' *Lingua Franca* (March 1999): 13–15.

Gussow, Mel. 'An Anglo-Saxon Chiller (With an Irish Touch): Seamus Heaney Adds His Voice to "Beowulf."' *New York Times*, 29 March 2000.

Hall, Jason David. *Seamus Heaney's Rhythmic Contract*. New York: Palgrave Macmillan, 2009.

Hart, Henry. *Seamus Heaney: Poet of Contrary Progressions*. Syracuse, NY: Syracuse University Press, 1992.

Hartwig, Julia. *Wybrańcy losu*. Warsaw: Wydawnictwo Sic! 2006.

Haven, Cynthia. 'A Sacred Vision: An Interview with Czesław Miłosz.' *The Georgia Review* 57.2 (Summer 2003): 303–14.

Haven, Cynthia, ed. *Czesław Miłosz: Conversations*. Jackson: University Press of Mississippi, 2006.

Heaney, Seamus. 'Brodsky's Nobel: What the Applause Was About.' *New York Times*, 8 November 1987: 7, 63.

– 'Current Unstated Assumptions about Poetry.' *Critical Inquiry* 7.4 (Summer 1981): 645–51.

– *Death of a Naturalist*. London: Faber and Faber, 1966.

- 'Earning a Rhyme.' *Poetry Ireland Review* 25 (Spring 1989): 95–100.
- *Electric Light*. New York: Farrar, Straus & Giroux, 2001.
- 'Envies and Identifications: Dante and the Modern Poet.' *Irish University Review* 15 (1985): 5–19.
- *Finders Keepers: Selected Prose, 1971–2001*. New York: Farrar, Straus & Giroux, 2002.
- 'Foreword.' *Selected Poems: 1931–2004*. By Czesław Miłosz. New York: HarperCollins, 2006.
- *The Government of the Tongue: Selected Prose 1978–1987*. London: Faber and Faber, 1988.
- 'In Gratitude for All the Gifts.' *The Guardian*, 11 September 2004: 4–6.
- *The Haw Lantern*. London: Faber and Faber, 1987.
- 'A Hyperborean.' *The New Yorker*, 18 January 1999: 56.
- 'Joseph Brodsky 1940–1996.' *Metre: A Magazine of International Poetry* 1 (Autumn 1996): 31–4.
- *New Selected Poems 1966–1987*. London: Faber and Faber, 1990.
- *North*. London: Faber and Faber, 1975.
- *Opened Ground: Poems, 1966–1996*. London: Faber and Faber, 1998.
- *Preoccupations: Selected Prose, 1968–1978*. London: Faber & Faber, 1980.
- 'Poetry's Power against Intolerance.' *New York Times*, 26 August 2001: 13.
- 'A Poet's Europe.' *A Poet's Europe: European Poetry Festival*, 156–61. Leuven: Europese Vereniging ter Bevordering van de Poëzie, 1991.
- 'Poets' Round Table: "A Common Language."' *PN Review* 15.4 (1989): 39–47.
- 'A Quality of Wisdom.' *The Guardian*, 9 April 2011: 20.
- *The Redress of Poetry: Oxford Lectures*. London: Faber and Faber, 1995.
- *Seeing Things*. London: Faber and Faber, 1991.
- *Station Island*. London: Faber and Faber, 1984.
- 'Views.' *The Listener*, 31 December 1970: 903.
- *Wintering Out*. London: Faber and Faber, 1972.
Heaney, Seamus, and Joseph Brodsky. 'Poetry and Politics: A Conversation between Seamus Heaney and Joseph Brodsky.' *Magill* 9.2 (November 1985): 40–8.
Herbert, Zbigniew. *Elegy for the Departure and Other Poems*. Trans. John and Bogdana Carpenter. Hopewell, NJ: The Ecco Press, 1999.
- *Poezje wybrane*. Warsaw: Ludowa Spółdzielnia Wydawnicza, 1973.
- *Selected Poems*. Trans. John and Bogdana Carpenter. Cracow: Wydawnictwo Literackie, 2000.
Herbert, Zbigniew, and Stanisław Barańczak. *Korespondencja (1972–1996)*. Ed. Barbara Toruńczyk. Warsaw: Zeszyty Literackie, 2005.

Herbert, Zbigniew, and Magdalena Czajkowska. *'Kochane Zwierzątka—': Listy Zbigniewa Herberta do przyjaciół, Magdaleny i Zbigniewa Czajkowskich.* Warsaw: Państwowy Instytut Wydawniczy, 2000.

Herbert, Zbigniew, and Jerzy Turowicz. *Korespondencja.* Ed. Tomasz Fiałkowski. Cracow: Wydawnictwo a5, 2005.

Hill, Geoffrey. 'Language, Suffering, and Silence.' *Literary Imagination* 1.2 (1999): 240–55.

Holub, Miroslav. 'Endangerment.' *Poetry Review* 85.3 (Autumn 1995): 22–3.

Hufstader, Jonathan. *Tongue of Water, Teeth of Stones: Northern Irish Poetry and Social Violence.* Lexington: University Press of Kentucky, 1999.

Janáček, Leoš. *Diary of One Who Vanished* [In a New Version by Seamus Heaney]. London: Faber and Faber, 1999.

Janion, Maria. *Czy będziesz wiedział, co przeżyłeś.* Warsaw: Wydawnictwo Sic! 1996.

– *Gorączka romantyczna.* Cracow: Universitas, 2000.

– 'Romanticism and the Beginning of the Modern World.' Trans. Aleksandra Rodzińska-Chojnowska. *Dialogue and Universalism* 10.9/10 (2000): 45–67.

– *Romantyzm i historia.* Gdańsk: Słowo/Obraz Terytoria, 2001.

Jarniewicz, Jerzy. *The Bottomless Centre: The Uses of History in the Poetry of Seamus Heaney.* Łódź: Wydawnictwo Uniwersytetu Łódźkiego, 2002.

– 'Eastern Recollections.' *Metre* 12 (Autumn 2002): 115–20.

– 'Reizm pozorowany: Herbert, Heaney i świat kamyków.' *Odra* 1.565 (January 2009): 33–41.

– 'The Way via Warsaw: Seamus Heaney and Post-War Polish Poets.' In *Seamus Heaney: Poet, Critic, Translator,* ed. Ashby Bland Crowder and Jason David Hall, 103–20. Basingstoke, New York: Palgrave Macmillan, 2007.

Jarzębski, Jerzy. 'Być wieszczem.' *Teksty* 4–5 (1981): 246.

Johnston, Dillon. *The Poetic Economies of England and Ireland, 1912–2000.* New York: Palgrave, 2001.

Kearney, Timothy. 'The Poetry of the North: A Post-Modernist Perspective.' In *The Crane Bag Book of Irish Studies (1977–81),* 465–73. Dublin: Blackwater Press, 1982.

Kermode, Frank. *The Romantic Image.* New York: Vintage, 1964.

Kijowski, Andrzej. 'Tematy Miłosza.' *Twórczość* 6 (1981): 44.

Kim, Hyung. '15 Questions with Seamus Heaney.' *The Harvard Crimson,* 8 October 2008.

Kinahan, Frank. 'An Interview with Seamus Heaney.' *Critical Inquiry* 8.3 (Spring 1982): 405–14.

Kinzie, Mary. 'Deeper than Declared: On Seamus Heaney.' *Salmagundi* 80 (Fall 1988): 22–57.

Kiślak, Elżbieta. *Walka Jakuba z aniołem: Czesław Miłosz wobec romantyczności.* Warsaw: Prószyński i S-ka, 2000.

Kosińska, Agnieszka. 'From East to West: Czesław Miłosz Interviewed by Agnieszka Kosińska.' *Dekada Literacka*, October 1997.

Leith, Sam. 'Return of the Naturalist' [Interview with Seamus Heaney]. *Daily Telegraph*, 2 April 2006.

Lerner, Daniel. Review of Czesław Miłosz, *The Captive Mind*. *American Sociological Review* 19.4 (August 1954): 488–9.

Lim, Shirley, and Amy Ling, eds. *Reading the Literatures of Asian America*. Philadelphia: Temple University Press, 1992.

Liu, Alan. *Wordsworth: The Sense of History*. Stanford: Stanford University Press, 1989.

Lloyd, David. *Anomalous States: Irish Writing and the Post-Colonial Moment*. Durham: Duke University Press, 1993.

Longley, Edna. *Poetry and Posterity*. Tarset, Northumberland: Bloodaxe Books, 2000.

– 'Putting on the International Style.' *The Irish Review* 5 (Autumn 1988): 75–81.

Lynch, Patricia, Joachim Fischer, and Brian Coates, eds. *Back to the Present, Forward to the Past: Irish Writing and History since 1798*. Amsterdam, New York: Rodopi, 2006.

Malcolm, David, and Ola Kubińska, eds. *Eseje o poezji Seamusa Heaneya*. Gdańsk: Wydawnictwo Uniwersytetu Gdańskiego, 1997.

Malinowska, Barbara. *Dynamics of Being, Space and Time in the Poetry of Czeslaw Milosz and John Ashbery*. New York: Peter Lang, 2000.

Matthews, Steven. 'The Object Lessons of Heaney, Carson, Muldoon and Boland.' *Critical Survey* 15 (2003): 18–33.

McCarthy, Conor. *Seamus Heaney and Medieval Poetry*. Rochester, NY: Boydell and Brewer, 2008.

McDonald, Peter. 'Difficulty, Democracy, and Modern Poetry.' *PN Review* 31.3 (Jan./Feb. 2005): 19–24.

– *Serious Poetry: Form and Authority, from Yeats to Hill*. Oxford: Oxford University Press, 2002.

Merchant, John. 'The Impact of Irish Ireland on Young Poland, 1890–1918.' *New Hibernia Review* 5.3 (Autumn 2001): 42–65.

– *The Impact of Irish-Ireland on Young Poland, 1890–1919*. Boulder: East European Monographs, 2008.

Mikołajczak, Małgorzata. 'Między kamieniem i wzruszeniem: O dylematach etyki i estetyki w twórczości Zbigniewa Herberta.' *Ruch literacki* 45.2 (2004): 205–21.

Miller, Chris. 'The Mandelstam Syndrome and the "Old Heroic Bang."' *PN Review* 31.4 (March/April 2005): 14–23.

Miłosz, Czesław. *Beginning with My Streets: Essays and Recollections*. Trans. Madeline G. Levine. New York: Farrar, Straus & Giroux, 1991.

– *The Captive Mind*. Trans. Jane Zielonko. New York: Vintage, 1953.

– *Eseje*. Ed. Marek Zaleski. Warsaw: Świat Książki, 2000.

– *Kontynenty*. Paris: Institut Littéraire, 1958.

– 'Mickiewicz and Modern Poetry.' *Slavic Review* 7.4 (December 1948): 361–8.

– *Native Realm: A Search for Self-Definition*. Trans. Catherine S. Leach. Garden City, NY: Doubleday, 1968.

– *New and Collected Poems (1931–2001)*. New York: Ecco, 2001.

– 'A Poet's Reply.' *New York Review of Books*, 21 July 1988: 42.

– *Prywatne obowiązki*. Cracow: Wydawnictwo Literackie, 2001.

– *Rodzinna Europa*. Paris: Instytut Literacki, 1980.

– *Second Space: New Poems*. Trans. Czesław Miłosz and Robert Hass. New York: Ecco Press, 2004.

– *To Begin Where I Am: Selected Essays*. Ed. Bogdana Carpenter and Madeline Levine. New York: Farrar, Straus & Giroux, 2001.

– *Visions from San Francisco Bay*. Trans. Richard Lourie. New York: Farrar, Straus & Giroux, 1982.

– *The Witness of Poetry*. Cambridge: Harvard University Press, 1983.

– *Zaraz po wojnie: Korespondencja z pisarzami 1945–1950*. Cracow: Znak, 1998.

Moretti, Franco. 'Conjectures on World Literature.' *New Left Review* 1 (January–February 2000): 54–68.

– *Graphs, Maps, Trees: Abstract Models for a Literary History*. London, New York: Verso, 2005.

Morgan, George. Interview with Seamus Heaney. *Cycnos* 15.2 (2008).

Murphy, Bruce F. 'The Exile of Literature: Poetry and the Politics of the Other(s).' *Critical Inquiry* 17.1 (Autumn 1990): 162–73.

N.a. [multiple authors]. 'Miłosz's World Today: ABC's to Road-side Dog.' *Partisan Review* 66.1 (Winter 1999): 100–14.

Nathan, Leonard, and Arthur Quinn. *The Poet's Work: An Introduction to Czeslaw Milosz*. Cambridge, MA: Harvard University Press, 1991.

Ni Anluain, Cliodhna, ed. *Reading the Future: Irish Writers in Conversation with Mike Murphy*. Dublin: The Lilliput Press, 2000.

Nieukerken, Arent van. *Ironiczny konceptyzm: Nowoczesna polska poezja metafizyczna w kontekście anglosaskiego modernizmu*. Cracow: Universitas, 1998.

– 'Czesław Miłosz wobec tradycji europejskiego romantyzmu.' *Teksty drugie* 3–4 (2001): 39–56.

Niżyńska, Joanna. 'The Impossibility of Shrugging One's Shoulders: O'Harists, O'Hara, and Post-1989 Polish Poetry.' *Slavic Review* 66.3 (Fall 2007): 463–83.

– 'Marsyas's Howl: The Myth of Marsyas in Ovid's *Metamorphoses* and Zbigniew Herbert's "Apollo and Marsyas."' *Comparative Literature* 53.2 (Spring 2001): 151–69.

Nycz, Ryszard. *Literatura jako trop rzeczywistości*. Cracow: Universitas, 2001.

O'Brien, Eugene. *Seamus Heaney: Creating Irelands of the Mind*. Dublin: Liffey Press, 2002.

– *Seamus Heaney: Searches for Answers*. London; Sterling, VA: Pluto Press, 2003.

– *Seamus Heaney and the Place of Writing*. Gainesville: University Press of Florida, 2002.

O'Brien, Peggy. *Writing Lough Derg: From William Carleton to Seamus Heaney*. Syracuse, NY: Syracuse University Press, 2006.

O'Donoghue, Bernard. *The Cambridge Companion to Seamus Heaney*. New York: Cambridge University Press, 2008.

– *Seamus Heaney and the Language of Poetry*. New York: Harvester Wheatsheaf, 1994.

O'Driscoll, Dennis. 'The News That Stays Poetry.' *Poetry Review* 77.3 (Autumn 1987): 14–16.

– 'The State of the Language.' *Poetry Review* 85.4 (Winter 1995–6): 32.

– *Stepping Stones: Interviews with Seamus Heaney*. London: Faber and Faber, 2008.

O'Leary, Timothy. 'Governing the Tongue: Heaney among the Philosophers.' *Textual Practice* 22.4 (December 2008): 657–77.

Oramus, Marek. 'A Poet of Exact Meaning: An Interview with Zbigniew Herbert.' Trans. Maria Szmidt. *PN Review* 8.6 (1982): 8–12.

Paine, Jeffrey. *The Poetry of Our World: An International Anthology of Contemporary Poetry*. New York: HarperCollins, 2000.

Parker, Michael. 'Changing Skies: The Roles of Native and American Narratives in the Politicisation of Seamus Heaney's Early Poetry.' *Symbiosis* 6.2 (Oct. 2002): 133–58.

– 'Fallout from the Thunder: Poetry and Politics in Seamus Heaney's *District and Circle*.' *Irish Studies Review* 16.4 (November 2008): 369–84.

– *Seamus Heaney: The Making of the Poet*. Basingstoke: Macmillan, 1993.

Parkinson, Thomas. 'Current Unstated Assumptions about Poetry.' *Critical Inquiry* 7.4 (Summer 1981): 659–65.

Paulin, Tom. *The Faber Book of Political Verse*. London: Faber and Faber, 1986.

– *Minotaur: Poetry and the Nation State*. Cambridge, MA: Harvard University Press, 1992.

Petković, Nikola. 'Kafka, Svejk, and the Butcher's Wife, or Postcommunism/ Postcolonialism and Central Europe.' In *History of the Literary Cultures of East-Central Europe: Junctures and Disjunctures in the 19th and 20th Centuries*, vol. 2, ed. Marcel Cornis-Pope and John Neubauer, 376–90. Amsterdam/Philadelphia: John Benjamins Publishing Co., 2006.

Picot, Edward. *Outcasts from Eden: Ideas of Landscape in British Poetry since 1945*. Liverpool: Liverpool University Press, 1997.

Pilny, Ondrej, and Clare Wallace, eds. *Global Ireland: Irish Literatures for the New Millennium*. Prague: Litteraria Pragensia, 2005.

Potts, Robert. 'The View from Olympia.' *The Guardian*, 7 April 2001.

Prendergast, Christopher, ed. *Debating World Literature*. London: Verso, 2004.

Ramazani, Jahan. 'Travelling Poetry.' *Modern Language Quarterly* 68.2 (June 2007): 281–303.

Reddy, Srikanth. 'The Bastion of Sensation: Stationing the Self in the Poetry of Seamus Heaney.' *Journal x* 5.1–2 (Autumn 2000/Spring 2001): 87–108.

Roe, Nicholas. *The Politics of Nature: William Wordsworth and Some Contemporaries*. Houndsmills, Hampshire; New York: Palgrave, 2002.

Rudman, Mark. 'A Calm and Clear Eye.' *The Nation*, 28 September 1985: 287–8.

– 'The Milosz File.' *The Kenyon Review* 20.1 (Winter, 1998): 126–43.

Saussy, Haun, ed. *Comparative Literature in an Age of Globalization*. Baltimore: Johns Hopkins University Press, 2006.

Scammell, William. 'The Singing Robes of Art.' *Poetry Review* 77.3 (Autumn 1987): 42–4.

Schuchard, Ronald. Introduction. *The Place of Writing*. By Seamus Heaney. Atlanta: Scholars Press, 1989.

Shallcross, Bożena. 'Zbigniewa Herberta podróż do zachwytu.' *Teksty drugie* 3[62] (2000): 19–78.

Shtern, Ludmila. *Brodsky: A Personal Memoir*. Fort Worth, TX: Baskerville Publishers, 2004.

Sławek, Tadeusz. 'Prawdziwość żwiru: Rozważania Heaneyowskie na motywach Szekspira.' *Literatura na świecie* 11–12 (2003): 401–23.

Smith, Stan. 'The Language of Displacement in Contemporary Irish Poetry.' In *Poetry in Contemporary Irish Literature*, ed. Michael Kenneally, 61–83. Gerrards Cross: Colin Smythe, 1995.

Sommer, Piotr. *Po stykach*. Gdańsk: Słowo/Obraz Terytoria, 2005.

– *Zapisy rozmów: Wywiady z poetami brytyjskimi*. Warsaw: Czytelnik, 1985.

Sorescu, Marin. *Selected Poems*. Trans. Michael Hamburger. Newcastle upon Tyne: Bloodaxe Books, 1983.

Spivak, Gayatri. *Death of a Discipline*. New York: Columbia University Press, 2003.

Stabro, Stanisław. 'O Zbigniewie Herbercie inaczej.' *Odra* 1 (January 2009): 42–8.

Tall, Deborah. 'Damned for Looking Back.' *Partisan Review* 53.3 (Summer 1986): 478–82.

Tell, Carol. *Part-time Exiles: Contemporary Irish Poets and Their Migrations*. Dublin, Bethesda, MD: Maunsel & Co., 2004.

Thomas, Harry, ed. *Talking with Poets*. New York: Handsel Books, 2002.

Tobin, Daniel. *Passage to the Center: Imagination and the Sacred in the Poetry of Seamus Heaney*. Lexington: University Press of Kentucky, 1999.

Toruńczyk, Barbara. 'Dukt pisma, dukt pamięci.' *Zeszyty Literackie* 17.68 (Fall 1999): 175–9.

Toruńczyk, Barbara, ed. *Zbigniew Herbert, Stanisław Barańczak: Korespondencja (1972–1996)*. Warsaw: Zeszyty Literackie, 2005.

Unterecker, John, ed. *Yeats: A Collection of Critical Essays*. Englewood Cliffs, NJ: Prentice-Hall, Inc., 1963.

Venclova, Tomas. 'Vilnius/Wilno/Vilna: The Myth of Division and the Myth of Connection.' Trans. Tatyana Buzina. Cornis-Pope and Neubauer, 11–27.

Vendler, Helen. 'From Fragments a World Perfect at Last.' *The New Yorker*, 19 March 1984: 138–46.

– *The Harvard Book of Contemporary American Poetry*. Cambridge, MA: Harvard University Press, 1985.

– 'On Three Poems by Seamus Heaney.' *Salmagundi* 80 (Fall 1988): 66–70.

– *Seamus Heaney*. Cambridge, MA: Harvard University Press, 2000.

– 'Seamus Heaney's Invisibles.' *Harvard Review* 10 (Spring 1996): 37–47.

– 'Seamus Heaney's "Sweeney Redivivus": Its Plot and Its Poems.' In *That Island Never Found: Essays and Poems for Terence Brown*, ed. Nicholas Allen and Eve Patten, 169–94. Portland, OR: Four Courts Press, 2007.

Walcott, Derek. *Conversations with Derek Walcott*. Ed. William Baer. Jackson: University Press of Mississippi, 1996.

Weissbort, Daniel, ed. *The Poetry of Survival: Post-War Poets of Central and Eastern Europe*. London: Anvil Press, 1991.

Williams, David-Antoine. 'Tête-à-tête, Face-à-face: Brodsky, Levinas, and the Ethics of Poetry.' *Poetics Today* 30.2 (Summer 2009): 207–35.

Wolff, Larry. *Inventing Eastern Europe: The Map of Civilization on the Mind of the Enlightenment*. Stanford: Stanford University Press, 1994.

Wood, Michael. *Yeats and Violence*. Oxford: Oxford University Press, 2010.

Wordsworth, William. *The Essential Wordsworth*. Ed. Seamus Heaney. New York: The Ecco Press, 1988.

Yeats, W.B. *The Faber Yeats: Poems*. London: Faber, 2004.

– *Selected Criticism and Prose*. Ed. A. Norman Jeffares. London: Pan Books, 1980.

– *W.B. Yeats: Poems*. London: Faber, 2000.

Zaleski, Marek. *Zamiast: O twórczości Czesława Miłosza*. Cracow: Wydawnictwo Literackie, 2005.

Index